Joke Farming

Joke Farming

HOW TO WRITE COMEDY AND OTHER NONSENSE

Elliott Kalan

The University of Chicago Press
Chicago and London

The University of Chicago Press, Chicago 60637
The University of Chicago Press, Ltd., London

Published 2025

Printed in the United States of America

34 33 32 31 30 29 28 27 26 25   1 2 3 4 5

ISBN-13: 978-0-226-82993-7 (cloth)
ISBN-13: 978-0-226-82992-0 (paper)
ISBN-13: 978-0-226-82994-4 (ebook)
DOI: https://doi.org/10.7208/chicago/9780226829944.001.0001

Library of Congress Cataloging-in-Publication Data

Names: Kalan, Elliott, 1981–, author
Title: Joke farming : how to write comedy and other nonsense / Elliott Kalan.
Description: Chicago : The University of Chicago Press, 2025. | Includes bibliographical references and index.
Identifiers: LCCN 2025019950 | ISBN 9780226829937 cloth | ISBN 9780226829920 paperback | ISBN 9780226829944 ebook
Subjects: LCSH: Wit and humor—Authorship | Comedy—Authorship
Classification: LCC PN6149.A88 K35 2025 | DDC 808.7—dc23/eng/20250512
LC record available at https://lccn.loc.gov/2025019950

♾ This paper meets the requirements of ANSI/NISO Z39.48-1992 (Permanence of Paper).

Authorized Representative for EU General Product Safety Regulation (GPSR) queries: **Easy Access System Europe**—Mustamäe tee 50, 10621 Tallinn, Estonia, gpsr.requests@easproject.com
Any other queries: https://press.uchicago.edu/press/contact.html

To my mom, who still thinks my brother
is the funny one
And to my dad, who's pretty sure
he's actually the funny one

Contents

Introduction

> Any great craft tends at last toward the conditions of a philosophy.
>
> —ROBERTSON DAVIES

HOWDY, FOLKS! Welcome to my joke farm. Lovely place, ain't it? Got a whole bushel of autobiographical jokes slowly ripening in the orchard. Over on that hill yonder is our topical comedy arbor. Gotta pay close attention to those jokes; they rot on the vine if you don't pick 'em fast enough. And if you listen by the barn, you can hear the soft mewling of newborn sketch premises.

(Look, I know this is a weird and possibly even confusing way to open a book about humor writing. But I'm trying to shake up your thinking about what jokes are and how they come into being, so bear with me for a little bit and eventually I'll drop the farm schtick. Though not just yet . . .)

I reckon this here joke farm is the first you ever did lay your eyes on. Heck, you've probably never even *heard* of a joke farm before. Well, it's much like any other farm, except for two things: (1) All it grows are jokes, and (2) it exists entirely in my imagination. Because writing jokes is a lot like sex: The first 90 percent of it happens in your brain, and the last 10 requires another person.

If you're reading this book, you're probably interested in the birthing and nurturing of jokes. Perhaps you're a comedy-curious youngster looking to be initiated into the world of humor. Or you're a current comedy professional looking for a way to write better jokes, write jokes better, or both. Maybe you have to give a funny wedding speech in three weeks and you are *flailing* (hint: skip to chapter 5!). Maybe you already think you're hilarious, but someone gave you this book as a gift, and you're just now starting to realize the message they're sending you. Sorry you had to find out this way, but I think I can help.

What Is Joke Farming and Why? (Not Necessarily in That Order)

There is a common misconception about how jokes are written, which I would like to illustrate in the form of a short play:

Setting: A coffee shop
(A Comedian sits in a coffee shop, staring idly out the window.)

COMEDIAN: Hmm, I see someone walking a dog.

(The Comedian stands as if electrified by a billion volts of creative genius.)

COMEDIAN: By Jove, inspiration has struck!

(The Comedian immediately walks onto a stage.)

COMEDIAN: What's the deal with saying "The dog needs to take a walk" when we're really saying "The dog needs to poop"? Are we worried about embarrassing the dog?

> "Master, please, don't mention the poop. I have to see these people tomorrow." Because let me tell you who's *not* worried about embarrassing the dog: the dog. Crowded street, bustling theme park, stadium Jumbotron, he doesn't care who sees. He's going to poop. Dogs probably just think "walk" is our word for "poop." A dog hears about "speed-walking," and he's thinking, "Tell me about it, my humans are always hurrying me along, too."
>
> *(Audience cheers and gives the Comedian a sitcom.)*

That's what I mean by the common conception of joke writing: A funny person notices something, inspiration strikes, and suddenly a joke arrives, fully formed, like a baby colt that can run within minutes of birth and then instantly gets jaded, loses its ambition, and doesn't do much else for the rest of its life.

It's true that sometimes jokes arrive that way. But believing that this is the *only* way a joke comes into the world can lead a comedy writer down an incredibly stressful path. When you believe creativity must come from unpredictable, unprompted epiphanies, it makes you dependent on that most uncontrollable of things: *inspiration*. Like the most famous person attending a meeting, inspiration only shows up when it feels like it, regardless of when you may prefer or need it to show up.

I've been writing jokes in one form or another for over twenty years, and I've found that the most important element in successful joke writing—the thing that I simply cannot do without—isn't inspiration. It's *reliability*. Reliability means writing quality jokes when they need to be written, not just when the jokes decide to make an appearance. Reliability is what shows the people who need jokes written that they can depend on you. Being funny is great and all, but being funny on command is what makes someone a serious joke writer.

This is where joke farming comes in.

Joke farming is how I describe using a methodical process to write funny jokes in an organic, sustainable way. Organically creative and emotionally sustainable, that is. It's very environmentally unsustainable. I go through a lot of paper.

The way I see it, every joke writer passes between stages of creative development analogous to those of human civilization itself. We begin as primitive people did, as *joke foragers* relying on our environment to provide the subsistence we need to create comedy. At this stage we're reliant on external circumstances that allow us to stumble onto funny things. Stick with joke foraging for too long and you'll inhibit your creative growth, because it's hard to push yourself to try new things (or even conceive of what new things to try) when you believe your work is dependent on something you have no control over.

The dream of most comedy writers is to turn from *joke foragers* into *joke machines* that can rapidly churn out uniformly hilarious jokes. But, civilizationally speaking, leaping straight from foraging to heavy industry ignores the most important stage of humankind's journey out of the trees and into the Starbucks coworking space: agriculture! It's not like humanity was gathering nuts one day and then serving billions of hamburgers the next. In between the nut-gathering and the billion-burgering stages came the development of a deliberate, reliable source of food.

So let's take a hint from our ancient ancestors (or, depending on what you believe, the aliens who taught our ancient ancestors) and recognize that the logical step after joke foraging is *joke farming*: working through a defined, repeatable process to plant premises, nurture them through the use of structure and wording, and ultimately harvest them as good jokes.

Achieving any goal requires understanding the process steps you need to follow to get there, and joke writing isn't any different. But—and I say this knowing full well that I am writing a book whose very existence implicitly argues the opposite point—there is no single, universal joke-writing process. Everyone's mind works a little differently, and if you're a creative person, then your mind might work a *lot* differently. So being a joke farmer involves designing a reliable writing process that specifically works for you. Not every crop gets farmed the same way. The purpose of this book isn't to say "Here's the only way to write jokes" but, rather, "Here's how jokes work, and here's how *I* write jokes, so now figure out your own method for doing it." After all, if you give someone a rubber chicken, they'll joke for a day. But if you teach them how to injection-mold their own rubber chickens, they'll joke for a lifetime.

I think that's how the saying goes.

What Is a Joke?

Often, books about humor start by asking the question "Why do people laugh?" Then they spend some time describing different psychological theories before shrugging their literary shoulders and saying, "We'll probably never know." I'd like to skip all that and get straight to the "we'll never know" part. Because if I'm being honest, my personal answer to "Why do people laugh?" is "I don't care." All I need to know professionally is that people laugh because jokes are funny. Having settled that, now we can move on from the unanswerable question "Why do jokes work?" to the incredibly answerable question "How do jokes work?"

A joke, at its most basic, is something deliberately created for the purpose of making someone laugh. It is the rudimentary element of comedy, though it would be a mistake to equate "comedy" (an art form that usually, but not always, accomplishes its goals through provoking laughter and usually, but not always, uses jokes to aid in that purpose) and "jokes" (a laughter-inducing technique). Not all funny things are jokes. Unplanned accidents can be funny, but they're not jokes. Tickling makes people laugh, but it's not a joke. To certain kinds of people (namely, me), a poorly made work of art can be funny. But it's not a joke. I believe nothing that is naturally occurring can be considered a joke, even though nature can be pretty funny sometimes. Just look at anteaters.

A joke must be deliberately constructed for a humorous purpose. In their book *Make 'Em Laugh*, William F. Fry and Melanie Allen describe jokes as "the humor inventions of comedy writers," which I like a lot. Jokes are thought machines for the production of laughter through the communication of ideas. (This is why tickling someone isn't a joke, but a moment in a narrative in which the audience laughs at seeing someone being tickled *could be*, if it's funny.) Jokes are an attempt to induce, on command, a naturally occurring spontaneous response to the unpredictable. If something someone has said on purpose makes you sincerely laugh—not in scornful derision at their idiocy but with actual appreciation—then it's a joke. And if you don't laugh at it, it's *still* a joke, just not a successful one. Laughter is the goal, even if it isn't always achieved. (And achieving laughter isn't necessarily an indicator of a joke's quality, morality, or worth. I've laughed at plenty of bad jokes, and I've laughed at things that I later felt guilty for laughing at. But I can't deny that they were jokes, because they attempted a joke's basic intention: to induce laughter.)

Of course, a joke can do more than make someone laugh. A joke can test a long-held belief. A joke can introduce a new perspective. A joke can express love. A joke can argue a point. A joke can reveal anger. A joke can demean. A joke can inflame. A joke can threaten. A joke can hurt. These are all things jokes *can* do.

But there is only one thing a joke *must* do. It must try to make someone laugh. If being funny isn't the intended effect, then it's not a joke. It may be something wonderful. But it's not a joke.

Hopefully this doesn't sound limiting. Because once a joke checks off the "trying to be funny" box, it can do just about anything else. Jokes are a strikingly effective form of communication, although they often confuse people. They create and sustain emotional connections between people, unless they're offending or dividing those people. They bring joy and make the world a better place, except when they bring pain and make the world a worse place. Sometimes you make money writing them, but usually you don't. For every practical reason for writing a joke, there's an equal and opposite practical reason *not* to write a joke. Don't let that stop you.

I'll be honest: I didn't get into writing jokes for *any* of the above reasons. I started writing jokes because jokes are funny, and I like funny things. I like them enough that I was willing to put a lot of time and work into getting good at making funny things of my own design.

Who Am I, Anyway?

At this point you're probably wondering who I am to act like some kind of comedy authority (especially if you didn't read the author bio on the back of the book, which doesn't seem like a lot to ask, but I get it, you're a busy person). As of the moment I type these words, I've spent the past twenty-two years in professional comedy. Most of my career was spent working at *The Daily Show with Jon Stewart*, a nightly topical comedy program, where I rose from college intern to head writer and picked up four Emmy Awards and a Peabody along the way. I also helped run the revival of the beloved cult-classic "robots make fun of bad movies" show *Mystery Science Theater 3000*, for which I received no awards of any kind. But really, those jobs are only the most easily braggable tips of my career iceberg. I've written comic books and prose essays, and I've hosted podcasts and untelevised late-night talk shows. I've scripted sitcoms for adults and written picture books for children. I've performed sketch comedy to an audience of two in a Times Square strip club and stand-up to an audience of soldiers in war-torn Afghanistan. (Honestly, the Times Square shows were scarier.)

I've been involved in one way or another with just about every form of comedy there is apart from mime. And I've still got plenty of life left to get into that.

For me, comedy has been less of a career than a calling—in the old-fashioned biblical sense of God demanding you do something even if it ruins your life. I've been fascinated with jokes ever since I was young. The kid who read joke books cover to cover as if they were novels? That was me. The teenager who amassed a library of VHS tapes of comedy shows, movies, and specials? That was me, too.

When other guys my age were decorating their rooms with posters of bands or athletes, I was covering my walls with magazine ads for my favorite shows like, well, *The Daily Show with Jon Stewart* and *Mystery Science Theater 3000*.

Am I saying I'm some kind of genius joke-writing savant? No. Absolutely not. And honestly, you don't want to learn from a genius. It's hard for geniuses to explain the brilliance that comes naturally to them. More importantly, if I were a genius, I wouldn't need the reliable joke-farming methods I'm going to describe in this book. While working at *The Daily Show* (where jokes were written quickly in the morning so they could be on TV that night) and *Mystery Science Theater 3000* (where hundreds of jokes had to be written over a few days), my job was to write laugh-out-loud material in stressful situations and on unforgiving schedules *without* burning out or having a nervous breakdown. Joke farming has allowed me to do just that, as well as to build a career on the promise of professional reliability. The people who hire me know I can deliver what they need when they need it. And I can do it with less anxiety and emotional stress because my creativity is a process I can operate consciously and deliberately.

Of course, I'd be a real jerk if I didn't own the privilege that has helped me in building that career. My economic and educational background made it easier for me to take the internship that launched my career, and many people went out of their way to help me as I progressed. I'm very aware that being a Jewish guy from New Jersey gave me an unfair leg up at a show hosted by a Jewish guy from New Jersey, where at one point the executive producer was a *different* Jewish guy from New Jersey who grew up literally one town over from where I did. I promise to do my best in this book to not make assumptions based on my background and to use examples from a variety of different kinds of comedy writers. At the same time, I'll be working within the unfortunate limits of my own frame of reference (more about frames of reference in chapter 4!). This book is by no means meant to be a comprehensive overview of the vast universe of comedy. It's merely meant to help you contribute your own light to that universe.

How To Use This Book

Joke Farming, the book, is built around the three central concepts of joke farming, the method of writing humor:

1. It's easier to write jokes when you have a defined work process for doing so.
2. All jokes are built out of the same foundational mechanical elements: **structure**, **premise**, **voice**, **tone**, **wording**, and **audience**.
3. There's a variety of different comedic forms and uses that jokes can be written for (such as **stand-up**, **narrative**, or **visual humor**), which operate differently but all rely on the same foundational mechanical elements.

In order to communicate those ideas, this book is split into three parts. First, I'll introduce you to the joke-farming process that I designed for myself and walk you through a real-life example of how I put it into action to write a joke for television. Then, once you've seen joke writing in action, I'll take a series of chapters to break down the foundational mechanical elements of a joke, as well as the guiding principles of **brevity**, **clarity**, and **specificity**. Finally, with that grounding in work process and joke mechanics under your belt, we'll look at different uses of comedy and some of the specific thinking that goes into writing for them.

Before we begin, however, I have a couple of provisos. In this book we'll inevitably stumble through some of my personal thinking about what is or isn't funny. These are opinions and not hard facts. Just as there isn't one food that everybody loves (just kidding, there is—it's called pizza, and it's amazing), there isn't one kind of "correct" comedy that works for everyone. Please take my opinions with a grain of salt (but not the pizza—it already tastes delicious, you don't need to put salt on it). I care a lot about comedy. Believe me, I don't want to. But I do. If you take issue with anything I say, that's a good thing. It means you care about comedy, too.

Also, I may make jokes, or use jokes as examples, that offend you—or, even worse, that you don't find funny. This is the danger that comes with producing any sort of creative work, but especially comedy, which often (though not always) gets its reaction through provocation. Please take me at my intention, which is to explain and clarify how jokes work and demonstrate the methods I've found for writing them. Comedy at its best is a personal expression meant for public consumption to induce a personal response: the work of individuals trying to connect with a mass of people who are, themselves, also individuals. That's the danger of it. But, as we'll talk about in chapter 7, that's also the excitement of it.

But how do you actually *do* it? Well, I don't know how *you* do it. But I know how *I* do it, and it's where we're going to begin our journey. So hop in the back of the hay wagon and make yourself comfortable. It's only a short drive to our first chapter.

Part 1

Down on the Joke Farm

IN THIS SECTION, YOU'LL SEE how I use a methodical, step-by-step thought process to go from creative intention to humorous idea to finished joke, which I'll illustrate through the example of a now ridiculously out-of-date piece of comedy. Once you've seen my farming method in action, it will hopefully provide a template or inspiration for you to begin building your own joke-farming process.

1
My Process

I APOLOGIZE, BUT THERE'S NO WAY to talk about how I write jokes without an autobiographical humblebrag. My joke-farming process is heavily influenced by my time at *The Daily Show with Jon Stewart*, where I spent thirteen years moving from college intern to head writer. While there, I learned many things, from how much effort you need to put in to get your first writing job (answer: all of it) to what title you need to attain before you can stop wearing shoes at the office (answer: head writer). But the most important thing working at *The Daily Show* taught me—and coincidentally, the most relevant lesson for this book—was the need to establish a writing process. As much fun as it is to write jokes for a living, it's also a job. I was paid to regularly and reliably write jokes at a consistent level of quality. This meant I needed a reliable joke-farming method. My starting point for developing one was the daily process used by the show.

Work Process Modeling Case Study: *The Daily Show*

Under host Jon Stewart, *The Daily Show* had a very clearly defined writing process. Each day began with a morning "writers meeting," at which we'd discuss what new stories we'd be covering on that night's show, what points Jon wanted to make about them, and some possible joke premises we could use to convey those points in a funny way. In addition to an interview and often a prerecorded video piece from one of our "correspondents," episodes generally had two written segments: a "headline" segment making a coherent, comedic editorial argument on a specific current event; and an "act 2" segment making sillier jokes about a less important story or a themed grouping of minor stories. These segments would be divided up after the meeting into assignments for writers to handle either singly or in pairs. On good days, the writers would have up to two hours to write their first drafts of, or "passes" at, the jokes.

These drafts would then be read by Jon, the executive producers (EPs), and the head writer, who would work together to select jokes to keep for the second draft, throw away the rest, and brainstorm the next iteration of the segment. This same group would also outline each segment's structure, which now had new ideas and prompts for jokes and a clearer overall flow for the larger argument. This outline would be split into assignments for the writers, so they could write their second drafts and try to sneak back in their jokes that got rejected in the first round (this never worked).

This second pass would go back to Jon and the top brass for another read, more thinking, and more refining. Then the head writer and one of the EPs would each take a segment to rewrite further. At that point, sometimes the script was in great shape and only needed a few tweaks. Other times, a combination of someone changing their mind at the last minute, ideas not working as intended, or the writers not following the outline for some damn reason meant massive script surgery was required. The head writer had between fifty and ninety minutes to perform that surgery, usually at the exact time lunch arrived. The resulting third draft was then rehearsed, followed by a final rewrite session in a much smaller room, during which Jon dictated most of the script word by word. When *that* was finally done, the show was performed and recorded, with minor edits if the episode ran long, and then it was finally broadcast across the country.

We did this four days a week, hitting every step of the process. As a result, there was always a show to broadcast at the end of the day, no matter what else might have been going on in our lives, how creative or funny we were or weren't feeling, or whether there'd been some sort of horrible tragic event in the news that morning. If we were ever unsure about where we were going, we *weren't* unsure about the process that would get us there. The reliability of the process enabled a similarly reliable level of quality in the material.

As I rose through the ranks of the show, I often found myself needing to write more jokes faster than I had before and with fewer opportunities for rewriting before showtime. I couldn't waste time waiting for inspiration to strike. I needed to be reliable and consistent on a time budget. I thought to myself: If a TV show's staff can have a process to produce consistent, reliable humor, then why can't I?

And so I became a joke farmer.

All Joke Writing Is Process Writing

The photographer Edward Steichen once wrote, "It takes a powerful generative force to produce a work of art in any medium. This force may be sparked by a spontaneous happening, intuitively perceived, but to become valid as truth, the intuition must be tested by intellectual processes of verification." I find this to be an incredibly insightful description of joke writing, despite being maybe the least funny thing anyone has ever written ever. To boil it down into joke-farming terms for us simple comedy agricultural folk, the inspiration for a funny *idea* may strike you anytime, anywhere. But to become a joke, that initial inspiration must be refined by your talent and skill into a form your audience will understand and find funny. For an idea to become a joke, it must be processed.

Sometimes this processing happens nearly instantaneously, like magic, as if the joke just popped into your head. I've seen it happen. I'll never forget performing stand-up with John Oliver on army bases in Afghanistan, when he would perform hilarious, fully written jokes about people he had just met minutes before going onstage. Or watching President Obama on TV say, "Just as Al Qaeda and its allies are constantly evolving and adapting their efforts to strike us, we have to constantly evolve and adapt to defeat them," and immediately thinking to myself, "If they grow talons, we will grow a thick shell." This is a joke that appeared in my head one morning and then aired on TV that night.

This kind of instant, unconscious joke writing is possible, but you can't always rely on it: Put simply, your brain can't be trusted to always give you the goods. If you're a professional joke writer, though, the clock is already ticking. The clock doesn't care if you're too tired, grumpy, or distracted to be naturally funny, or if you're just plain out of ideas. You need a way to replicate your brain's sudden digestion of joke inspiration as a deliberate, conscious, reliable process. Let me tell you how I do it.

My Process

Let me show you how I joke farm. First I'll name each step of my process, and then I'll go over those steps in more detail, showing you how I used them to write a specific *Daily Show* bit that I've always been unreasonably proud of. (And then, of course, we'll tackle the steps one by one in the chapters that follow, albeit in a slightly different order.)

Here is my process, as simply as I can state it:

1. Identify the absurdity I've recognized in a subject: the seed of what's funny about it. Then consider how this absurdity would be viewed from the perspective and frame of reference of the comedic **voice** for which I'm writing.
2. State that absurdity in plain language in order to clarify the purpose of the joke: in other words, the **point** I hope the audience will take away from it.
3. Select a humorous way to communicate that purpose: the conceptual **premise** that will lead the audience toward seeing the point.
4. Apply a concrete **structure** to that premise in a first draft. Joke structures tap into familiar patterns that help to bring out the humor of the premise.
5. Think "oppositely" to find a twist in the **structure** that yields another, even funnier layer to the joke. (I know, I know . . . structure gets two points in the process. It's *that* important, though it still only gets one chapter to itself.)
6. Finesse the joke's **tone**, making sure its emotional attitude gives the audience the proper cues for how to feel about it.

7. Put a final polish on the **wording** with an eye toward brevity, clarity, and specificity, as well as capturing the voice of whoever is telling the joke.
8. Deliver the joke for an **audience** that laughs so hard you become instantly rich and famous. (Results may vary.)

Stated so bluntly, those steps may seem a little abstract. Admittedly, I've delivered my point without illustrating it through a premise. So let's go through each step again with a specific, real-life, ripped-from-the-headlines-of-a-decade-ago-or-possibly-much-longer-depending-on-when-you-read-this-book example.

It was January 19, 2015. At the time I was *The Daily Show*'s head writer, which meant I didn't get my typing fingers on the script until the third draft. The amount of time I had to write varied depending on the day, but it was a good rule of thumb that I couldn't allow myself more than six minutes for each individual joke—and any jokes I wrote in *less* time afforded me surplus seconds I could spend on particularly tricky premises. That day's news featured then–Secretary of State John Kerry going to France on a sympathy "charm offensive" (that's what the reporters called it) after the horrific *Charlie Hebdo* massacre in which terrorists had shot twenty-three people working for a famously boundary-pushing French humor magazine. Even across the Atlantic Ocean, the massacre had hit the comedy community hard. There was a real worry that a show like ours could also be a target, but we couldn't let that worry stop us from writing jokes about what happened.

You may ask, why *didn't* we not write jokes about it? Partly because as a topical comedy show we were beholden to writing about the news that felt most relevant to our audience, who wanted to know Jon Stewart's thoughts on these things. But we were also drawn to address stories that were difficult to make jokes about. Jon often told us to "steer into the skid" of uncomfortable material rather than avoiding it. The aspect of a news story that we felt the most discomfort about addressing—the aspect we had the strongest emotional reaction to—could, if handled with care, lead to the funniest and most powerful material. Jon referred to that care as "active intention," a concept that encompassed working with deliberate, conscious purpose and self-interrogation rather than rote, passive, or complacent comedy hackwork. The challenge of all this was that without the right jokes, our work ran the risk of being unenjoyably depressing, upsettingly offensive, or unentertainingly dry. All three risks cropped up literally in this case because the shooting was a fresh tragedy and John Kerry was—let's face it—a very boring person.

I began by trying to identify an absurdity in this situation. The first idea that came to mind was the sheer boringness of John Kerry, a former senator, losing presidential candidate, and person you'd least expect to go on a "charm offensive." Stiff and dull, he had all the energy of a dying man under heavy sedation. If you watch the segment we eventually produced, you'll see that we *do* have a joke about the disconnect between John Kerry and the idea of charm. But there had to be more than that to say, though, because in 2015 everyone already *knew* he was boring—there was nothing surprising about that angle.

Ah! But there was a *second* possible absurdity! This one was buried in a cable news sound bite (a lot of the jokes on *The Daily Show* came as reactions to sound bites) in which CNN anchor Wolf Blitzer noted that John Kerry "speaks French, loves France, studied in France." Of course! We could make fun of John Kerry's slightly less cliché reputation for being too French! (This was a facet of his personality that, alongside the aforementioned boringness and with a little help from a shameless smear campaign involving his record as a Vietnam veteran, had sunk his presidential run.) I'd identified my absurdity: that this wooden man was such a big fan of maybe the sexiest country in Europe. The next step was to state it to myself in plain language that pointed in the *direction* of a joke: John Kerry is in love with France.

I then brainstormed premises that would communicate what's absurd about that idea. To save time, I would think about premises in terms of the forms and/or structures that *The Daily Show* tended to use for delivering jokes. Jon could make a direct comment on the situation, perhaps by making a pop culture reference ("The most boring man in the world and the sexiest country in Europe. Opposites do attract. You were right, MC Skat Kat"). He could reply to the speaker of the sound bite as if in conversation with them ("OK, we get it, he's Frenchier than a cigarette wearing a beret! If a mime had a baby with a really long loaf of bread, it'd be John Kerry!"). He could continue the sound bite as if finishing the speaker's thought (". . . eats France, excretes France"). He could act out a scenario using a funny voice ("I, Young John Kerry, will now embark on a voyage of French self-discovery . . ."). He could illustrate the point with an analogy ("He's so French he makes Pepe le Pew look like Pete Pewerson of Cleveland, Ohio!"). Or he could reference a made-up thing for which we could mock up a graphic ("In high school, John Kerry was named most likely to fall in love with a nation with which he had nothing in common," illustrated with a fake yearbook page).

None of these felt right to me. They were communicating the point, but as we'll explore more in chapter 3, the *premise* of a joke should force the audience to make a leap of understanding over the gap between what the joke says and what it means but doesn't say. I felt these premises didn't involve the right amount of audience leaping. For some, the leap was too big (John Kerry's self-discovery voyage), for others, too small (the yearbook page). Returning to the original sound bite, Blitzer's rhythm ("speaks French, loves France, studied in France") pointed me in the direction of doing some kind of joke list of other specific things Kerry admires about France. And if it's an absurd concept that John Kerry is in love with France, how much more absurd is the premise that John Kerry loves everything that's *called* "French"?

Now *that* was a funny idea to me, and it opened up a second level to the joke that I really liked: pointing out that there are a lot of random things that have "French" in their names, regardless of whether they're actually French. Now I had a real premise, and I could start applying it to a structure: in this case, Jon doing a self-call-and-response, where the audience could make the mental leap of intuiting what the second half of the call-and-response would be. "Favorite type of fries? French! Favorite type of bulldog? French! Favorite type of kiss? French!" Adding the silliness of Kerry having a favorite kind of bulldog or there being any kind of fries *other* than French, the joke was now about something more than just John Kerry: our culture's arbitrary use of the prefix "French."

The pattern had been set, and now that the audience could understand it, the joke could have stopped there or kept going forever ("Favorite kind of bread? Favorite kind of horn? Favorite kind of press?"). Actually, it couldn't have gone on forever, because that would have gotten tiresome. Once the joke did its business, it needed to end. But what if it wasn't done doing its business? I wanted to see if I could go further and provide a final twist that would disrupt the pattern I'd set in a funny way. It was time for me to *think oppositely* to see if I could surprise the audience and add another level to the joke. Thinking oppositely is how I describe shaking myself out of a pattern of thought to find new avenues for ideas. To do it, I have a personal ritual that is as silly as it is helpful to me, and it involves a small stuffed fox.

The Story of the Fox

Once upon a time, when my wife and I were first dating, we loved a particular expensive curio shop in the Park Slope neighborhood of Brooklyn (RIP Cog & Pearl). One of the objects on display was a small, red stuffed toy fox about four inches long that was so beautifully made that the stuffing inside really mimicked the natural musculature of a real fox. It had a sort of smug look on its face, like it was patiently waiting for you to realize something important that it'd already known for a long time. I really wanted to own this fox despite it being ridiculously expensive for a small, smug stuffed fox. My then-girlfriend/now-wife bought it for me because we were still at the stage of our relationship where you buy stupidly overpriced stuff for each other for no particular reason. I decided to keep the fox on my desk to justify the expense by making it somehow work related, and I came to find that the fox had a strange, mystical hold on me. Not in a scary "You must kill anyone who would come between us" way, but in a productive "Let me help you unlock imaginary doors" way.

I found that when I was stuck on an idea that wasn't working, I could look at it and be reminded to think like a fox and find a novel, clever way to approach the material. I would do this by imagining the exact opposite of my original idea. "What if," that smug little face seemed to whisper, "instead of doing *this*, you did *that*?" *That* usually didn't work any better than *this*, but those two poles would establish the boundaries of imagination that I was working within, creating a continuum along which a new, more surprising and funnier thought could be found. Whenever I find myself writing something that feels predictable, I visualize the fox to remind myself that surprising elements can be discovered by imagining the opposite.

You obviously don't need a stupidly expensive stuffed toy fox to do this. You may already have, or you can easily create, your own way of tricking your brain into jumping its rails and reaching something unexpected. TV and film writer Ruth Flippen described a non-fox approach when she said, "When you're in trouble with a script and a scene won't work, try writing it backward. Or take the lines the girl is saying and give them to the boy—for that matter take an old joke and switch it." But that's not systematic enough for me. I'll say about the fox method the same thing I'll say about my joke-farming process: You don't have to do it this way. It's not the only way to get there. But this is my way of doing it, and for me it works.

Back to 2015, Already in Progress

To return to where we left off, I had my John Kerry joke pattern and was looking for a way to twist it and subvert the audience's expectations. So I thought oppositely about the situation. I'd established the premise that John Kerry loves everything with the word "French" in its name. What if I could end on something called "French" that John Kerry *doesn't* love? This is when I remembered two things:

1. There is a brand of mustard called "French's."
2. John Kerry is married to Teresa Heinz Kerry, a woman who owns a piece of the condiment company Heinz, a key competitor of French's mustard.

With these facts, I was applying my personal frame of reference (which apparently includes knowledge of condiment brands and John Kerry's personal life) to probe every angle of the subject for humor.

Thus, for the last beat of the bit, I'd have Jon seemingly continue the pattern by saying "Favorite mustard?" The audience, knowing their mustards and understanding the pattern we'd set up, would assume the answer was "French's," but Jon would surprise them with "Heinz. Come on, he knows what side his bread is buttered on!" I liked this a lot. It felt like an elegant and, even more importantly, *specific* way to break the pattern. This joke that had started with a premise about John Kerry and become a joke about things with "French" in their name had returned back to being a joke specifically about John Kerry—and in a way that the audience wasn't likely to see coming.

Now that I had the basic structure and content of the joke worked out, I went back to finesse the wording and find the best specific examples. "Fries" would have to be first, because it was the clearest and most obvious example of a thing with "French" in the name. It had the most potential to set up the pattern and premise quickly. I put "bulldog" next because it's slightly less obvious than "fries," but not the most hilarious example. It works as a transitional bridge for this section. It isn't really heightening much to go from "fries" to "bulldog"—*heightening*, a concept we'll delve into later, means building a joke by going from "funny" to "funnier" to "funniest"—but I decided not to be a heightening purist for the greater good of the joke as a whole.

Then I changed "Favorite type of kiss?" to "Favorite kind of maid?" because it seemed funnier to me that someone would specifically have a favorite kind of maid. (Looking back now, I wish I'd cut "bulldog" and gone "fries," then "maid," and then "horn." But if there was ever something not worth expending energy on regretting, it's this.) For additional clarity, I changed "He knows what side his bread is buttered on" to the clearer, "He's not going to jeopardize his marriage over mustard!" Not only does this make the point more clearly, it also doesn't run the risk of confusing the audience by mixing metaphorical butter with literal mustard.

Finally, I went back over the joke to make sure it sounded as much like the voice of Jon Stewart, the person who'd be delivering it, as I could. This usually meant cutting out unnecessary words to get Jon's characteristically casual New Jerseyan rhythm.

Once that joke was finished, I was on to the next one. I handed in my script, the rest of the process proceeded as normal, and I ended up very gratified by the audience's reaction. This joke got solid laughs from the early beats, and then a big laugh and applause at the mustard reveal. How long did I spend on the actual work of writing this joke? Hardly more time than you spent reading about it. Probably no more than eight minutes. But that was only possible because I'd spent years developing my farming system.

More of My Process: A Mid-chapter Appendix

The example of my working process above involved a situation where it didn't take much time to pick up on an absurdity in the material I was working from. But there are times when it's not so easy to identify that original absurdity. What do you do when you want or need to write a joke, but you can't see what kind of joke it should be—or even what it should be about?

In a situation where I'm writing jokes based on a specific piece of material, it helps me to start by recognizing the *shape* the joke needs to be, or rather the shape of the blank space in the script or routine that the joke is meant to fill. When I wrote for the animated sitcom *HouseBroken*, we would often need to find replacements for jokes that weren't quite working. I'd look at what was happening in the scene *before* the joke and then what needed to happen *after* the joke. What kind of joke would comfortably bridge the gap between these two moments? What would fit the voices of the characters in the scene? What kind of joke wouldn't be too distracting from the emotional action the audience needed to follow? Similar thinking can help with writing jokes for stand-up routines, sketches, or movies. If you know the shape the joke needs to fit to, then you can immediately eliminate everything that the joke *can't* be on the way to finding out what it *has to* be.

Fitting a joke to the available shape was a key concept for me when I was writing for *Mystery Science Theater 3000*. Every episode of the show is the length of a movie, and the vast majority of the jokes are comments riffed over a film as it's playing, so we were hemmed in by the preexisting material that had to serve as the basis for our jokes. For example, we might have trouble finding the right joke to fit, say, a seven-second slot between two lines of dialogue. One thing that helped me to spark ideas was another form of thinking oppositely: deliberately pitching jokes that definitely *wouldn't* work. Professional writers will often spend long periods of time pitching jokes that they know are too elaborate, obscure, clunky, hacky, or vulgar to be used. We do this mostly because it's fun, but also, believe it or not, because pitching real jokes is an anxiety-inducing, high-stakes activity: You're not only being judged on your idea but also on what that idea says about what *you* think is *funny*. You worry that inadvertently pitching the wrong joke could get you fired. If you advertently pitch a deliberately unusable joke, however, you're establishing that you understand the general contours of what will or won't work and just haven't found the right specific joke to fit those contours. Not only that, but one of those wrong approaches may even contain the kernel of the right approach if worded, structured, or conceived slightly differently. And if it doesn't work, at least you've made the other writers in the room laugh, which is half the job.

Of course, there will still be times when you're stuck on a joke. Perhaps you're having trouble figuring out a premise that communicates what you find funny about the idea, or you know your premise but have trouble thinking of the specific example that best illustrates it, or the wording is clunky but you can't find a way to make it flow naturally. When you're writing under a tight deadline, you can't afford to spend too much time untying those knots. So part of joke farming is knowing when to hit the pause button, move on to something else, and pass the troublesome joke on to your subconscious. Often I find that when I leave a joke, work on something else, and then return to it later, the back of my mind has continued working on the problem and found a solution. Even if it hasn't, at least the neurons dedicated to that joke have had time to rest and refresh themselves for another bout with it. By letting that part of the joke-farming field lie fallow, the nutrients in the soil have been allowed to replenish themselves, and often the answer seems clearer.

Mercy Is for the (Comedically) Weak

I already regret that subheading. It could easily be misinterpreted as me saying that a joke writer can't have mercy *toward the subject of a joke*, which is very much not the case. Part of any writing process (hopefully early on, before you've done all the work) should be figuring out whether the subject you're joking about deserves the ridicule or criticism you're about to heap on them. What I mean with this subhead, though, is that a joke writer can't afford to be too merciful to their work.

Because what's the first thing I do after I write a joke? I go back and rewrite it. This is why I saved all that time while writing it the first time! So I'd have time left over to rewrite it! Every second I didn't spend clawing through the rubble of my brain to *find* a joke is a second I can now spend *polishing* the jokes I farmed so that they'll shine like prizewinning watermelons in the summer sun. When I wrote for the sketch comedy show *The Who Was? Show*, I wouldn't hand in a script until I'd done a quick second pass on it. I could finesse my wording, double-check the connections between my setups and payoffs, make sure my patterns were clearly introduced and disrupted, and cut the sketch shorter, tighter, and sharper, because every comedy sketch can be shorter.

Rewriting your work this way isn't only about improving your jokes but also about excising jokes that are less than your best. At *The Daily Show* I knew it was incredibly unlikely that every joke I submitted would actually make it onto the show. So unlikely, in fact, that it never happened. Over time, I became better at identifying which jokes were less likely to make it. So, like any good keeper of livestock, before handing in my drafts I'd cull the weakest of the herd, giving those stronger jokes a better chance to survive. After all, a great joke at the end of a subpar script never really has a shot. This made my scripts stronger, shorter, quicker to read, and therefore less likely to wear out their welcome. It also kept my jokes' submitted-to-broadcasted ratio higher.

Killing an innocent joke to improve the chances of its siblings may sound heartless, but joke farming can be a brutal business. If you don't have what it takes to pick up one of your own handcrafted, personally meaningful jokes, turn its face toward the setting sun, and swiftly crush its windpipe for a quiet, merciful death, then maybe go into a line of work for softer hearts, like investment banking.

Our Processes, Ourselves

Maybe you read this explanation of my joke-farming process and thought, "That's brilliant!" Or maybe you read it and thought, "I put up with all of the introduction's strained barnyard-based metaphors for *this*?!" Both are fair responses! My method is not a universal, guaranteed approach to joke writing. It's merely the process that works for me, modeled on my past experiences and based on an attempt to understand how my brain's natural, subconscious creative process operates. It aspires to achieve what Ralph Waldo Emerson described as "a certain control over the spontaneous states, without which no production is possible."

When I first set out to design a writing process for myself, I began with the assumption that the jokes I came up with quickly must have been the result of some inner thought process happening faster than I was consciously aware of. My joke-farming methods may have originated with the *Daily Show* production model, but they truly developed in earnest when I actively, intentionally practiced reverse engineering my internal thought process. I would take jokes that I'd written quickly (such as the Barack Obama "talons" joke mentioned earlier in this chapter) and attempt to think through how I got from A (the sound bite) to B (the joke). "Ah," I'd think, "my brain must have identified an absurdity in the word 'adapt,' as if terrorism followed the rules of natural selection, and my brain then identified that as a funny premise with which to exaggerate and highlight that absurdity."

It was very difficult, thinking about my own thinking—a little like trying to see the back of your head in the mirror. But once I had a general sense of the steps of a process, I could test them out. When I was struggling to come up with a joke, I'd run the prompt through this process and see if it helped speed up my inspiration and writing. It did. And the more I used the process, the faster I got at using it. Now it feels natural to go through those steps. I wish I could show you examples of jokes in this book where I used my joke-farming process, but to be honest, there were so many of them that if I started to pick them out, I'd never finish. This was especially true for the chapter subheads. You think "As Opposed to a Living Pan" in chapter 5 just happens?! (Trust me, it's hilarious in context and you'll laugh when you get there.)

Of course, your brain—like your social security number and the degree of your love for 1960s Czech cinema—is likely different from mine. The best process for you might also be different. Where you find inspiration, and what intellectual processes of verification you apply to it, should follow your natural ways of thinking rather than fight them. As comic-book creator Scott McCloud says, referring to comics but speaking in a way that applies to humor as well: “A lot of pure instinct goes into making comics. These ideas are meant to supplement and inform those instincts, not replace them.” The specifics of your process are less important than *having* a process to fall back on when you need it. Your joke farm should reflect who you are, how you work best, and what results you hope to achieve. Setting up that joke farm will take work, as well as periodic revision, because we all change during our lives and our processes should reflect that. Quoting McCloud again: “Every technique we use begins its life as conscious process and, with luck, gradually becomes second nature. But not every technique works to our advantage in the long run and it pays to consciously separate good instincts from bad habits once in a while.” As with cleaning out your storm drain and researching your brother-in-law’s cryptocurrency investment offer, a little work now will save you a lot more trouble later. (The examples in that last sentence are another joke I had to spend some time farming.)

Now that you’ve seen how my personal *joke farm* works, it’s time to take a deeper look at how *jokes* work. You’ll be relieved to know that every joke is built from the same basic mechanical elements and works from the same principles of humorous engineering. So let’s put our metaphorical lab coats on *over* our metaphorical overalls and take the metaphorical shuttle bus to the metaphorical agricultural humor program at the metaphorical local community college. It’s time to start dissecting things!

Part 2

Elements, Mechanisms, and Other Obviously Hilarious Things

ALL JOKES, NO MATTER THEIR FORM, message, or SSQ ("side-splitter quotient," a statistic nobody has ever used) operate according to a set of elements and mechanisms that interact in not-unpredictable ways. In this section, we'll walk through the essential parts from which jokes are constructed and discuss how to go about assembling those parts (also known as "writing"). My hope is that by the end of this section you'll be able to look at a joke and understand its inner workings—in other words, the exact opposite of what happens when I lift the hood of a car and just see a bunch of incomprehensible tubes and stuff. With this knowledge, you should be able to approach your joke writing in a deliberate, efficient, and reliably productive way. You'll have a better sense of why a joke is or isn't working and how to adjust it (or scrap it) as needed. Which sounds like it will make joke writing less fun, but trust me, it'll still be really fun.

2
Structure

IN 2001, WHEN I WAS STILL A callow young college student, I attended one of the world's premier comedy events, the Just for Laughs Festival in Montreal. While there I saw a number of performers who would impact my life in various ways, including Jon Stewart, who didn't know I would start working for him a year later. But it was during the festival's "Best of Canada" show that I had a moment of comedic enlightenment, like a silly Buddha sitting under a hilarious bodhi tree.

The comedians in "Best of Canada" understood that few Americans were likely to show up at the "Best of Canada" show, and as a result their comedy was incredibly ultra-specific to Canada and its various regions. As I am from New Jersey, which is not part of Canada, their references were entirely lost on me. But even though I didn't get the references, I still got the jokes.

There's a *reason* I got these jokes. The key to a properly farmed joke—perhaps the most important element of writing a joke that *works*—is structure. The structure of a joke tells us how to understand it and what about it is meant to be laughed at. Just as a paratrooper airdropped into an unfamiliar landscape can find their way to safety if they have a map, a joke's structure will lead your audience to its humor even if the specifics of its content are inscrutable.

Without proper structure, though, it won't matter how well your audience recognizes the references. They'll still end up confused.

What Is Structure?

Structure is the form, construction, and/or mechanical design of a joke—the way you put together the joke's *parts* to make an *idea* seem funny. You'll notice that while working on my John Kerry joke described in the previous chapter, I spent a good amount of time trying out the point of my joke on various types of structures to actually help me figure out the joke's premise. If you believe, as I do, that a joke is a sort of humorous idea machine, then having a firm grasp of structure is like having a firm grasp of basic engineering: It's the place to start, because it plays such an overwhelming rule in triggering the response you want in an audience.

A well-structured joke can take a funny concept and raise it to higher heights. John Hodgman's book of invented trivia, *The Areas of My Expertise*, includes a list of "Seven Hundred Hobo Names," which is exactly what it sounds like. It's funny because the individual hobo names either sound silly ("1. Stewbuilder Dennis," "25. Normal-Faced Olaf," "318. Thanatos Koch") or are funny references to things ("125. Zaxxon Galaxian," "127. Terry Gross," "399. Applebee O'Bennigan McFridays"). It's also funny for the mock-intellectual feat of actually coming up with seven hundred hobo names. But what makes it worthwhile for the reader to continue reading through this long string of silly names—something that might feel tedious around, say, the 150th or so—are the moments of structure that occur at various points in the list, such as organized subsections ("139. Robert the Tot," "140. Robert the Child-Size," "141. Robert the Minuscule," "142. Robert the Wee," "143. Robert Fits-in-a-Case," "144. Robert Eats-for-Free") and running gags (like the reappearance of names with states in them, such as "226. Texas Emil," "409. Mississippi Barry Phlegm," and "607. Maine-iac Leonid"). These surprising moments of structure are like towers reaching past the fog of goofy monikers, delight-inducing goalposts incentivizing and motivating us to read all seven hundred of these things.

Alternatively, poor structure can sink a promising concept. Henry Alford's *New Yorker* humor piece "Reentry Talking Points" works off the excellent premise that after the COVID lockdown, the narrator is having trouble making normal conversation, and each joke is written as a couplet of "What I Said" and "What They Heard." In theory this is a solid format, because it signals to the audience that they should expect a classic one-two structure of jokes with setups and punchlines. Unfortunately, the way Alford structures his jokes fails to fulfill the promise of that format. At first it seems that the joke will be the narrator attempting to say normal things and either blurting out weird things instead or being misunderstood by his conversation partner. ("What I Said: It's weird being back at parties, huh? What They Heard: Do your anxieties ever lead to internal screaming?"). However, the narrator then begins to actually say weird things, and the listener is hearing *different* weird things ("What I Said: Did you read that there's a party in New York called Pheromone, for armpit fetishists who don't wear deodorant? What They Heard: In what ways have you tried to hurt your mother recently?"), and eventually the narrator is making long comments that the listener hears as unrelated short comments ("What I Said: All of literary New York is here. I saw Colson Whitehead in the stairwell and Jennifer Egan on the roof. The critics Christian Lorentzen and Lauren Christensen just arrived—if they got married, they'd be Lauren and Christian Christensen-Lorentzen. What They Heard: It's weird how 'lonely' has an 'e' in it, but 'only' doesn't"), and so on. The relationship between the "said" and "heard" lines doesn't fit into any recognizable system from one joke to another, and by the time I finished reading it I was convinced I'd had a stroke. I worried how I'd tell my wife about my potential neurological condition until later that day, apropos of nothing, she mentioned she'd just read a *New Yorker* piece that made no sense. A perfectly solid premise had been completely flushed down the toilet through inconsistent structure—in this case, a refusal to follow the single most important concept in joke structure: patterns.

The human brain loves to identify and predict patterns, a habit that humor preys on like a reverse-mortgage salesman eyeing an elderly widower. Jokes operate by introducing a pattern and then either fulfilling that pattern in a ridiculous way or disrupting that pattern in a ridiculous way, playing on what early TV comedy pioneer Ernie Kovacs referred to as the "suppressed desire to logical ending." Jokes proceed in steps, and structuring a joke is about making sure those steps lead the audience to an understanding of the logic underpinning the ultimate illogic of the joke.

In the John Kerry joke from the last chapter, I'd set the pattern of "things with 'French' in the name" (favorite fries, favorite bulldog, favorite maid), and then disrupted it (favorite mustard). But imagine if instead I'd gone from "Favorite fries: French" to "Favorite bulldog: French" to "Favorite potato salad: German" to "Favorite 49ers quarterback: Montana." The audience would be confused. Is the pattern things named "French"? Or things with country names in them? Or things and *people* named after places? And if I'd then, ignoring the total incomprehension on the faces of the audience members, heedlessly persisted in continuing on to "Favorite mustard: Heinz," it would have meant nothing. You can forget about building a whole chapter around a nonjoke like that. Failing to build the right structure means failing to build the right expectations in the audience's mind, destroying the fun of seeing a pattern playing out and then seeing it twisted in new (but rational) ways.

A simple example of a joke pattern is this line from Jane Wagner's play *The Search for Signs of Intelligent Life in the Universe*: "I worry if peanut oil comes from peanuts and olive oil comes from olives, where does baby oil come from?" The pattern here is clear. Two oils named after the things they're made from, followed by an oil named after the thing it's used on—the breaking of the pattern—whose place in the sequence implies a logical relationship to the previous examples, which the audience picks up on: Maybe they make baby oil out of babies.

This most simple pattern of humor—two not-funny things followed by a funny thing—is known as the "rule of threes," which is often taken to mean that three is just an inherently funny number of things. But much like cavemen watching day turn to night and assuming the moon ate the sun or something, comedians have traditionally vastly overstated the connection of the literal number three to the actual principle the rule of threes is describing. Legendary improv teacher Del Close once wrote "We have three brains—the neo-cortex, the mammalian cortex, and the reptilian cortex. My theory is that each brain gets a joke at a different rate. Of course, it might be something else entirely!" And he was right: It *is* something else entirely.

Three is not a magic number. Three isn't even a funny number. Three is just the least number of things you need to establish a pattern and then disrupt or exaggerate that pattern. That's it. That's the whole deal. For example, take the most annoying joke in the world:

> Knock knock.
> Who's there?
> Banana.
> Banana who?
> Knock knock.
> Who's there?
> Banana.
> Banana who?
> Knock knock.
> Who's there?
> Orange.
> Orange who?
> Orange you glad I didn't say banana?

My kids love that joke. I hate it. But it's a great example of setting up a pattern and then subverting it in a semilogical way (one fruit, same fruit, different fruit). And the joke would work equally well if you said "banana" five or ten or fifty times. Which is to say, it would still suck, just not for structural reasons.

Let me break it down again with an example I actually like, a bit from the Marx Brothers movie *Horse Feathers* where Harpo Marx, the brother who doesn't talk, tries to play a pay phone as if it's a slot machine:

1. He puts a coin in and dials; nothing happens. This establishes the situation.
2. He puts another coin in and dials; nothing happens. The pattern is set.
3. The phone rings, he answers it, and coins shoot out of the return slot. The pattern has been disrupted.

Moreover, this bit is actually the third in a *series of successive bits* that show Harpo first winning coins at a slot machine, then releasing all the coins from a train conductor's change belt, and finally, as we see here, attempting to win coins from the phone. The pattern isn't disrupted in this set of three bits, though. Instead, the logic of "increasingly unlikely ways for Harpo to get money" is stretched from lucky break to theft to freak occurrence—an example of *heightening*, something we'll return to later in this chapter.

Even jokes that don't introduce a complete pattern involve some degree of disrupting or exaggerating existing patterns. Jokes that seem to be made out of a single, discrete event (sudden slapstick gags, one-panel cartoons, absurdist one-liners) are actually disrupting or stretching the patterns we've internalized from our time living in reality. Comic creator Scott McCloud describes something similar when he notes that "in our daily lives we often commit closure, mentally completing that which is incomplete based on past experience." For example, if you only see the front half of the Nike swoosh logo on a billboard because the other half is obscured by a tree, you instinctively know what the other half looks like and that it doesn't end in a mermaid tail or a giant sperm. In many jokes, the disruption of a pattern is enacted by hijacking that experience-based closure.

Take the wordless one-panel comic by the legendary cartoonist Sam Gross in which a maid sweeps up severed heads piled around a guillotine. The comic doesn't set up a pattern within itself, but it does play off our own assumption of what maids do based on the pattern constructed by our experience of seeing or being a maid. Gross's cartoon then stretches that pattern to a ridiculous point (i.e., sweeping up heads). Looking ahead to the chapters after this, you could say that our **perspective** and **frame of reference** are basically just our way of observing and internalizing patterns in reality and that the creation of a premise is a way of examining what *part* of that reality pattern can be disrupted or stretched to get a funny idea across. Or, alternately, if that doesn't make sense because you haven't

This Sam Gross comic plays off the viewer's instinct for closure, making a joke by stretching an experiential pattern to a ridiculous point.

S. Gross / CartoonStock Ltd.

read the chapters after this one yet, you could *not* say that. I'm not your boss.

How to Structure a Joke

I know this chapter has already been a nonstop roller-coaster thrill ride, but hold on to your hats, because here's the most exciting thing about structuring a joke: There are many ways to do it . . . *as long as* you fulfill the two needs of joke structure. First, give the audience the information they require to get the joke; in other words, set the pattern. Second, fulfill or deny the expectations raised by that information; in other words, finish the pattern.

You're probably already familiar with the most basic, binary structure of a joke, in which a setup is followed by a punchline. The setup and punchline exist in symbiotic balance, each completely worthless without the other's existence. The setup is the introduction of information that the audience needs to get the joke. (As Mel Brooks writes, "Without information, there is no joke. You've got to set things up.") The punchline then fulfills this preparation.

A great example of this is a joke by the comedian Michelle Buteau:

> Setup: "It's been a very interesting year for me, because a lot of my guy friends have come out."
> Punchline: "As predators."
> Tag: "Like, I always knew, but it was really *their* journey to figure it out."

(Don't worry, we'll get to tags later in the chapter.) First, notice how Buteau subverts our expectations from the setup in a way that still fulfills the information she's given us. We make an assumption based on the reality pattern we're familiar with regarding the phrase "come out." Then the punchline disrupts that assumption with a new piece of information that skews what we've heard before without invalidating it. Steve Allen, arguably *the* inventor of the late-night talk show, describes the mechanism of a joke like this as "leaping outside what had appeared to be the rules of the game at the moment."

Buteau's joke is also a beautiful example of one of the principles of strong joke writing: **brevity**. Brevity in comedy writing is exactly what it sounds like: taking as little time as possible to communicate a joke, both to avoid overstaying your welcome and because the quicker you finish the joke, the quicker the audience can make the intuitive leap that's fundamental to humor (something we'll get into in greater detail in the next chapter). The audience needs to jump quickly. Have you ever tried to jump slowly? You just fall down. Brevity is the reason the rule of threes has stuck around for so long. The power of the number three isn't in its mystical threeness but is, as I said above, because it's the least number of things you need for pattern-setup-and-disruption purposes. The least amount of information (whatever's necessary and no more) is almost always the best amount of information. Even when the premise of a joke is "What if this joke went on for a long time?" (such as the well-known *Family Guy* bit where Peter Griffin rubs his injured knee for nearly half a minute of TV time), the setup should get the audience to that premise (this is funny precisely *because* it's taking so long) as quickly as possible.

If a joke's setup doesn't give us all the information we need for our brains to connect it to the punchline, then the joke will fail: "A customer walks into a bar, and the bartender says, 'Why the long face?' Oh, right, I forgot to tell you the customer is a horse." But if the setup gives us too much information, then our brain is busy trying to figure out which part of what we're being told is relevant to the punchline, and the joke will also fail: "A horse walks into a bar called Hinterlands, in the Kensington neighborhood of Brooklyn, and it's a bar known for having a pretty laid-back vibe, and the bathrooms are wallpapered with pages from old fantasy role-playing game manuals, and the bartender, whose name is Stuart, says, 'Why the long face?'" I don't even remember what this joke was about, and I'm the one telling it!

One method you can use for testing whether your joke is too long or too brief is to examine how balanced the information in the setup is with the payoff in the punchline. Ask yourself, does each piece of information in some way connect directly with the punchline? And then ask, is each piece of information in the setup *necessary* to the punchline? Is each *word* necessary for communicating this information to the audience? If the answer is no for any individual fragment of the joke, then eliminate that fragment and look at the joke again. Most of the time the result will be a funnier, more effective joke.

Setup and punchline. It's a simple, balanced, and—yes—brief way to structure a joke. But, personally, it's not enough for me. You see, I prefer to write comedy not with two parts to a joke—*but with THREE! BUM BUM BUMMMM!*

Jokes and Three-Act Structure

A joke is basically a story. It has a beginning, a middle, and an inevitable end, just like life, snakes, and Democratic control of Congress. In storytelling this is called three-act structure, and I personally prefer it as a model for jokes.

Why? I can't fully explain. It just feels right to me, and part of joke writing—as I mentioned before—is finding the method of doing it that feels right to you. Because how far will you get creatively working in a way that feels *wrong* to you?

Let me explain how three-act joke structure works by taking you through an example from my old stand-up act. **Act 1** creates the world the joke inhabits and announces the premise:

> I had a child. How did I do it? You know the Death Star scene at the end of *Star Wars*?

Act 2 is the bridge that develops the premise further and gets more specific. It takes the statement of act 1 and turns it into a pattern, establishing the relationship that connects each link in your chain of joke logic:

> I had to pilot my craft down this narrow trench, then fire my torpedo at just the right moment to get through the opening . . .

We've established a pattern—using *Star Wars* as a metaphor for sex—and **act 3** fulfills the premise in a funny or surprising way:

> . . . and an old man was giving me advice while I was being chased by a guy in a mask.

The pattern has now been stretched (and disrupted) by introducing *Star Wars* elements that make my sex life sound pretty strange.

"But," you might say, trying to trip me up, "there's more than one funny moment in that bit. Surely a *single joke* doesn't break down into three acts!" That's where you're wrong, defiant voice I am unfairly attributing to the reader! Let's look at a joke from the all-time great stand-up Rita Rudner:

> I broke up with my boyfriend. He wanted to get married, and I didn't want him to.

You could break it down as "setup/punchline" structure, like this:

> Setup: "I broke up with my boyfriend."
> Punchline: "He wanted to get married, and I didn't want him to."

Or this way:

> Setup: "I broke up with my boyfriend. He wanted to get married,"
> Punchline: "and I didn't want him to."

But to me, it feels more elegant to break down the structure like this:

> Act 1: "I broke up with my boyfriend." (establishing a premise)
> Act 2: "He wanted to get married," (bridge, providing new information)
> Act 3: "and I didn't want him to." (payoff, with surprising, but logical, information)

Of course, now your need to challenge me has only increased. "Surely, you can't break down a single sentence into this structure!" you shout, hurling the book against the wall before hurrying to pick it up again so you can read my response. And surely, I can. For example, take the beloved joke in the opening line of Jane Austen's novel *Pride and Prejudice*:

Act 1: "It is a truth universally acknowledged" (establishing the premise that we're about to get some heady wisdom)
Act 2: "that a single man in possession of a good fortune" (the bridge, providing new information)
Act 3: "must be in want of a wife." (payoff, bringing us down from a universal truth to the level of gold-digging matchmaking)

As with the piece of food stuck in your blind date's teeth, once you see how three-act structure works you'll have a hard time not seeing it. Three-act structure can even be found in the individual acts of a joke, creating a sort of fractal joke structure. Let's break down my *Star Wars*/conception joke from above even further:

Act 1.1: "I had a child."
Act 1.2: "How did I do it?"
Act 1.3: "You know the Death Star scene at the end of *Star Wars*?"
Act 2.1: "I had to pilot my craft down this narrow trench,"
Act 2.2: "then fire my torpedo at just the right moment"
Act 2.3: "to get through the opening . . ."
Act 3.1: ". . . and an old man was giving me advice"
Act 3.2: "while I was being chased"
Act 3.3: "by a guy in a mask."

After I write something, I break it up into smaller parts and analyze them to make sure they can be organized into three-act structures. Jokes, stories, scenes, dialogue stretches: Everything can be broken down into a setup, a bridge, and a payoff. It gives a sense of unity and cohesion to a piece of writing that won't necessarily be noticed by the audience but will help them subconsciously feel it's a satisfying whole.

This may seem like I threw out one rule of threes ("Three is the funniest number") for another rule of threes ("Everything needs to have three acts"), but I would balk at calling three-act structure a rule. I'm not saying this is the only, or even the best, structure for a joke. As I said above, the three-act structure is simply the technique for organizing information that feels most comfortable to me personally. If structure is the skeleton of a joke, it's good to remember that the skeletons of different animals look different. All a skeleton needs to do is keep the animal from collapsing into a gross, wet bag. As long as your structure prepares the audience, then fulfills that preparation in a way the audience finds surprising, understandable, and delightful, then it's a good structure. Find the structural technique that best expresses your voice. As Gerald Mast writes in *The Comic Mind*, "'Good' structure is not a fixed quality but a function of the whole work's intentions." The old design maxim "form follows function" applies to jokes just as much as it does to skyscrapers and expensive chairs.

Structural Technique 1: Do the Height Thing

Once you've got a basic structure for your joke, there are techniques you can use to strengthen that structure for maximum comedy. One of the simplest is the concept I've mentioned before, **heightening**, which is literally ordering the progression of your joke so that each step increases by whatever metric is important for the premise of the joke—size, vulgarity, randomness, or what have you. Richard Schickel, describing the silent comedy star Harold Lloyd, calls this "the basic law of his art, which is that the end must be funnier than the beginning." In simple terms, this means the joke's clauses should go from funny to funnier to funniest. In the movie *Kung Fu Hustle*, there's a scene in which two hapless thugs attempt to bully a crowd by challenging members of the crowd to fight. In trying to find an opponent they're sure they can overpower, they call out a short guy—who, it turns out, was sitting down and is actually ridiculously tall. Then they challenge an old man—who steps forward to reveal he's ridiculously muscle-bound. So they challenge a little kid—who reveals he's *also* ridiculously muscle-bound. The heightening has gone from believable reveal (short guy is tall) to less believable reveal (buff old dude) to unbelievable reveal (buff little kid), heightening the surprise factor of each reveal. Then, following the principle of brevity, the joke ends. After the buff kid, they don't challenge anyone else, like a woman who turns out to be a centaur or a baby who pulls out a gun, because why keep going when the joke's mission has been accomplished?

Heightening in a joke should always follow a clear, logical progression. If, while I'm walking down the street, a bird poops on my head, then a skydiver poops on my head, and then an airplane empties the contents of its bathroom tanks on my head, that's a logical progression of increasingly larger amounts of poop falling on my head. If, however, we change that order so that while I'm walking down the street, a bird poops on my head, then a plane unloads its bathroom on me, and then a skydiver poops on me, we've failed to properly heighten. The step between airplane and skydiver is an anticlimactic one, failing to create a sense of progression. Even worse, if a bird poops on my head, then I win the lottery, and then the earth is hit by a meteor, that's just three events that, while increasingly big, have no consistent relationship to each other, so there still isn't a sense of progression.

Adding to the complexity of heightening, it's not just the direction your examples move that matters (big, bigger, biggest) but also the distance between each step (five feet tall, ten feet tall, five hundred feet tall). Each time you go from one bit of the joke to the next, the distance traveled should be appreciably bigger. From a bird to a person is one magnitude of difference in amount of poop. From a person to an airplane is an even larger magnitude of difference. If I were to continue the sequence I might go to a space shuttle jettisoning one of its enormous booster rockets, but have it labeled "septic tank." And after that there's pretty much nowhere to go but God taking a dump on my head. Each increase in size must be a bigger stretch than the previous increase was. To put it in terms that make no sense out of context: When you heighten you've got to heighten the heighten.

It works in the other direction as well. If I were writing a joke for a sitcom in which someone was trying to annoy their roommate with their physical presence, I could probably have them sit closer and closer to the roommate with increasingly smaller and pettier movements. The annoyer would go from sitting across the room from their roommate to sitting on the other end of the couch from their roommate. Then they'd go from the other end of the couch to right next to their roommate. Then they'd move one more inch so that they're pressed up against the "increasingly irritated" roommate. My example here is pretty basic, to be fair, but there are three *types* of incremental steps going on in this bit—the increasingly small *distance* of the moves, the increasingly *intrusive closeness to* the roommate's personal space, and the increasingly irritated *reactions* (or the classic "pretending not to be irritated" reactions) on the part of the roommate.

Even jokes built on illogic are stronger when there's a logical, heightening progression that an audience can follow. Consider TikTok comedian Petey's video "Strongest baby ever maybe," in which three dudes (all played by Petey) find a child's handprint in the sidewalk and go from assuming the print is "some sort of fossil" to deciding it's evidence of a prehistoric "strong baby" who could break cement with their hands because "babies were a lot stronger back then"; in the end, the men are thankful they're alive at this point in history because "strong babies so scary." Each incorrect assumption made by these characters leads to the next, heightened, even dumber assumption. The chain of logic is strong despite every link in it being completely stupid.

Structural Technique 2: Come On, Reader, Let's Do the Twist

Heightening is a way of reinforcing structure, but you can also make a joke more interesting by twisting and distorting its structure slightly. In this way you can subvert the pattern you've set up so that it increases the amount of surprise for the audience, without subverting the pattern so much that the whole thing falls apart. The twist could be as simple as finding a slightly less straightforward way of getting across the last act of the joke. Returning to my extremely highbrow hypothetical poop joke from the previous section, if the joke starts with a bird pooping on my head and then continues with a larger bird pooping a larger poop on my head, it might then involve an elephant skydiving above me, causing me to run for cover because I know what will happen next. In this case, rather than stretch the pattern, I've disrupted it by refusing to be pooped on a third time.

Or, alternately, I could be pooped on by a bird, then pooped on by a larger bird, and then when a skydiving elephant passes over my head *without* pooping on me, I could get mad and chase after it, demanding it finish the job the others started. Here I've twisted the structure by disrupting the pattern of action *and* my character's expected reaction to those actions.

A beautiful example of this type of heightening twist appears in the *Looney Tunes* cartoon "Zoom and Bored." Director Chuck Jones describes the gag: "The Coyote has built a rickety construction all the way up the side of a hill" in order to roll a bomb down onto the Road Runner. The camera spends nearly ten seconds panning up the hill to show the entire contraption. . . . "When we reach the top," Jones continues, "we find the Coyote putting a lighted match to a bomb, getting ready to send it on its way—and it immediately blows up, before it can utilize the long, carefully designed ramp. The bomb explodes in the audience's face as much as in the Coyote's." In this joke, Jones plays with the audience's expectations by structuring the gag as if it will involve this long, rickety ramp—only to deny us the structural fulfillment we expect, giving us a funnier, more surprising finish in exchange (though one that still plays off the expected pattern of the Coyote's plans always backfiring).

Structural Technique 3: The Joy of Deheightening

Another way to twist your structure is to do the exact *opposite* of what I advised at the beginning of this section: ***de*heightening**, or deliberately arranging the steps of your joke in a seeming progression followed by a sudden regression. Canny audiences may *expect* heightening but will probably not expect a drop in extremity. My favorite example of this technique is an off-the-cuff comment made by my grandmother, Geraldine "Gerry" Kalan, after she'd moved from New York City to suburban Connecticut: "Connecticut is boring. You look out the window, and there's a tree, there's a rock, there's a bush. But in New York, you look out the window and there's a theft, there's a murder, there's a delicatessen. . . ." While the central premise of this joke is my grandmother's wistful appreciation for violent crime, she adds a second level of humor by giving us not a third New York example that's even more violent but, instead, something completely nonviolent. Why does this work when the example of bad heightening I gave earlier ("bird poop, airplane poop, skydiver poop") didn't? Because in this case it isn't just a drop in severity between examples (like "theft, murder, jaywalking," which wouldn't work here) but a complete change of category to something so innocent that it disrupts the pattern enough to really surprise us.

Perhaps the most famous example of deheightening is the old "Why did the chicken cross the road?" joke, in which the setup preps you to expect a funny reason, only to give you the most literally obvious explanation possible, "To get to the other side." It's not a great joke, since the premise is basically "What if I wasted your time?," but it's also a surprisingly sophisticated case of deliberate anticlimax. I find it incredibly ironic that the first joke many children learn is entirely reliant on a preexisting expectation of joke structure. In fact, the first person who ever heard the joke probably thought it was very surprising and laughed at it. OK, I've come around on it. It *is* a great joke.

Similar to deheightening is **nonheightening**, a form of repetition in which the audience's expectation of different joke specifics is foiled by repeated delivery of the same specifics. An example of this is the TikTok sketch by @geemcgwee in which an offscreen voice (@geemcgwee herself, I assume) asks a series of young New Yorkers what they do for a living and always gets the reply "I lay eggs." Nobody she asks does any other job, and the repetition of not just the same answer but the same exact phrase takes us on a slightly-less-than-one-minute-long journey of laughing at the strange answer, then laughing at hearing the strange answer a second time, then laughing as it dawns on us that every answer will be the same. You might call it the surprise of not being surprised.

Tagging a Joke

There is a final, optional piece of joke structure known as the **tag**: a little comedy epilogue that provides an extra payoff without weighing too heavily on the joke's overall structure. Usually, a tag is an additional thought or extrapolation of the premise that follows the real punchline with a bonus bite of comedy. It's the humor equivalent of a fancy restaurant rounding off your hearty meal with a single handmade potato chip.

We've already seen one example earlier in this chapter, in Michelle Buteau's "friends came out as predators" joke.

Another example of a tag is a piece of dialogue in the movie *The Naked Gun* in which the main character sums up his tragic romantic history with this joke: "It's the same old story. Boy finds girl. Boy loses girl. Girl finds boy. Boy forgets girl. Boy remembers girl. Girl dies in a tragic blimp accident over the Orange Bowl on New Year's Day." This is already a complete joke, but when the woman he's talking to asks, "Goodyear?" he responds, "No, the worst." The "boy meets girl" routine could exist without this tag, but it gets another final laugh from the premise that's been set.

Ideally, a tag to a joke will carry the feeling of a genuine thought added in the moment—or discovered organically in the creative process—rather than something forced or labored over. When tags are successful, they add not only an extra laugh to a joke but also a jolt of energy and closure. I think of nonsense essayist Robert Benchley as the master of these sorts of tags, as in this essay opening: "The social season in our city ends up with a bang for the summer when the Strawberry Festival at the Second Congregational Church is over. After that you might as well die. Several people have, in fact." That last sentence feels like a thought he's just realized, a sudden aside that he couldn't help but interject.

When writing tags, my advice is to see what pops into your head when you reread (or, if you're a stand-up, perform) your joke. If nothing occurs to you in that moment, then it isn't worth racking your brains to shove a tag onto the end of a joke. A tag is the enemy of brevity, since it asks the audience to keep thinking about something that's otherwise over, and so a forced tag really overstays a joke's welcome. But if the idea of the joke sparks another idea in your mind that you hadn't fully anticipated while you were writing it, then it may give the audience the same unexpected delight. The tag is therefore not a load-bearing piece of a joke's structure but an extra dash of flavor-enhancing spice to be used prudently.

Structure: A Power for Good or Evil

Remember at the beginning of the chapter, when structure helped me to understand jokes from a strange, alien, Canadian culture? It certainly seemed to imply that structure is a force for communication, interpersonal connection, and all-around goodness. Perhaps joke structure, used wisely, could bring humanity together and solve the ills of our fractured world!

Well, I've got bad news for you. Structure doesn't only work for sharing truths. It also shares lies, making it easier for an audience to laugh at ideas that are at best inaccurate and at worst harmful. The love of patterns, and the thrill we get from seeing those patterns disrupted, is so hardwired into the human brain that it can do an end run around conscious thought, smuggling new ideas into our thinking. When that's used to help us break down inaccurate assumptions, it's great. When it's used to implant new inaccurate assumptions, that's not great.

Let's look at an example that's hopefully antiquated enough that we can analyze it without being distracted by the toxicity of its message. It's a joke I laughed at as a youngster when I first encountered it in *Isaac Asimov's Treasury of Humor*, and it's the kind of "story joke" still told by uncles and grandpas but not really used onstage by professionals anymore.

In this joke, God is traveling the ancient world looking for people who will follow his commandments. He first asks an Arab, who gives a speech taking issue with the commandment "Thou shalt not kill" because his livelihood depends on killing travelers and confiscating their goods. Next, he asks a Babylonian, who gives a speech taking issue with the commandment "Thou shalt not steal" because he is a dishonest merchant and his livelihood depends on cheating his customers. Finally, a discouraged God encounters Moses. Asimov tells the rest of the joke like this:

> God called to him. "Moses," he said, "would you like to follow My commandments?"
> And Moses said, "How much do they cost?"
> "Why, nothing," said God. "I'm giving them away for free."
> "In that case," said Moses, "I'll take ten."

For all its old-fashionedness, and my clunkiness in trying to summarize it succinctly, this is a well-structured joke. The premise is clear, and the progression is structured as a pattern of "people take issue with individual commandments," which is then disrupted by Moses's focus on the price rather than the actual content of the divine law. After the longer responses from the first two figures, Moses's short, matter-of-fact response changes up the joke's rhythm in a funny way—and it plays off a common frame of reference, because the fact that there are ten commandments is widely known even among people who may not believe in them.

It's also pretty clearly a racist joke, playing off deep-seated and harmful slurs about Arabs being murderers and Jews being obsessed with money. Even the seeming randomness of calling Babylonians thieves plays into the stereotype of the unscrupulous Middle Eastern trader. I don't think Arabs are more violent than any other kind of person, nor that Jews think about money more than any other kind of person—but there's part of me that still finds this offensive, hoary, hacky joke funny. Why? The structure. The structure is a funny structure. I don't want to like this joke, because the things it's saying are horrible to me, but just as you can't help tapping your toe to a catchy song you don't actually like, I can't help responding to the structure.

There are times when you laugh at a joke, then feel bad afterward because that laugh has forced you to recognize something unpleasant in yourself. People often defend those jokes by saying your laughter proves that "it's funny because it's true." But honestly? A lot of the time the situation is actually "it's funny because it's structured." Laughter isn't proof of accuracy.

What this means for an audience is: Don't get seduced by structure. What it means for a joke writer is: You have to be aware of what your joke is actually saying, not just whether it "works" on a technical level. I've seen writers on a deadline come up with jokes that are funny mechanically but carry a point they end up regretting. I've been guilty of it myself. Start with the premise you want to communicate and then use structure to make it work as a joke. Don't start with structure and fill it up with whatever random, lazy premise happens to fit in it. Then you're no better than Moses buying commandments in bulk, sight unseen.

But about this thing I just mentioned, what did I call it? A "premise"? What's that? Why is it so incredibly necessary? And how do you use it to get the world to listen to the idea you think is so worth saying that it deserves to be a joke? Ask me no more questions! Merely turn the page, and all shall be revealed!

3
Premise

WHEN YOU WRITE A CHILDREN'S PICTURE BOOK, you learn that the actual writing of picture books is only a small fraction of the work of a picture book writer. The real work is parading into rooms full of children (usually in schools and bookstores, but restaurants or bounce houses will do) and reading your book to them so that they'll annoy their parents into buying it. I write picture books, and as part of those readings, I talk to kids about how to be a writer—much as I'm doing in this book, albeit with shorter words and more silly voices. I do, however, always ask the kids if they know the one thing you need to be a writer. And they never guess it. They always say "Paper!" Or "A pencil!" Or "A computer!" They don't realize that the only thing you absolutely *need* if you're going to write is an idea.

In comedy, we call the final form of that idea the **premise**. You have to start somewhere when you write, and the premise is that somewhere.

What Do I Mean by Premise?

You may be familiar with "premise" as another term for a story's basic situation or plot. The author has something they want to express—a message, a feeling, a thought—and stating it plainly would be boring. The premise is how they dramatize it, dressing it up with spaceships or murders so we pay attention. Similarly, every joke has a point—a message, feeling, or thought—that it's communicating to the audience. The premise is the comedic situation or mini story the joke uses to get that point across.

Now, in ordinary conversation, some of these words get used a little interchangeably. So before we go any further, let me define the most important terms I'm going to use in this chapter: idea, point, and premise. To me, you can differentiate them as follows:

An **idea** is the first inkling that something might be funny. In terms of my *Star Wars* sex joke from the last chapter, the idea was something like "It would be funny to talk about fathering a child as if the audience didn't know how it worked and needed to have it explained to them." (Literally the first part of the joke that came to mind was "I had a baby. How'd I do it? Well . . .")

The **point** is the message or concept that the joke is communicating beneath the humor, even if you may not fully understand the point of your joke until you're done writing it. Once I'd started playing with that initial joke idea about fatherhood, I hit on a point I liked (and felt was, if anything, hitting a little *too* close to home) about being so enmeshed in commercial geek culture that it was the only frame of reference I had for something as natural and eternal as human reproduction.

The **premise**, finally, is how you express that idea and intention in a funny way—in this case by implying, through a *Star Wars* metaphor, that my sex life is way more interesting than it is.

So that's how I'll be using each of those terms in this book. The idea is the initial thought, the point is the message, and the premise is the developed conceptual story of the joke.

"Elliott," you're probably saying, "can I have a complicated metaphor for how a premise works?" I'm glad you asked, since I happen to have one right here. I think that a joke works a lot like a synapse, the space between nerve cells that electrical impulses travel across when they leap from one neuron to the other. Similarly, when you tell a joke, you are on one side of a gap and the audience is on the other. The premise is the bridge that carries your joke idea from one side of the gap *almost* all the way to the other, but not completely, forcing the audience to take the last, final leap that makes the connection. The great movie director Billy Wilder learned this concept from the also-great movie director Ernst Lubitsch: "If you say two and two, the audience does not have to be told it's four. The audience will find it themselves; let the audience find the joke." In other words—if you like letters more than numbers—the joke should provide the audience with "ABC" and "E," allowing them to intuit the existence of "D."

A very straightforward illustration of this idea is the Rita Rudner joke I mentioned last chapter, which, to remind you, is "I broke up with my boyfriend. He wanted to get married, and I didn't want him to." Here, Rudner is giving us some information (she and her boyfriend disagreed about getting married) followed by a new piece of information (but not about marrying each other) that allows us to figure out the unspoken piece of information (Rudner is the "other woman" in an act of infidelity). Think how much less funny this joke would be as "I broke up with my boyfriend. He wanted to marry someone else—his actual fiancée—and I didn't want him to." Fully communicating the idea—that is, bridging the entire gap between the speaker and the audience—leaves no aspect of the story unsaid for the audience to discover, which stops it from being a real joke. Whereas by using the premise "What if I talked about an affair as if it weren't an affair?" Rudner forces the audience to make the cognitive leap of understanding to "Oh! He wanted to marry *the person he was cheating on with Rita*!" That moment of understanding is what provokes the audience's laughter.

I've heard people describe the secret of humor as surprise, but it's not really a pure surprise. People don't like pure surprises. If you've ever been at a surprise party, you know what I'm talking about. Before the surprisee starts smiling politely, there's always a moment of dismay that crosses their face as the primitive lizard part of their brain thinks, "I wasn't expecting this! Is this a threat?!" What makes jokes work is a surprise that the audience can quickly make sense of. In that moment of sensemaking, we get the joke and laugh at this new connection or idea that we didn't foresee but now understand.

That leap of understanding is where the joke lives, and the purpose of a premise is to give the audience everything they need—and as little else as possible—to take that leap into the waiting arms of comedy. This connection between comedy and understanding is beautifully illustrated in stand-up Tig Notaro's routine about repeatedly running into the singer Taylor Dane. The two of them do not know each other, and Notaro is increasingly amazed that (a) they keep coincidentally being in the same space, and (b) Notaro can make the exact same comment to Dane every time with Dane never remembering they've met before. The joke here isn't the audience's surprise that Notaro keeps seeing Dane again but rather their growing understanding that it will keep happening. In the version of this bit on her album *Good One*, my favorite laugh comes when, after establishing the pattern, she tells the audience, "You are not going to believe who was sitting there." Notaro waits a moment so that someone in the theater can say out loud, "Taylor Dane?" And she confirms it: "Yeah, it was Taylor Dane. That's exactly who it was." The joke is in the audience getting there first, not because Notaro has tipped the joke (a comedy way of saying "given away the punchline early") but because she has deliberately given them everything they need to make the leap on their own.

A successful audience leap is only possible when a joke is written in accordance with the second principle I'll introduce you to in this book. In the last chapter we talked about the need for brevity, and in this chapter we'll talk about the need for **clarity**. The comedic premise of a joke must be clear to the audience. It's hard to achieve a successful synaptic leap if the audience has to puzzle out the joke they're being told. This means every joke requires both *clarity of communication*—giving the audience everything they need to identify your premise without confusing them—and *clarity of premise itself*, by which I mean having a premise that is understandable in the first place. Clarity will come up repeatedly in this book (it's really very important!); for instance, another form of clarity is having a clear idea of who your audience is, something we'll talk about much later. But in this chapter we'll focus on the principle of clarity as it relates to building a premise.

Mighty Premises from Little Points Grow

If the premise of a joke is how you lead your audience to the point, it stands to reason that your joke *has* a point. Let's think of some points you might want to make in your comedy, thoughts you might want to express. "Rich people are inbred morons." "Living with roommates is difficult." "Stereotypes are destructive." I don't hear you laughing at these, and not just because you can't hear through books. I don't hear you laughing because they're not funny. And when a point isn't funny, audiences aren't interested in hearing it (unless they already agree with you, which kind of defeats some of the purpose, as we'll see later in the chapter on satire). Like a clear structure—which can be used for good or evil in comedy—a strong premise can make the audience laugh, opening their heads to whatever thoughts you want to pour in there. As actor and improv legend Joe Flaherty said, "It was always most important to make the audience laugh. After that you could make social comments, or make a point, anything, but first and most important make sure it's funny."

To make a point funny, it goes without saying that you need to find a humorous way of expressing it to the audience instead of just stating it baldly. Take that bald point and put some comedy hair on it! And by "comedy hair" I mean one or more of the basic techniques of humor construction. Which sounds boring, I know, so you can see why I called it "comedy hair." These basic techniques include the following:

Exaggeration: Taking something out of proportion to a funny extreme. Example: humorist Jean Kerr explaining how she and her husband prepare to write together by saying, "We first of all locate the four children and threaten them with violence and sudden death if they come near us." It's clear that she's speaking hyperbolically and wouldn't really kill her children.

Congruity/incongruity: Juxtaposing or combining two unrelated things, thus forcing us to find a connection between them, *or* juxtaposing two seemingly related things, forcing us to see the difference between them. This is the technique that underlies most wordplay and is what Samuel Johnson must have meant when he described wit as "the unexpected copulation of ideas." Example: Groucho Marx in *Duck Soup* telling Margaret Dumont, "You can leave in a taxi. If you can't get a taxi, you can leave in a huff. If that's too soon, you can leave in a minute and a huff." Here, Groucho takes the idea of leaving "in" something, and the not-quite-homonyms "huff" and "half," to force our brains to make sense of phrases that sound like they *should* make sense together but don't.

Revelation: Holding back a piece of information that changes the meaning of the information we already have. Example: last chapter's Michelle Buteau joke. Another example: in the film *The Goat*, when Buster Keaton, running from the police, hops aboard a train caboose—only for the rest of the train to pull away, revealing the caboose isn't connected and Buster isn't going anywhere. Our expectations have been thwarted in a way writer Nell Scovell describes as "the twist you never saw coming, but once it arrives, it makes total sense."

Reversal: A subset of revelation, when something we're shown or told is followed by new information that disproves or undercuts the previous information. Example: on the sitcom *Abbot Elementary*, when a self-serious character tells us about how important the work of local news is . . . *right before* we're shown a local news broadcast about a dog riding in a remote-control car.

Shock: A surprise that upends our expectations either because something truly unpredictable happens or a taboo topic is addressed. Example: the short film/ TV experiment *Too Many Cooks*, in which the bland opening sequence of a seemingly generic TV sitcom is continually transformed in ways that seem random (it suddenly becomes a cartoon) and disturbing (the cast is hunted down by a machete-wielding cannibal).

Comedic dramatic irony: The old chestnut where the audience is aware of information that the joke teller or character is seemingly ignorant of, allowing us to laugh at the character's misunderstanding and anticipate the moment when they'll learn what we already know. Example: the picture book *Sam and Dave Dig a Hole* by Mac Barnett and Jon Klassen, in which Sam and Dave keep digging *around* increasingly large diamonds they don't realize are buried near them but which we, the readers, can see clearly.

Recognition: Playing off a shared frame of reference by describing something we recognize from real life. Example: Robertson Davies in the novel *Tempest-Tost* describing "a couple of janitors who were, as school janitors so often are, mopping at something invisible in the corridors." Or a reference to a thing we at the very least have heard of. Example: Samantha Irby writing, "And, when your dad corners me to talk about sports, I'll win him over, because I've seen enough of Skip Bayless to fake my way through a convincing conversation about Ezekiel Elliott's rushing yards last season."

Repetition: Imbuing something with humor—or heightening the humor of a joke—by repeating it. Example: when Sideshow Bob on *The Simpsons* steps on a rake, causing it to hit him in the face, to which he reacts with a grunt of annoyance. This is mildly funny on its own. But it becomes very funny when it happens multiple times in a row and he reacts with the same annoyed grunt each time (which segues into a revelation-based joke when the camera pans out and we see that he's walking through an area simply covered in rakes).

The list above is exhausting without being exhaustive. It's very likely I've forgotten, or never even heard of, some other comedy techniques. (Comedy writer Scott Dikkers has his own list of such techniques, for example, which he refers to as "Funny Filters.") Jokes are works of human imagination, though, so I'm happy if they elude the rigidity of taxonomic systems. Still, my point—which I've failed to make funny—is that these kinds of techniques can be applied to just about any point you'll want to make in order to create a premise that communicates that point in a funny way. Which technique do you use? The one that will express your idea the most clearly.

Remember those points that we wanted to make earlier but didn't know how to make them funny? The members of Monty Python applied exaggeration to express the point that "rich people are inbred morons" in the premise of their "Upper Class Twit of the Year" sketch, in which grotesque men compete in tests of idiocy and entitlement ranging from walking in a straight line to backing their car over an old lady. The writer/performers Taika Waititi and Jemaine Clement applied congruity/incongruity to the point that "living with roommates is difficult" to create the premise of *What We Do in the Shadows*, wherein the roommates are also different types of vampires. Filmmakers Vera Chytilova and Ester Krumbachova took the point "stereotypes are destructive" and applied exaggeration and shock to create the premise for their satirical 1966 film *Daisies*, in which two young women rampage through Prague feigning coyness so they can con older men into buying them expensive meals.

In each of these cases, the premise of the work illustrates the point for its audience without coming out and saying the point, leaving a gap in understanding for the audience to fill in themselves. While they fill that gap, they laugh. One practical method for generating such premises is to take a point and start asking "What if?" questions. "What if those rich morons competed to see who was the best at being the worst?" "What if the roommates were literally bloodthirsty?" "What if women weaponized the stereotypes that confine them?" Pretty much any comic premise can be reverse engineered into a "What if?" question. For example, if we look back at my *Star Wars* sex joke (which I'm sure is *not* getting old by this point), we can see that I might have asked myself, "What if I had to describe how babies are made? What if the only frame of reference I felt comfortable with was *Star Wars*?" A good way to brainstorm premises is by asking yourself "What if?" questions about the point you want to make.

A Disclaimer on Points, Premises, and Chronological Order

Before we get too deep into this chapter (he said, already quite deep into the chapter), let me be clear that when you're writing a joke, you may not always start out knowing the point you want to make. You may just see something and think, "That's funny." A premise may pop into your head before you know what the premise is communicating. Chuck Jones talks about being inspired by Mark Twain's description of a coyote to create the character of Wile E. Coyote. He didn't think, "How do I illustrate the theme of repetitive overconfidence leading to failure? A coyote!" But a funny joke always ends up having *some* point to it, even if it's an obscure point that's hard to dig out, or a point so basic that you're reinforcing something everybody knows already.

Even the zaniest jokes have points. Take the scene in the parody western *Blazing Saddles* where a group of cowboys sit around a campfire eating beans and farting a lot. It seems pointless, but it's one of many instances in which the film makes the point that traditional westerns leave out the ugly aspects of the past. Most of the joke premises in the movie make this point in regard to racism; this joke just happens to make it through flatulence.

There's a great book about playwriting called *The Art of Dramatic Writing* by Lajos Egri, who's mainly known for writing that book and having an amazing name that sounds like a deadly Caribbean virus. In his book, Egri talks about how every play has a theme, and so authors start with a theme and come up with a plot to illustrate it. As someone who comes up with plots professionally, let me tell you that this is almost never how it happens. In my experience, you think of a story or character, and then as you work on it a meaningful theme develops. But I think that Egri starts with theme because it feels more logical to say "A writer wants to talk about X, so they say Y" than to say the more realistic "A writer starts saying Y and realizes eventually that they're talking about X." But it's more than OK to start with Y and work backward to X. Not only that, it's natural.

This is all to say that when you read this chapter, keep in mind that joke writing doesn't always happen as "point, then premise, then joke." Sometimes it goes "premise, then joke, then, ah, I see what I'm trying to say here, then rewrite joke." But this is all very theoretical. Let's talk about how developing a premise works in practice.

Developing a Premise

Let's walk step by step through the process of developing a premise for a joke. Personally—as you saw in chapter 1—I *do* like to start with a point and then build a premise from there, because I have a better of sense of how to make a joke work when I know what I want to say through it. Finding what you want to say can feel difficult, but it's really just a matter of identifying something you feel is strange, frustrating, or illogical about the world. As the stand-up Bob Newhart said regarding the way his work undermined things like advertising and military bravado, "It was in my gut; these things upset me." So identify something that bugs you, and don't worry about whether it's a funny thing to feel that way about.

For my part, I'll start with "Humans are destroying the planet," which is something that infuriates me. This is a pretty basic point that many people know right now, but it certainly bears repeating because for my audience—humans—it's so much easier to go through life and do everyday stuff if you *don't* think about it. It's also not particularly funny. Perfect!

So my mission is to figure out how to communicate or illustrate this point in a funny premise, because I can't just say "We're destroying the planet" and keep anyone's interest. The first thing I do is look at different aspects of the situation to come up with ideas for possible premises. Not full-blown jokes, but just the ideas for jokes: How do I think God would feel about this? We only have one planet; or do we? What do the other animals think of the way this one animal (us) is messing up the place?

Concepts in hand, I then begin auditioning the kind of "What if?" questions mentioned above. What if humanity was like a teenager wrecking the house while God was away and worried about what He was going to say when He got back? What if this was just our "training earth" that we were learning on so we would know how to handle the "grown-up earth" we'd actually live on one day? What if the rats and cockroaches of the world were envious of us because we're so much better at being destructive vermin than they are?

I like that last idea because it's the least straightforward. It's not stating my point outright, but if I can get the audience thinking about humans from a different perspective—using the congruity/incongruity between human habits and the habits of animals we see as gross and destructive—then maybe I can induce them to make the leap to my point on their own. In addition, giving animals a chance to talk and complain opens this premise up to a silliness that counterbalances the preachiness of my point. But is there a way to develop that idea even further? To make it more of a comic situation that gives me more angles in which to find jokes? I'm now imagining a situation where one species might feel envy for another species—which is to say, a situation that is surprising or incongruous when applied to animals but carries an emotional dynamic that the audience will grasp quickly. This is how I land on the idea of awards shows. I can reasonably assume that my particular audience (American, media-savvy, and, let's face it, probably as middle-aged as I am) will be aware of how big, glitzy awards shows work. I'll make the premise that rats and cockroaches have lost to humanity yet again in the annual Earthy Awards for Outstanding Vermin.

Now this premise isn't just a point I'm trying to make, or a basic idea, but a scenario that I can see in my head and ask even more "What if?" questions about as I build further jokes off it. What would humanity's proud acceptance speech say about how we wreck everywhere we live? What if the runners-up were resentful? What if the rats were badmouthing us and accusing us of sleeping with Mother Earth to win? What if the cockroaches were acting like yes-men, telling us how great we are, that they voted for us even, in an attempt to get on the winning side? What if Mother Earth hosted the event from her deathbed and ended it all by saying how proud she was of all the contestants: "I'll see you at next year's Last Living Microbe on a Now Barren Rock Floating Silently in Space Awards!"

A little heavy-handed? Sure. But if I were writing it for real, I'd take time to work out the jokes so they didn't all feel like they were so on the nose. The point is, I tried to develop my premise systematically, and then I picked it up, turned it over, and even shook it a little to see if anything fell out in order to get every extra idea from it that I could.

Once you have your premise, don't be afraid to write up a very rough draft of your joke (or routine or sketch, since the preceding example snowballed into a multijoke beast). But then take a moment to ask yourself some more questions about it: Is this premise really expressing the point that I mean to express? If so, am I expressing my point clearly? Or am I expressing it *too* clearly, without leaving that gap for the audience to comprehend the joke in?

Weak Premises; Or, Sometimes I Waste Time on Ideas That Stink

Usually, a weak premise's problem is a lack of clarity. Often this can happen when a writer confuses a clever *idea* for an actual joke premise with an understandable point behind it. When I was a younger, less weathered man, I spent more time than I'd like to admit trying to work out an audio-only bit about a radio show featuring a performance by a mute ventriloquist. I had learned that *The Edgar Bergen/Charlie McCarthy Show*, starring ventriloquist Edgar Bergen and his puppet Charlie McCarthy, had been a hit radio show for many years. This seemed weird to me, since the whole point of ventriloquism is to be able to see the ventriloquist *not* moving their lips when they talk. I wanted to take this a step further and have a performance by a ventriloquist who couldn't talk at all, meaning the audience at home would hear stretches of silence, followed by the clacking of the puppet's wooden mouth, and then more silence, followed by occasional laughs and bursts of applause from the studio audience at the radio station.

I could never get this idea to work, partly because "Ventriloquism is a weird fit for the radio" is a point not particularly worth making. It was also partly because I couldn't find a way to clearly communicate the premise without just having an announcer stating it outright, in which case the description "mute ventriloquist" would already be the whole joke and anything after that would be unnecessary. At best, the concept was a semiclever idea, but without the qualities it needed to be a complete premise. I realize now that a stronger premise would have been a ventriloquist who *can* talk but explains that his puppet is mute, allowing the audience to fill in the understanding that he's just doing this to make his job easier. Now the joke is actually about something: the shortcuts people take even though they ruin the thing they're doing.

Ultimately, of course, the joke was actually on me because years before I was born, Albert Brooks had already done a far more hilarious routine about a terrible ventriloquist act that made a very similar point about the empty illusions of show business. Absorbing a lot of comedy is a good way to figure out your premises, too, by learning what's already been done and therefore doesn't need to be bothered with.

Keep in mind, though, that *clarity* of premise doesn't have to mean *simplicity* of premise. A premise can be complicated as long as those complications are communicated clearly to the audience. A great example of this is the sketch "Pre-taped Call-In Show" from the HBO series *Mr. Show*. In this sketch, the host of a television call-in show that tapes its episodes one week in advance becomes enraged when the people calling in can't understand that they shouldn't be asking him about the topic on the episode they're watching right now, which was taped last week, but should be asking instead about the topic of the episode they're taping now, which will air next week. That description may be confusing, but the sketch's writing is handled so deftly that its premise is clear from the beginning. The name of the show-within-the-sketch is "The Pre-taped Call-In Show" (not something jokey but unhelpful, like "United States of Talkmerica" or "Next Week Tonight"), and the show's host opens by saying, "We tape all our shows a week in advance." With things set up so clearly, we can enjoy seeing the host dealing with callers tripped up by the premise ("What's going on? I mean, you're doing a show about pet care, but everyone's talking about racism") without getting tripped up by it ourselves. We can also see clearly that the ultimate joke isn't the confused nature of the show's premise but the host's furious inability to understand why his callers are confused. Not knowing how the sketch was written, I have to assume the writers took great pains both to understand how the premise would function and to communicate that understanding to the audience.

Finally, there's one last question to ask yourself about your premise, one phrased well by *Mr. Show* cocreator Bob Odenkirk: "Is it funny? Really, truly *funny*? Or do we just *think* it's funny because we really *want* it to be funny?" To answer this requires finding that balance in yourself between being brutally honest and also having faith in your own sense of humor. If you have faith, then even a complicated premise's humor can be realized fully. If you're being honest, when an audience tells you the premise doesn't work, you have to listen. And if you're being *brutally* honest, a mute ventriloquist just isn't very funny.

Where to Find Premises

Let's say you want or need to write a joke, but you don't have some big point that you desperately need to share with the world or an idea for something that could be funny. This is a situation professional comedy writers will often find themselves in: "I need to write, and I have a deadline, but don't know what to write about." This is fine. As fancy-pants historian Jacques Barzun once wrote, "No writer has ever lived who did not at some time or other get stuck." When I'm having trouble generating premises, I reflect on two things comedian/banjo player Steve Martin says in his memoir *Born Standing Up*:

> I laugh in life . . . so why not observe what it is that makes me laugh?
>
> Comedy is a distortion of what is happening, and there will always be something happening.

In those two lines he's boiled down the art of identifying potential premises. The seeds of premises are planted by what you observe and how you feel about it, based in who you are. (We'll go further into who *you* are in the next chapter. And I'll say it now: You should be ashamed of yourself.) The long-running satirical newspaper *The Onion* makes regular use of premises based on shared, fairly universal experiences in headlines like "Dad Hands Phone Off to Mom Immediately After Being Wished Happy Father's Day" and "Neighbor Arriving Home at Same Time Offers Brief, Beguiling Glimpse Inside Apartment." With each of these articles the basic premise is "What if the news reported on the mundane things that many of us have experienced?" It's a combination of recognition, incongruity, and exaggeration that works really well over and over again. *Onion* headlines are, in essence, well-stated premises, and a good place to look to get the hang of premise building.

On the other hand, premises can also be based on offering unique, individual perspectives to audiences who might not share that experience. In her 2009 stand-up special *I'ma Be Me*, Wanda Sykes builds a premise from her specific experience of being Black and gay, saying, "It's harder being gay than it is being Black. . . . I didn't have to come out Black. I didn't have to sit my parents down and tell them about my Blackness." Sykes then acts out a hypothetical "coming out as Black" conversation with her parents, as well as their horrified reaction: "The Bible says Adam and Eve, not Adam and Mary J. Blige!" By using incongruity (forcing one type of experience to seem like another) and recognition (playing off the audience's familiarity with the hateful "Adam and Eve, not Adam and Steve" slogan), Sykes creates the clear premise "What if I'd had to come out as Black the same way I did as gay?" in order to communicate a point, based on her personal experience.

Because we contain multitudes, the following will fly in the face of what I said earlier about Albert Brooks already covering the topic of ventriloquism: It's OK to make a point that another joke has made before. It's rarely acceptable to repurpose a preexisting joke premise (unless it's incredibly old and you're adding a knowing spin, like how people keep taking Shakespeare's plots and setting them in space or on the West Side or whatever). But because each of us sees the world differently, similar points can be said and resaid through very different premises, resulting in different jokes.

For example, the stand-ups George Carlin and Ismo Leikola both built jokes around the basic point that the American rules for vulgar language are illogical. In the hands of Carlin, a native English speaker with a lot of aggression inside him, it becomes the premise of his "Seven Dirty Words You Can't Say on Television" routine, in which he goes after the idea that a word can be "bad" ("Those are the ones that'll infect your soul, curve your spine, and keep the country from winning the war") and shows how arbitrary and illusory the line is between polite and rude language ("You can prick your finger, but don't finger your prick"). Ismo, on the other hand, being a Finnish native who seems more befuddled than angry, develops a premise about the confusing use of the word "ass" ("Sometimes if you add 'ass' to something it can actually reverse the meaning of the original word. . . . 'Bad' is bad, but 'bad-ass?' Good.

But not always. Like, 'dumb-ass' is still dumb! So how can you know?"). Both of these routines have the same basic point: that the rules of language are a self-contradicting fiction. But because their different premises develop from different voices, nobody would say they're the same joke.

Many of these premises boil down to a simple question: "What if this thing that bothers me, hurts me, or seems curiously illogical to me were looked at *differently*?" The joke is illustrating or answering that question in a way that shares that bothered/hurt/illogical feeling with the audience but makes the audience do a little of the work of understanding, which spurs them to laugh at it. This is the alchemy of comedy and one of its great powers: helping us process the frustrations of the world collectively. Or, as the science fiction and fantasy author Gene Wolfe writes way more eloquently than I ever will, "so powerful is the charm of words, which for us reduces to manageable entities all the passions that would otherwise madden and destroy us." This is the job done by a good premise.

The Truth, Some Truth, and Often None of the Truth

Each of the examples in the previous section deals in some way with a shared or individual sense of the nature of reality. In a way, they can be seen as expressing a feeling of truth held by the joke writer. "This is a thing that exists. Here is one way of processing it." But how beholden is a joke's premise to expressing an objective, factually accurate truth? Every year or so, a debate about this very issue reignites in the world of comedy. Some comedians argue that the premises of their jokes are only meant to express emotional truths and shouldn't be held to the standards of literal truth. Others assert that a joke's job is to confront the world with uncomfortable truths, but they defend themselves when they are challenged for being offensive or fudging specific facts by saying they are "just telling jokes."

Nobody has asked my opinion about any of this. I am, however, going to give it to you anyway, because it gets at the heart of my thinking about when premises work and when they don't.

For a joke premise to work, it must connect at least a little bit with the audience's understanding of reality. It has to relate in some manner, even a skewed one, to something that feels true. The stand-up Mitch Hedberg told a joke I love about how it takes way too long to cook a baked potato, saying, "Sometimes I'll just throw one in there, even if I don't want one, because by the time it's done, who knows?" Do I think Hedberg ever actually did that? No. But I do agree that potatoes take a long time to cook. I also enjoy this tweet from @KimmyMonte:

> football and soccer are like gimme the ball i want that ball but baseball is all like fuck this ball get rid of it i hate it

Is this literally true? No, the fielding team in baseball desperately wants to get that ball. And once a soccer or football player has the ball, they want to get rid of it into the goal. But this very silly joke is somewhat true enough for me to laugh at it. And even though neither this joke nor Hedberg's is literally true, the points they make ("It's hard to plan ahead" and "Sports rules can be confusing") *feel* true.

Jokes don't have to be factually accurate in order to make someone laugh. The funny thing that a comedian said they saw "the other day" didn't actually happen the other day. It may not have happened at all. That's OK. Comedy isn't reporting, no matter how often it's called upon to perform that role when actual quality journalism is unavailable. But at the same time, the potato- and sports-based examples above are silly jokes meant purely for amusement. They have the same function as fictional entertainment and don't deserve to be fact-checked, just as you wouldn't fact-check *Star Wars* (or any *Star Wars*–based sexual practices I claim to indulge in). But there are other jokes, which I would refer to as "serious jokes," that are intended to make serious, actionable, persuasive, and often political arguments. In my mind these play by slightly different rules and must stand up to a level of fact-checking. The degree of truth necessary for a premise is directly proportional to the intended purpose of the joke.

A silly joke is inconsequential. It doesn't really matter if the audience walks away thinking Mitch Hedberg would just throw a potato in the oven at random. But if a joke is intended to change your mind—to convince you to think a certain way or vote a certain way—then the joke writer has a greater responsibility to accurately represent true, factual reality, and the audience has a greater right to expect to be able to verify those facts. This is a matter of basic honesty, which is another form of clarity. Laughter can be built on air, but more serious emotions—not to mention more serious intentions—require firmer foundations.

Of course, some kinds of truth *are* subjective. They depend on your personal experience of the world—where you're from, what you've been through, the things you've learned and hold in your head. These are also the elements that may be motivating you to start writing jokes in the first place. So now that we know a little about the hard sciences of structure and premise, let's take a dive into the soft science of the intangible soul that lies at the heart of every joke: voice.

4
Voice

WHEN YOU'RE A WORKING JOKE WRITER, you end up writing for many different kinds of people. Late-night comedians. Game-show hosts. Medieval peasants. Robots. Easily confused cats. Spider-Man. A pirate's severed head. Various guys from New Jersey. Doing this well requires two things: (1) a fairly loose grip on reality and (2) the ability to recognize and work with the most fundamental element of comedy: voice.

What Is Voice?

Every joke has a teller, which we can define as "whoever tells the joke." (Let me know if I'm going too fast for you.) The way that teller tells a joke, their choice of what to joke about, and what the joke tells us about the way they see the world—these are the things that make up a **voice**. So the first question you have to ask before you write a joke is, "Who is telling this joke?" And before we go any further, don't assume "telling a joke" or "having a voice" means "talking." Buster Keaton has a different voice from Harpo Marx, who has a different voice from Mr. Bean, who has a different voice from Charlie Chaplin's Little Tramp, who has a different voice from Teller, and none of them ever talk all that much.

The *Garfield* strip from April 14, 2023, expresses a clear comic voice.

To get a better sense of what voice is, let's pretend we're scientists and look at two examples of voice while eliminating as many variables as we can. For example, take two print cartoons about owning a difficult pet. One will be the *Garfield* comic strip by Jim Davis for the day I'm writing this, April 14, 2023. In three panels, we see Garfield the cat looking on as his owner Jon Arbuckle hangs upside-down from the ceiling while talking to Liz, Garfield's vet (and possibly Jon's lover? I don't know why else a vet is hanging around her client's house). Jon says, from the ceiling, "You're probably wondering how this happened." Liz replies, "Not really," and Garfield thinks, as he looks at us, the audience, "She's catching on to this place."

Now, yes, *Garfield* is the most mainstream, down-the-middle comic strip there is—endlessly merchandised, its edges smoothed. But that doesn't mean it doesn't have a specific comic voice. The characters are deadpan but unsubtle; the drawing style is plain, undetailed, and cute; Jon is embarrassed but unharmed; and even though we don't know exactly how Jon ended up suspended from the ceiling (the premise's element of missing information that lets the audience leap to comprehension), the story of the cartoon is pretty straightforward.

"His final Internet search was 'insane monkey how make calm down.'"

This Edward Steed cartoon published in *The New Yorker* on January 17, 2022, exemplifies a very different comic voice from that of the *Garfield* cartoon shown earlier. Edward Steed / *The New Yorker* Collection / The Cartoon Bank.

Now let's compare that to the one-panel *New Yorker* cartoon by Edward Steed from January 17, 2022. It shows a pair of detectives surveying a room that has been completely ransacked, where a man with torn clothes and scratches lies on the floor, apparently dead. The caption is "His final Internet search was 'insane monkey how make calm down.'" This cartoon is still somewhat deadpan, but the drawing style is rough, scratchy, and cluttered. Steed's style has been described as "primitive savagery, as if the cartoonist himself were enraged as he drew the cartoon"—in no way cute or easily merchandisable. His pet owner has been murdered, and it takes a moment for us to put together what's happened when we view the cartoon. I personally find this cartoon to be the funnier of the two.

In both cartoons the teller is expressing a cynical message about the power dynamic between pet animals and their owners, in which the animals rebel violently against their human jailers. But the tellers have different personalities and different ways of expressing their point—in other words, different voices. The result is that they affect their audiences differently, or they affect different audiences similarly—it's unlikely the same reader is chuckling over both of these cartoons, even though they're both basically saying, "Pets hate us!" Each has a specific voice expressed in a specific way to tell a specific joke. And if it seems like I'm using the word "specific" a lot, it's because before we can talk about the nuts and bolts of voice, we've got to discuss the importance of specificity. And for that, I'm going to need a new subheading.

What, Generally, Is Specificity?

Pick a blade of grass and look at it. No, *really* look at it, the way characters talk about in comedies about drugs. The closer you look, the better you see that you're not just holding a generic "blade of grass." You're holding one specific blade of grass with individual qualities and features that set it apart from all the other trillions of blades of grass in the world. Reality, it turns out, is specific.

And since comedy functions best when it reflects reality, something specific is typically funnier than something vague. Details make things funnier. This concept is called **specificity**, and it hangs over all good joke writing like your late uncle's vengeful ghost demanding you catch his murderers before you can inherit his fortune. See how specific that analogy was? So much easier to understand than if I'd said something like "specificity suffuses comedy as a general principle."

It's just plain easier for an audience to understand and digest something specific. And so, paradoxically, as comedian Cristela Alonzo has described it, "The more specific you are, the more universal it can be." Vagueness obstructs understanding. This might feel counterintuitive, but let's try it out. Picture a shirt. Now picture a red button-down shirt with ruffled sleeves and little hearts all over it. The second one was easier to see, wasn't it? The same concept explains why it's less funny to say "Have you ever eaten so much that your tummy hurt?" than it is to say "You ever sadness-chugged so much Ben & Jerry's Chocolate Fudge Brownie that you felt like you might be pregnant?"

In writing a joke, you should be taking advantage of every opportunity to be specific. Any word that *can* be referring to a specific thing *should* be referring to a specific thing. Take this line from author Sarah Vowell's book *The Partly Cloudy Patriot*, in which she describes the people of Gettysburg, Pennsylvania, ignoring the anniversary of the Gettysburg Address: "Around the corner, the citizens of Gettysburg stand in line at the Majestic Theater for the 2:10 showing of *Meet the Parents*." If she'd just said "People are going to the movies," it would have expressed the same basic point, but what makes this sentence *funny* is the specific details of that scene—that these people are "citizens" possessing certain civic responsibilities, the aggrandizing name of the theater, and, most exquisitely, "the 2:10 showing of *Meet the Parents*," because nothing is more unlike President Lincoln honoring the Union army's hallowed dead than watching Ben Stiller launch a champagne cork into the urn containing his future father-in-law's mother's ashes, which a cat then pees on.

Specificity doesn't just make jokes funnier; it also makes jokes easier to write. This also sounds counterintuitive. After all, shouldn't it be easier to write something basic like "shirt" than to have to come up with a bunch of specific details like "ruffled sleeves and little hearts all over it"? Well, not really. Because, at least in my experience, thinking in specifics has the effect of charging up your imagination—one specific detail inspires another, which inspires another—whereas thinking in generalities leaves my imagination cold. In fact, if you're ever having trouble working out a joke, I find it helps to start plugging in specific details. The first ones that come to mind may not end up being the best choices, but they'll help you shape your joke, allowing you to replace them with the second or third or even fifty-eighth ones that come to mind, if that's how many attempts it takes to get the joke right.

Which brings us back to voice. It's hard to write a joke without having a specific voice in mind. If I say, "Write a joke for a psychotic gerbil" (something I've done), it means briefly putting yourself into the mindset of a psychotic gerbil, which you've probably never done before. But at least you've got "psychotic" and "gerbil" to point you in the right direction for a subject (something a gerbil would deal with) and an attitude (psychotic). If I say, "Write a joke for somebody," it means briefly putting yourself into mindset of "somebody." "Somebody" doesn't have a mindset. There's nothing specific about them. They don't exist, and that gives you no foundation, no direction, and ultimately no jokes.

The Sub-elements of Voice

Voice is the unique, specific way that a joke teller expresses themself (or itself) when telling a joke, and it emerges from the combination of a few different factors. Let's take the concept of "voice" and fire a champagne cork at it so we can crack that sucker open and see everything inside before a cat pees on it. Voice is made up of these components:

- frame of reference
- perspective
- sensibility
- style

Each of these aspects of a voice answers a vital question about the voice's specifics, and those answers combine to answer the biggest question: "Who is telling this joke?" Asking yourself these questions is a good way of defining the voice within which you're writing.

Frame of reference answers the question "Where is this voice coming from?" It's the world the voice emerges from and exists within, informing the voice's assumptions about reality. When Homer Simpson demands that his brain explain to him how a twenty-dollar bill can buy peanuts, the joke is operating from a frame of reference that takes for granted certain assumptions about capitalism and how brains work. When Bugs Bunny's plummeting airplane stops just before hitting the ground because he's out of gas thanks to his "A" ration card, the joke is operating within a frame of reference that assumes a certain familiarity with government control of private gasoline use on the American home front during World War II. And in *Reservation Dogs*, when the spirit of Elora's newly dead grandmother warns her not to give away her blue willow dish set, the joke is operating in a specific Indigenous cultural frame of reference in which communicating with a spirit is less notable than the spirit's attachment to a (specific) set of dishes.

In each of these cases, the joke teller doesn't take time to explain the joke's frame of reference to the audience. Why would they? A frame of reference is built on assumptions—things accepted by the teller as true, or at least commonly understood by them and their intended audience. Every successful joke has a frame of reference embedded within it, one that contains the conditions that make the joke's humor possible. The movies *Waiting for Guffman* and *What We Do in the Shadows* are very similar movies: mock documentaries about cringey but endearing characters with whom the audience is led to sympathize while also laughing at their absurdity. But one of them exists in the world of small-town community theater and the other exists in the world of vampires. From those two different frames of reference spring very different sets of jokes (and also different premises, if you want to drag the previous chapter into it). Whether an audience responds to those jokes depends in large part on their familiarity with those frames of reference.

That familiarity can't be taken for granted. We'll talk later about knowing your audience, but a big part of that is having a sense of the frame of reference they may be bringing to your work. If an audience member doesn't "get" a joke, it's often because the joke failed to adequately communicate an assumption the audience member doesn't already share. But that doesn't mean jokes can only be told to audiences with the same frame of reference as the joke writer. Two of my favorite sketches from the TV show *A Black Lady Sketch Show* depict the "Basic Ball" and "Funeral Ball," drag-style competitions that showcase performances of "realness" in portraying unglamorous people ("too depressed to leave the house," "barbecue daddies," "running errands"), or the types of people who show up at Black funerals ("I just came for the food at the repast," "we thought you'd die way before him," "secret wives"). Part of the joke is in seeing the competitors preening and being judged as though at a drag ball, but most of the joke comes from the ultraspecific types of people or behaviors they're referencing. Some of the references in these sketches don't apply to my personal frame of reference. But the jokes are written with such clarity (remember our old friend *clarity* from last chapter?) that their ultraspecificity becomes part of the humor. By being so specific, the sketch is communicating—and to a certain sense universalizing—assumptions the audience (in this case, me) may not share but can still understand when given the information to understand them.

One of the unfortunate stereotypes about humor is that the older a joke is, the less funny it becomes. It's more accurate to say that the older a joke is, the less likely it is to speak to a modern audience's frame of reference. But a well-written old joke can still overcome this obstacle. There's a joke in Laurence Sterne's 1759 novel *Tristram Shandy* that I love, even though I have no idea what the narrator is talking about:

> A man's body and his mind . . . are exactly like a jerkin, and a jerkin's lining;—rumple the one—you rumple the other. There is one certain exception however in this case, and that is, when you are so fortunate a fellow, as to have had your jerkin made of gum-taffeta, and the body-lining to it of sarcenet, or thin persian.

I barely know what a jerkin is, and I have no idea what gum-taffeta, sarcenet, or thin persian are. But it's very funny to me that the narrator almost immediately undercuts his serious metaphor about body and mind with a very literal exception that obviously means something *to him*, a man who knows what jerkins are made of. Sterne is making a pointed joke about this self-defeating narrator by using a specific reference to clothes, and the specificity still makes the joke funnier even if those specifics lie outside our frame of reference. Just as structure tells an audience how to laugh at a joke they may not fully understand, your audience will also better understand what you're joking about when *you* understand what you're joking about. And that brings us to the next part of constructing a comedic voice.

A voice's frame of reference begets its **perspective**, the element that answers the question "How does this voice see the world?" Perspective is the angle from which a voice looks at and judges the world, informed by its specific frame of reference. To put it more simply, if the joke teller is an escapee from a lunatic asylum, and frame of reference is the Burger King dumpster they're hiding in, then perspective is their view of the parking lot as they peer out from under the lid of the dumpster. OK, maybe that wasn't the simplest way I could have put it.

Let me try again. If your joke teller is a lighthouse, then the frame of reference is the rocky shore it stands on, and perspective is the beam of light it uses to illuminate the surroundings for passing ships (i.e., the audience). It's the way a voice sees things, and that act of illumination requires applying your perspective to a topic so you can generate a new, interesting, or funny thought about it. In their book *Only Joking*, Jimmy Carr and Lucy Greeves describe perspective like this: "A comic goes through life constantly on the lookout for the funny angle. . . . Jerry Seinfeld describes the comedian as a person with a 'third eye,' constantly watching the proceedings with a certain ironic detachment." That detachment from a subject is necessary in order to see it clearly enough to find the funny thing about it. Which means a comic voice has to create distance between itself and the topic—even if that topic is the comedian themself—in order to see it more clearly and find the funny aspect of it that everyone else has missed. After all, how useful is a lighthouse that's only a couple of inches from the thing it's pointing its light at?

Film historian Gerald Mast wrote about how comic detachment allows us to "make connections, see parallels, become aware of ironies, [and] perceive contradictions, consequences, causes and effects." In some ways, the work of a comedy writer is to use detachment to find, and then show to the audience, a new way of seeing things. One of my favorite examples of this is a line from Douglas Adams's novel *The Hitchhiker's Guide to the Galaxy*, in which he works from a cosmically expansive frame of reference to gain a perspective outside of human civilization, writing about Earth:

> Most of the people living on it were unhappy for pretty much of the time. Many solutions were suggested for this problem, but most of these were largely concerned with the movements of small green pieces of paper, which is odd because on the whole it wasn't the small green pieces of paper that were unhappy.

If there's any aspect of life most of us take for granted, it's the importance of money (that's why it's funny that Homer needs his brain to explain it to him). By taking a galactic-scale perspective, Adams gets outside of that taken-for-grantedness to make a joke that invites the audience to see just how arbitrary this supposedly important thing is.

At the same time, however, Adams doesn't create so much distance from the humanity that he doesn't notice the green pieces of paper at all. A lighthouse isn't useful if it's too close, but it isn't useful if it's a hundred miles from the shore, either. In writing jokes about a topic, one of the parameters to work within is figuring out the distance from the topic that best allows you to see it in full while keeping it in focus. Too much detachment or too little detachment will both cause you to overlook the real idea or point of a joke—as well as creating too big a disconnect between you and your audience. Remember, Adams was well aware that though he was writing about the galaxy, he was writing about it for an audience of humans with human frames of reference and perspectives. When you're working on a joke, step back far enough from the topic to see what other people miss about it, but not so far that you lose sight of the topic, or of how other people relate to it, entirely.

Detachment in comedy often comes from some form of alienation on the part of the writer. Some people are born alienated outsiders, some people achieve alienation, and some people have alienation thrust upon them, as Shakespeare would have said if he'd written this book. For those truly excluded from the social, cultural, or economic mainstream, ironic detachment may come more naturally. But you don't have to be a literal outsider to apply your perspective from outside of a topic in order to generate new insights or ideas. The human mind is powerful enough to analyze anything, even itself. It's how I was able to develop the joke-farming process I explained in chapter 1. You may not notice *every* funny aspect of something, but if you approach a topic from genuine investigative curiosity, rather than relying on commonly held assumptions, you're likely to find the funny aspect that your perspective can highlight.

It may not be the funny aspect that someone with a different perspective would find. But one of the exciting things about perspectives is that there are so many of them, which means the variety of jokes is potentially endless. As we saw, two people from different countries can look at American English vulgarity and find totally different jokes in it.

So we know where a voice comes from and how it sees the world. When are we going to talk about "What does this voice think is funny?" Right now, because that's the question answered by a voice's **sensibility**. You could say sensibility is a voice's taste in jokes—the kind of joke a voice tells most naturally, which develops into a disposition for certain types of material that end up defining what that voice "does" for the audience. For example, *I Love Lucy* and *Girls* are both sitcoms about women dealing with the limits that reality sets on their ambitions, but the jokes on *Girls* rarely take the form of shouted one-liners, and the characters on *I Love Lucy* rarely have loud sex (I'd say never, but I haven't seen all the episodes). Both shows' voices have their own specific sensibility that is shaped by, and also constrains, the subject matter of their jokes and how those jokes are told.

Finally, **style** answers the question "How does this voice express itself?" How does it use the formal elements of communication to share the perspective informed by its frame of reference and defined by its sensibility? This is the surface level of voice, the thing most of us probably would think of most immediately when we hear the word "voice." It can be something as straightforward as how a voice uses vocabulary and grammar, as we see in this clash of voices from Percival Everett's novel *I Am Not Sidney Poitier*: "The bully, his name was Clyde, asked me at what I was staring, his precise words being, 'What you starin' at, li'l motherfucker,' the 'li'l motherfucker' saving him from ending a sentence with a preposition." We can pick up a lot about who the narrator and Clyde are from the way Everett has them handle their words—their styles become indicators that we can use to pick up clues about their frame of reference, perspective, and sensibility. And the joke of these clashing styles, the application of the narrator's educated frame of reference to Clyde's vulgar voice, helps us to understand the sensibility of the *novel*'s voice, which finds humor in miscommunication.

Even though I've listed style as the last subelement of voice—with the implied value judgment that it's the least substantive of those elements—it's usually the first impression an audience gets of a voice. Think back to the *Garfield* and Edward Steed cartoons from earlier. Before an audience reads the words, it sees the pictures (cute or disturbing) and forms an expectation of what kind of joke (cute or disturbing) they're about to experience. Before an audience processes what your joke is saying, they'll pick up on how you're saying it, just as we judge a stranger by the way they dress (admit it, you do). It's worth making sure your joke's style is an accurate indicator of its purpose—that a joke's packaging is truthfully advertising the kinds of concepts an audience will find inside it.

Writing for Voices: The Adventure Begins

Since it's a lot easier to write for a specific voice than a generic voice, the first step of writing comedy is to know whose voice you're writing for. (Or, as our inadvertently grammatical friend Clyde would have it, "whose voice you're writing for, li'l motherfucker." That's a kind of joke called a **callback**, a term that I think is pretty self-explanatory.) There are two categories of voice you can write for: "you" and "not you." "Not you" is the larger category.

Writing for Voices: Not You

Here's a rule I like to follow when I'm writing a joke: If I'm writing for a real person, I think of them as a character. If I'm writing for a character, I think of them as a real person. Now let's clear off some counter space so I can unpack that. Writing jokes for a real person requires you to pay close attention to that person's frame of reference, perspective, sensibility, and style—and then flatten it all into a joke unencumbered by all the extra stuff that makes that person human. In writing for Jon Stewart, the host of *The Daily Show with Jon Stewart*, I didn't just write jokes in my own voice and hope he'd like them. I started by trying to understand Jon's voice, spending many hours observing how he performed, but also how he spoke in real life, paying special attention to words and phrases he used frequently and the rhythms of his speech. I'd write down things he'd said that weren't necessarily funny but that gave me a piece of his voice to utilize when I wrote for him. I realize how creepy this may sound, but I didn't invent most of it. I stole these techniques from Robert Schlesinger's book *White House Ghosts: Presidents and Their Speechwriters* when I realized that I was essentially a speechwriter for the president of a TV show.

My ultimate goal was to understand what Jon found funny about the world so that I could replicate that perspective. But along the way I was also seeing that the way Jon spoke in regular life wasn't exactly the same way he spoke onstage. People feel different moods at different times. They often act out of character. Characters, however, never act out of character. (That's why it's called "out of character.") A character's voice must remain consistent and reflect what the audience has accepted as the voice's sensibility, frame of reference, or perspective. You may think of a really funny quantum physics pun, but it would ring false and unfunny coming out of Homer Simpson's mouth. Similarly, I could write a great joke about someone being afraid to tie their shoelaces because they might be little snakes, but it would be weird and off-putting coming from Jon Stewart.

But like I said, in real life people aren't always as consistent as a fictional character must be. If I thought, "How would Jon feel about this as a person?" I could get lost trying to account for every aspect of his personality. But if I thought to myself, "How would 'Jon' feel about this as a comedy persona?" the answer was simpler. (We'll talk more about the way a real-life personality is flattened into a **persona** in chapter 8.) He had established the boundaries of his on-screen voice, and I could work within those.

Of course, when writing for another person you have to be careful not to flatten them *too* much and end up caricaturing them. I was guilty of doing this when I wrote jokes for comedian and *Daily Show* contributor Lewis Black. The boundaries of his angry, impatient, smart-but-not-intellectual voice were very clear, and it was easy to stick to the simplest, most straightforward version of that voice. But perhaps it would have been better if I'd strayed toward those boundaries more often—not crossing them but testing them. Then maybe he would have felt like he was being treated like a person instead of a character and wouldn't have looked annoyed so often when he read my scripts.

When writing for a real person, you have to take a full human being and distill them to the funniest, clearest version of themself. You have the opposite task when writing for a fictional character. You have to take the few distinct characteristics that have been invented for them and make them feel like they belong to a fleshed-out, complicated individual. Just as you would for a real person, when writing for a character, put yourself in their specific mindset and imagine how they would see things if they actually existed—which means filling in the not-yet-imagined gaps by drawing on some of your own experience and emotion. As Chuck Jones said of writing for Daffy Duck, "We mine ourselves, dredge the Daffy in us to the surface, become Daffy, look at the world through Daffy's eyes, speak with Daffy's voice, move with Daffy's peculiar and unique musculature."

A guideline I use in writing jokes for voices other than my own is to remember that almost nobody thinks that they, themself, are weird or irrational. No matter how strange or misguided the character you're writing for is, write for them as if *they* think what they're saying or doing is the most sensible option. One of my favorite types of character is the weird person who thinks they're the only person who *isn't* weird. This category includes Kramer on *Seinfeld*, Tati on *Los Espookys*, Orla in *Derry Girls*, and every member of the Marx Brothers except for Zeppo. Their jokes work best when written with a certain sort of respect, on the part of the writer, for the bizarre, erroneous nonsense the characters are indulging in.

Take, for example, a scene I wrote in the comic book *Spider-Man and the X-Men* no. 2, in which Spider-Man learns that Sauron (a half-man, half-pteranodon with vampire powers—don't worry about it) is turning people into dinosaurs. Spider-Man points out, "With tech like that, you could cure cancer!" to which Sauron replies, "But I don't want to cure cancer. I want to turn people into dinosaurs." The joke here is that Sauron, honestly stating his wants, feels like he is being completely reasonable. It's the rest of the world that's not being reasonable by *not* being dinosaurs! The joke is entirely built on allowing him to state his personal perspective in a way he doesn't see as funny. Because as long as the audience knows the character is telling a joke, it's often better that the character doesn't know that's what they're doing.

Of course, it's possible, and often desirable, to write jokes that test the limits of a character's or a performer's voice—jokes that introduce a new stylistic twist, or a unique addition to their frame of reference, or a surprising nuance to their perspective. *The Simpsons* frequently gets laughs from characters expressing unexpected knowledge (as in Bart's classic defensive line "I am familiar with the works of Pablo Neruda"). But you can't stretch every element at once. Think of voice as a restaurant table that rests on four legs. One of the legs can wobble and you can still eat off that table. But if two or more legs wobble, then dinner is ruined. You can futz with one aspect of voice as long as the other three aspects of voice remain consistent with the teller. On *The Daily Show* we worked within Jon Stewart's frame of reference—which was why there were so many jokes about the New York Mets and the movie *Goodfellas*—but there were times when expanding that frame of reference was extremely welcome, provided the joke in question still fit Jon's sensibility, style, and perspective. In these instances, I thought about writing for Jon as "I am writing the jokes he would have written if he knew this specific thing I know." Early in the Obama presidency, I wrote a joke responding

An unreasonable character doesn't have to know they are telling a joke for the audience to appreciate that joke. From *Spider-Man and the X-Men* no. 2, Marvel Comics, January 28, 2014, written by Elliott Kalan with art by Marco Failla.

to a news report claiming that the children of presidents become social trendsetters, by saying that young Willie Lincoln "got all of America started on the hot new craze, dying of typhoid fever." Did Jon know that Abraham Lincoln had a son named Willie who died of typhoid fever during his father's presidency? I don't know. But it fit the other elements of his voice and wasn't too far outside his frame of reference. And now that I've made that joke *again*, it's probably a good time for me to apologize to the ghost of Abraham Lincoln. I'm sorry, Mr. President. If it'll make you feel better, I give you permission to dunk on one of my kids sometime.

Writing for Voices: You

When I started writing jokes, I found it more challenging to write for my own voice than for someone else's. It was harder for me to step back and get distance from my own ways of thinking and speaking and identify the characteristics that made them unique. An easy *mistake* to make while doing this is to assume your comedic voice is the same as your regular, everyday voice, and so you should just write the way you talk. But while your regular, everyday voice is a good place to start (after all, it's right there waiting for you to use it), through active thought you can mold it into a voice that is funnier and more effective.

To begin, stop thinking of yourself as a person and start thinking of yourself as a character. After all, you're not writing jokes for you, the living person, so much as "you," a version of yourself who exists to create jokes. As memoirist David Sedaris describes it, "In real life, you're a person. Once you're on paper, you're a character—and you have to behave like a character." We'll revisit how this operates in the realm of stand-up in chapter 8, but until then let's sit with the idea of writing for yourself as a specific character with a specific voice that has qualities you can take note of and craft specific jokes for.

Ask the questions about this "you" character that you'd ask about any other comedic voice's frame of reference ("Where do I come from?" "What assumptions do I carry in my thinking?") and perspective ("How do I view the world around me?" "What do I see that others might miss?"). Those questions may feel hugely all-encompassing, but answering them is kind of fun because it essentially calls for you to free-associate your memories, knowledge, and opinions—like therapy, but less expensive. It also invites you to *add* to that store of memories, knowledge, and opinions, which is to say that the more you know and experience, the more fodder you'll have for writing jokes, not to mention the more fulfilling your life will be. After all, as much as I hate to admit it, there's more to being alive than just writing and telling jokes. This is the moment where I implore you to fight the temptation to live always within the ironic detachment needed to identify subjects for humor, lest it become a total detachment from life.

Identifying your sensibility takes similar focused self-examination. It may seem obvious, but literally ask yourself "What do I think is funny?" and answer that question in all its different facets. One way is in broad philosophical terms. What kinds of things are or aren't acceptable to you as subjects for humor? What kinds of jokes are you comfortable or uncomfortable telling? Some comedy professionals will tell you that you aren't truly making comedy if you're not constantly busting taboos and stepping on toes. But your sense of right or wrong, your comedic moral compass, is a valuable part of your sensibility. A concept that gets mentioned a lot in comedy is "punching up" rather than "punching down," that is, telling jokes about people more powerful than you, who deserve to be brought down a peg, rather than the opposite. As writer Lindy West describes it, "The idea is that people in positions of power should avoid making jokes at the expense of the powerless. That's why, at the company party, the CEO doesn't roast the janitor." Not everybody subscribes to this principle. A lot of people tell cruel jokes about the powerless. We call those people "bullies," and sometimes they punch down all the way from the White House. The ugly truth is that sometimes those cruel jokes can be written and told in a way that is funny. But this doesn't mean the teller isn't still a jerk for telling them or that you aren't kind of a jerk for laughing at them.

Considering your conscience in your work, even if only to test it, isn't just acceptable, it's necessary. If you write jokes that you feel questionable or queasy about, then your work becomes something you can't stand behind. The audience's laughter, rather than being a source of pride, becomes a source of guilt. Of course, the situations that call for your moral compass to be consulted aren't always as simple as the CEO/janitor dynamic. Personally, I would recommend navigating it by trying not to hurtfully joke about anyone who would want to hurtfully joke back at you but lacks the power to do so. And I have no qualms telling mean jokes about animals, because they don't care anyway. Ultimately, I stand with what comedy writer Nell Scovell says: "I truly believe that if you're a comedy writer and have never been told 'You've gone too far,' then you haven't gone far enough. I also believe that if you're constantly told 'You've gone too far,' then maybe you're an asshole."

Phew, heady stuff! Let's get less serious! Because you should also ask yourself the hopefully less fraught question "What comedy that already exists makes me laugh?" Make a list of those funny things and look for the common links between them. Those links are keys to your sensibility. Once you know what they are, then, as comedy-writing legend Merrill Markoe describes it, you can "analyze *why* you like what you like. When you can isolate and put your finger on the mechanism, you can try to duplicate it in an original way and then apply it."

There's a dichotomy here that's worth parsing: *duplicating* something, but in an *original* way. That seeming paradox applies not only to sensibility but also to style, and to the question of "How do I communicate these things?" Whether they're just starting out or fine-tuning their voice, nearly every comedy writer will at some point imitate the voice of someone or something else they think is funny. There's nothing wrong with you doing this as long as you're not literally stealing the jokes of others and passing them off as your own. It can even be a useful tool for creative evolution. I often think about a quote attributed to Pablo Picasso that outlines a certain artistic evolution: "You should constantly try to paint like someone else. But the thing is, you can't! You would like to. You try. But it turns out to be a botch. . . . And it's at the very moment you make a botch of it that you're yourself." In other words, if imitation is the sincerest form of flattery, then originality is the sincerest form of imitating something and failing in a way that is specific to you.

In crafting a comedic voice for yourself, it makes sense to start with your actual voice, then temper it with the things you think are funny in others. The more you write in that voice, the more you'll see what aspects of it fit your personal sensibility and style. For example, when I was young and dabbling in stand-up comedy, I would try to write jokes along the lines of what the other comedians I saw were performing. In an attempt to match the sort of "adult" humor I was hearing around me, I wrote jokes like "Lately, I've been doing a lot of sex work. Let me rephrase that, I've been doing a lot of work for sex." But these jokes never went over well for two interrelated reasons. First, they were fairly weak because, second, they didn't feel comfortable or natural coming from me. I'd also tried writing the sort of elaborate, biting sociopolitical jokes I admired, and I realized that while I could write them for others—such as in my day job—they didn't feel quite right for my own voice.

The more I allowed myself to drift from those original influences, the sillier my stand-up routines got. Rather than skewering politics, I developed a bit in which I "revealed" the secrets of performing baby magic tricks like "got your nose" and "peekaboo." When I wanted to experiment with being edgier or profane, I had to figure out how to write jokes to fit the whimsical, goofy sensibility and style that felt right to me, while also still reflecting my frame of reference and perspective.

How did I square that circle? With a joke called "Fantasy," in which I told the story of my wife asking me in bed to tell her my biggest, weirdest fantasy, the fantasy I was always too embarrassed to share with anyone else. I would then launch into a long, half-improvised prologue for a *Lord of the Rings*–style epic: "A shadow hangs over the land of Kal-Kazar! From the Iron Mountains of the North, where rings eternal the sound of elvish hammer, to the Southern Swamps of the Lizard Men. . . ." I would go on and on like that as a few members of the audience laughed and the rest sat in baffled silence. Eventually, I would end the prologue and pause. Then I'd say, "Chapter the first," and pick up the story again. Every single time, at that moment, I'd get an enormous laugh from the entire audience. It turned out that this was the kind of sex joke that fit my comedic voice's sensibility: the kind that wasn't really about sex at all.

As this story illustrates, understanding your voice and how it works—not to mention whether or not it belongs to an asshole—isn't a quick and easy process. It takes time, practice, patience, thought, and work. And even after that, you may still find yourself being misunderstood if you're not careful about the subject of our next chapter: tone.

5
Tone

MOST HUMAN BEINGS will go nearly their entire lives never needing to write a joke. This may fool them into thinking they don't need a joke farm, because they'll always be in the audience and never on the stage. But there is a singular situation in which the tables will be turned, the clown shoe will be on the other foot, and suddenly they will need to be funny in front of the people whose opinion of them matters most.

At some point, these civilians may have to speak at a wedding—which means thinking, in advance, of something funny to say.

With This Joke, I Thee Laugh

I am known within a very small, very judgmental circle for the quality of my wedding speeches. Oft told is the legend of the reception at which I brought the audience back after the previous toaster had spoken, unscripted, for forty-five consecutive minutes. Thanks to the power of joke writing, I turned the mood around in about seven minutes. And I didn't even use my most cherished wedding speech maneuver, in which I introduce a joke idea at the top of the speech and then circle back to it at the end of the speech. This *never fails* to amaze the attendees. Structure! Is there anything it can't do?

I approach wedding speeches the same way I approach writing jokes professionally. I clearly delineate the point I'm making—how I feel about the couple in question—and then look for a funny premise to express that. Unfortunately, humor has a tendency to want to "go too far," overstepping the invisible boundaries between "Ha! I can't believe you said that!" and "You monster, how could you say that?!" Jokes (and, let's be honest, many comedians) are like junkyard dogs straining at their chains to get close enough to bite. It can throw an audience when a joke goes too far at a comedy show. But at a wedding, it can destroy a family. One way to keep that from happening is by being conscious of your tone.

What Do We Mean by Tone?

For all the thought that goes into writing a joke, comedy is ultimately an art built on emotion. Structure can trick us into laughing at things we don't agree with, because laughter is an emotional response, not an intellectual one. As Steve Allen says, "We do not *decide* to laugh at a joke; we simply respond automatically, in much the same way that we blink if we look at the sun or duck to avoid a blow." If your joke sparks the right emotional reaction, your audience laughs. If it sparks the wrong emotional reaction, they don't. No amount of further explanation of the joke will change the outcome. This means that for a joke to succeed, it needs to convey the proper tone.

Tone, in basic terms, is the "vibe" of a joke, its emotional texture. What a middle-aged comedy writer trying and failing to sound young might call a joke's "feels." As *Bob's Burgers* creator Loren Bouchard puts it, "Tone is everything. Tone is partly your ethics and your morality and your, sort of, decency. . . . Some of it is also just what I would call likability." Tone is all those things and more: a quality of mood that expresses a joke writer's intentions through what their sentiment, sincerity, and overall attitude imply behind the explicit words of the joke. Tone can feel amorphous, but in practice it's a tangible aspect of a joke that the writer can test and adjust. Tone may also seem to be another aspect of voice, but just as a person is capable of expressing more than one emotion, a voice can operate in a variety of tones depending on the intention of the joke.

Tone can radically impact a joke's received meaning. The same words mean very different things depending on the audience's sense of the person saying them, the situation in which they're being said, and the varying levels of intensity or irony that are put behind them. Sometimes tone is what makes something a joke in the first place. For instance, writer George Saunders's short story "I Can Speak!" finds its humor in a passive-aggressive tone. The story takes the form of a written reply to a complaint letter sent to the manufacturer of a mask for babies to wear in order to create the illusion that they can speak. As strange as this product is, the jokes of the story are only partly in the details of this deeply disturbing mask. For me, the real humor comes from the tone, which is trying to express professional positivity ("We at KidLuv really love what kids are, Mrs. Faniglia, which is why we want them to become something better as soon as possible") but can't hold back moments of irritable petulance ("And so I thought I would take some of my personal time [I am on lunch] and try to address the questions you raised in your letter").

The attitude of the story is an ironic one, because George Saunders is clearly *not* on the side of putting talking masks on babies or letting people use "I have to do my job" as an excuse for immoral or inhumane behavior. He is telling us, "Don't be like this person." But he doesn't do this through a straightforward method like having the plot punish the character. That would be less funny. He just uses a tone of voice that draws out the reader's unpleasant associations with people who *use* that tone of voice. The tone is petty, officious, and prickly—to put it another way, it's very specific. And that makes it much funnier.

Degrees of Irony: Like a Thermometer for Joke Meanings!

The job that tone does in Saunders's story is a job it does in nearly all humor: It helps the reader to decode the joke's degree of **sincerity** or **irony**. Once we know that degree—basically, how much the person writing this joke *means* what's being said on the surface—we can begin to grasp the implied intention of the joke. And that intention, what the joke teller is hoping to communicate through the joke, is the whole point of telling this joke in the first place.

In some jokes, the balance between sincerity and irony leans more heavily on the sincere side. In a routine about eliminating the Confederate flag, stand-up Roy Wood Jr. asks, "But if we get rid of the Confederate flag, how am I gonna know who the dangerous white people are? . . . Stopping for gas at a strange place at two in the morning, you see that flag hanging from the window, you know this is not the place to get gas." There's a little bit of irony in the idea that Wood, a Black man, wants to keep the Confederate flag around, but the thrust of the joke—that this flag is something to be avoided—is meant sincerely and unironically.

Other jokes have what we might call "medium irony," where a sincere feeling is being communicated through an insincere statement. Take, for instance, stand-up Patton Oswalt's routine about how if he had a time machine he'd go back to the early 1990s "and kill George Lucas with a shovel" to stop him from making the *Star Wars* prequel films, saying, "That's how I would try to save history." Oswalt acts out his disappointment with George Lucas's concept (on seeing Darth Vader as a kid: "I don't really care about him as a little kid. At all. *At all!* At all") before screaming, "I don't give a shit! Where the stuff I love comes from! I just love the stuff I love!" Oswalt is doing all this to make a sincere point (he really is disappointed in those movies, *and* in himself for caring so much about them) by saying something ironic (i.e., he's not really going to kill somebody with a shovel).

Finally, some jokes are completely ironic, wherein the joke teller is communicating literally the exact opposite of what they're saying. In comedian Sara Schaefer's memoir *Grand*, she describes her teenage irritation at receiving tragic news from her parents, saying, "I realized that we were in the middle of a massive family crisis, but as Viking #3 in a musical adaptation of the famous comic strip *Hagar the Horrible*, I was the bedrock of an entire theatrical production." You don't need me to tell you Schaefer is making the point that she was wrong to prioritize her school play over her family, because she's established an ironic tone through specificity (contrasting "a massive family crisis" with being an unnamed Viking in a high school musical), structure (mentioning the family crisis first, so we feel the anticlimax of "Viking #3"), and exaggeration ("the bedrock of an entire theatrical production"). Instead of saying something directly, like "At the time I was wrong to think this," she uses an ironic tone to make that point abundantly clear to any reader who's not a psychopath or a teenager, which, to be fair, are kind of the same thing.

In the two examples from stand-ups above, much of the tone is communicated by the way in which the routine is performed, which is missing when the words are reprinted on a book page. Performance is a huge part of tone—and such a huge topic that attempting to cram it into this book would be like a picture I once saw of a snake that had attempted to swallow an alligator and subsequently burst open, resulting in a perfectly healthy alligator wearing a snake as a scarf. So I won't get too deep into performance here.

But, come to think of it, I bet you picked up the tones of those stand-up jokes even when you only saw the jokes on the page. Partly because human brains are pretty good at picking up subtle emotional tones, since our ancient ancestors needed to figure out which Neanderthals were just pretending to be our friends so they could later steal our stone tools or whatever. But also because tone is not exclusively the purview of live performance. Although tone is more about feeling than about thinking, it can still be written, and it still operates through understandable mechanics and guidelines. I guess what I'm saying is, get ready for a lot more written words in this chapter.

Crafting Tone: Keep Your Friends Close, and Your Audiences Less Close

At first glance, the idea of crafting tone can feel anywhere from improbable to impossible. It's the sort of thing that can be hard to describe in writing, like the color blue or why we have the Electoral College. But there are tools you can use to craft your tone in order to guide an audience's emotional response. To simplify matters as we talk about them, I'm going to talk about tone in the very broad categories of **aggressive** and **passive**, and, nestled between those two poles, our old friend from "I Can Speak!," **passive-aggressive**.

As we discussed last chapter, all jokes come from a voice doing the telling. That voice has a relationship with the audience, and establishing the right relationship lays the foundation for how your tone will be perceived. Are you an outsider to the audience or an insider? Friend or challenger? You can't really change the level of belonging you share with your audience, but you *can* leverage that relationship (and how you want the audience to interpret it) to calibrate the level of **aggression** your joke expresses toward its subject or its audience. Patton Oswalt's joke above is aggressively hostile to its *subject*, but he doesn't turn any of that hostility toward the *audience* by, say, accusing them of secretly being evil *Star Wars* prequel–lovers. When a joke directs all of its aggressiveness toward its subject, it gives the audience the opportunity to share that feeling, implying not just "I hate this thing" but "I know you agree with me in hating this thing." In this way, a hostile tone can bring the audience closer to you.

But sometimes you don't want that. You want to push the audience farther away. If you're writing a joke whose emotional goal is to shock or discomfort the audience, you need to direct your aggression toward *them*. Writer Samantha Irby does this in her essay "Milk and Oreos," in which she aggressively and sarcastically (in other words, ironically) expresses her "love" for the problems she has with the white readers she's addressing:

> I love that you're so fucking fancy. You don't cram yourselves into a sticky booth at IHOP to shovel four dollar pancakes from a box mix down your throats, no, *you* stand huddled against the cold for three hours waiting for the hotly anticipated opening of that adorable new brunch place that serves bald eagle omelets and tiger milk pancakes with cinnamon butter. . . . You love that I can teach you things about black culture and our current sociopolitical landscape, and I love that you have no idea that I don't know what the fuck I'm talking about.

Irby wants the reader to understand that they aren't there to laugh at her joke's subject but to *be* her joke's subject. By directing her hostility and aggression at the reader, she pushes them away from her emotionally. What makes it funny is her using the language of love to describe something she actually hates, providing that gap in meaning for our brains to leap over. I have pulled the same trick many times, writing comedy pieces where the overriding joke is expressing ironic support or appreciation for something I'm clearly saying stinks. Irby has some very funny jokes here, like the specificity of "tiger milk pancakes" and the reveal that "I don't know what the fuck I'm talking about." But the aggression she uses, and her repeated sarcastic use of "love" communicates a tone that says, "You may be laughing, but I'm genuinely feeling this anger." As a result, waiting in line for brunch manages to come off as far more devastating than the idea of killing George Lucas with a shovel.

Imagine how different these jokes would feel if they communicated a different relationship with the audience, like if Samantha Irby were using her jokes to confide feelings of inadequacy rather than offense (thus bringing the audience closer) or if Patton Oswalt were accusing his audience of loving something terrible (thus pushing them away). The jokes would probably still be funny, but their tone would communicate a different intention to the audience and spark a different emotional reaction. It's the comedy equivalent of how a nursery rhyme sung jauntily by a group of children is delightful, but a nursery rhyme sung slowly by one child is the scariest thing in the history of the world.

As Opposed to a Living Pan

Let's talk about aggression's less threatening yet somehow more frustrating opposite: **passivity**. Though the examples of aggression above have different intentions and spark different responses, they both involve a fairly high level of emotional sincerity. In ordinary life, people are usually more overtly emotional when they're less guarded and more sincere. As a result, comedic passivity contributes to a tone of ironic insincerity. Sure, some jokes are so cartoonishly aggressive that they reach levels of irony (as in the work of legendary insult comic Don Rickles), but comedic insincerity more often lives in tones drained of emotion, especially in the nonemotional state known as deadpan.

Deadpan is the refusal to display emotions, creating both a distance between the teller and the audience and a distance between the teller and the subject of the joke. In other words, deadpan is building a relationship with the audience by refusing to build a relationship with the audience—an emotional tone of detachment.

A classic example of this is the work of silent-film actor and director Buster Keaton, known as the "Great Stone Face" for his trademark lack of visible reaction to the dangerous or bizarre things that happen around him. Of Keaton's Civil War–set movie *The General*, Gerald Mast writes, "Keaton's presence makes *The General* take place in a comic world—despite the fact that the film is full of adventure, suspense, war, and death." Now it's not true that Keaton shows *no* emotion, but by displaying emotion almost entirely through his body while limiting his face to a muted palette of mild irritation, frustration, or confusion, he creates an ironic tone that communicates to the audience, "I'm refusing to take this too seriously, and so should you."

This Keaton example is an instance of communicating a deadpan tone through performance—though I'd argue that his lack of reaction is so necessary to his humor that it is, in fact, a written element of the jokes. But a deadpan tone can also be expressed through language alone when the language is sufficiently drained of emotion. It's something writer Richard Brautigan used to great effect in his work, such as this line from one of his short stories: "The Beach Boys were singing a song about California girls on the radio. They liked them." The measured, deadpan tone of the narrator's understated summing-up of the Beach Boys' exuberant wish—that literally every single girl could be a California girl—signals a clear emotional remove from the situation, and perhaps even from emotion itself.

No, I'm Still Not Done Talking About Tone

Keeping in mind the examples we've looked at about these tones, a good rule of thumb is that an audience is more likely to be drawn to your joke emotionally if it carries a tone full of emotion. They may not react *happily* to a joke (surely some of the readers of the Irby piece didn't), but a tone high in emotion will invite an emotional reaction from your audience. You can craft a joke so that the audience shares that emotion by, for example, aiming your aggression at something in a way that lets the audience share that feeling. It doesn't have to be aggression, though. You can also craft a joke so that you aim a high-energy, high-intensity beam of appreciation, envy, or lust at something, allowing the audience the chance to feel those same feelings.

If you want to push *away* the audience, maybe because they're the butt of the joke and you want them to recognize something they've done, then aim your emotional intensity *at* them. Again, this doesn't have to be purely a matter of hostility. Stand-up Atsuko Okatsuka tells a joke in which she appeals to the audience about the wasted space in their homes: "When was the last time you touched your ceiling? Don't let it collect dust, you paid for it! At least feel it!" It's an aggressive friendliness, which pushes the audience and gets an emotional response from them without being an attack.

Most of my examples have been from stand-up or humor writing, forms of humor that involve a direct address from the joke teller to the audience. But the same ideas apply to jokes told by a character in a narrative scene. Take two of the classic lines from the 1984 movie *Ghostbusters*. In one, our heroes explain to New York's mayor why they need to go out ghostbusting. Describing the consequences of inaction, the character Peter Venkman histrionically suggests the city will see "human sacrifice, dogs and cats living together—mass hysteria!" The basic joke here is using "dogs and cats living together" as an example of disaster, but what makes it truly funny is the emotional intensity of "mass hysteria," implying that even though Venkman is saying a silly thing, he's also kind of being sincere about it.

We can see the opposite tone at work in the following back-and-forth from the same scene, when another ghost-buster, Ray Stantz, refers to their bureaucratic nemesis Walter Peck as "dickless":

> STANTZ: Everything was fine with our system until the power grid was shut off by Dickless here.
> PECK: They caused an explosion!
> MAYOR: Is this true?
> VENKMAN: Yes, it's true. This man has no dick.

Here, the joke carries the opposite tone, communicating a deadpan, low-emotion, and deeply insincere insult. You could say that in both cases the joke's audience is really the character of the mayor, with Venkman, in one instance, using high emotion to elicit an emotional response and, in the other, directing aggression at a third party in a bid to bring the mayor over to Venkman's side. Whatever the case, the movie audience instantly picks up on the emotional implications of both jokes' tones. And though that tone is assisted by performance, it's also entirely present in the writing of the jokes.

Which emotional tone should you strive for? Well, whichever best achieves the aim of your joke. And *that* depends on what you're trying to say, who you're telling the joke to, and an element that you'll never fully control: the circumstances in which the joke is experienced.

Context Creates Subtext (in a Text)

Jokes are like cartoon chameleons, unconsciously taking on the tonal influences of the world that surrounds them. An audience can't help but factor the situation in which they encounter a joke into their reaction to that joke. A joke about killing a man named George Lucas with a shovel means one thing at a late-night comedy show and something else entirely at a political rally where it's followed by chants of "Shov-el! Shov-el! Shov-el!"

In the largest contextual sense, the zeitgeist in which you tell a joke will inevitably affect the tone the joke is conveying. No work of comedy exists in a timeless, universal space of primal humor, and changes in society, culture, or recent events may completely throw off the effect you intend to have. Some topics for joking may be too close to the audience's feelings to joke about. Other jokes may be too out of step with the way people think or feel for them to even see what's intended to be funny. We'll talk about that in more detail in chapter 6. For now, let's just say there are myriad examples of legendarily transgressive humor that seem tame and boring now despite the dangers they held at the time, as well as vast swaths of older comedy that wasn't intended to offend but which is so suffused with bigotry that it's become unwatchable for audiences today who are newly (finally!) empathetic toward different kinds of people. This is a context you, the joke writer, cannot control but can only be aware of and adjust to. There's no beating reality.

The same thought and understanding should be applied to an audience's second biggest context clue (after "all of contemporary reality"): the identity of the joke's teller. The teller's identity—not just its voice, but who that voice is attached to—is the first step in building a joke's relationship with the audience and will affect how the joke's tone comes across. In practice, this means that not everyone can tell the same joke in the same way. I don't mean this in a political "Only certain people are allowed to say certain words" sense but in a very real, you'd-be-foolish-to-ignore-it "Audiences will infer different meanings and tones from different people" sense.

For example, comic Charlie Hill, a member of the Oneida Nation, when asked on a 1970s talk show if he had played "cowboys and Indians" as a kid, responded, "No, we never played cowboys and Indians. But we did play Nazis and Jews. The rules are the same." This is a funny, hard-hitting joke coming from an Indigenous comedian. The teller's identity creates a context for the audience that helps them understand the tone as one that forcefully, though not necessarily aggressively, presents a critical analogy comparing racist institutional violence. That identity also makes clear that the intention of the joke isn't to downgrade "Nazis and Jews" to the level of a childhood game but to lift the concept of "cowboys and Indians" out of childhood play and into lived historical reality. Now that I've sucked all the humor out of a joke I admire, let's see how it might carry a different tone—and a different meaning—from a different speaker.

What if the same joke were told by Sarah Silverman, a Jewish stand-up whose style is known for an ironic tone that mixes deliberately provocative subject matter with a sort of innocent, naive glee? I don't think the audience would reject the joke, but it wouldn't necessarily carry the same undertone of seriousness that Hill's identity lends to it. Instead, it would probably feel like a piece of naughty silliness, along the lines of a chapter heading in Silverman's memoir: "Summer Camp: The Second Worst Kind of Camp for Jews."

And it probably goes without saying that because Silverman is Jewish, a reference to Jews and Nazis—like Hill's mention of "cowboys and Indians"—feels less off-putting than it might if, say, a comic like the white, non-Jewish

Anthony Jeselnik told the joke. Jeselnik specializes in humor that is often cruel and violent, but with a deadpan edge that, again, carries an ironic tone. From him, this joke wouldn't carry Hill's tone of "I'm making a point" or Silverman's (hypothetical) tone of "I'm pretending I don't realize this is offensive" but, rather, a tone of "I know this is wrong to say, and the humor is in my challenging you to have a problem with it." Many in the audience would reject this joke from him, but others would enjoy it, their emotional response stimulated by the taboo-ness of a guy like Jeselnik telling a joke like this. The joke would no longer be about historical injustice but about the dare-based relationship between the comic and his audience. It would still be funny, probably, but for a different audience in a different way.

Now what if, say, Jim Gaffigan—a white, gentile, famously "clean" comic—told this same joke? In recent years, Gaffigan has become slightly edgier in his comedy, but he is better known for jokes about being a very pale, overweight dad. What would it be like if he told this joke? I can't imagine a scenario in which it would go over well. Gaffigan's usual tone is built on a certain kind of sincerity, and I think that this joke, told by him, would lose any sense of irony and just sound like he thinks it's funny to play a game about Nazis. This joke, while still *being* a joke, would mean big trouble for this hypothetical, not-at-all-real-especially-for-defamation-lawsuit-purposes concept of Jim Gaffigan.

Even worse, what if comedian-turned-fascism-adjacent-podcaster Joe Rogan told this joke? Regardless of his intention, the tone, purely informed by the identity the audience understands as his, would be perceived as one of aggressive insensitivity. It would feel like the kind of joke certain guys tell each other in hushed tones after looking to make sure nobody is close enough to hear them. The wording would be no different from how Charlie Hill told it, but because of the different context it wouldn't *feel* like the same joke. And feelings are what tone is all about.

If it seems like I've been portraying tonal context as if it's always a laugh-killer, know that this isn't always the case. For one thing, being aware of the current social climate can open up opportunities for jokes that reflect on, react to, or play with the feelings of that climate. But setting aside big contexts, humor can also be built from creating a joke's own little contexts.

In the same way a painter lays down a background color to provide the right context for the foreground—or the way your more pretentious postcollege friends painted one "accent wall" of their apartment to provide the right context for pretending they had a sense of style—you can use one emotional tone as the setup to a second emotional tone's punchline. The joke then becomes the conflict between *what's* being said and *how* it's being said. You see this frequently in comedy songs, where one emotional tone can provide a context for a contrasting emotional tone. The musical comedy duo Garfunkel and Oates (Kate Micucci and Riki Lindhome) rely heavily on this dynamic, either by juxtaposing upbeat *music* with cynical lyrics (as in their song "Pregnant Women Are Smug") or juxtaposing upbeat *lyrics* with other, more downbeat lyrics (as in "29/31," where alternating verses stage a clash between a woman's optimistic twenty-nine-year-old self and pessimistic thirty-one-year-old self). This deliberate clash of tones has a really nice effect—a sense of irony that still manages to feel sincere to the audience.

Perhaps my favorite achievement in the realm of "sincere irony through clashing tones involving context" (which is somehow still not an Olympic event) is the song "Always Look on the Bright Side of Life" from the film *Monty Python's Life of Brian*. It's a jaunty tune about staying positive that does include some funny lyrics ("Life's a piece of shit / when you look at it") but is otherwise, context-free, a sincere message. Its performance in the film, however, comes from a cast of characters who have just been crucified. And this is the *end* of the movie—those characters will not be saved, and the audience knows it. The humor of the joke—and the ultimate meaning and tone of that humor—doesn't come from the music or the lyrics but from the setting where those things are being performed.

When I first saw this movie as an adolescent, I was blown away by the audacity of writer/performer Eric Idle admonishing the audience not to sweat the small stuff while he himself is experiencing a lingering death. However, when Idle repurposed the song decades later in the musical *Spamalot*, for a scene in which a disappointed King Arthur is cheered up by his squire, it lost all that contextual tonal power. The joke, a product of its original context, had evaporated. It's hardly funny to tell someone to look on the bright side when there *is* an actual bright side for them to look on. Alas, context giveth and context taketh away. All we can do as joke writers is look on the bright side—and if that's the side that's throwing our joke's tone off, either rewrite the joke or look for another side to deliver it on.

Case Studies: Toasts vs. Roasts

If you've been to a wedding, you know what the toasts are like—heartfelt, slightly teasing, filled with references many of the attendees won't understand—and you can see how they rely on the same tonal factors we've been talking about. If you're the one speaking, you'll consider the closeness of your relationship to the couple and the audience's awareness of that closeness; the level of hostility or tenderness, sincerity or irony, that you intend to convey; and the context of the event itself, from whether the bride's parents didn't show up to how loud your drunk aunt Sharlene is being when you're trying to talk. All of this influences how your tone will be perceived by your audience and what emotional reaction you'll receive in return.

Ironically, a wedding toast's sincere show of affection operates on the same mechanics as comedy's most insincere show of hostility: the roast. In a roast, comedians honor someone by telling the meanest, most personal, and least sensitive jokes they can think of. Both wedding toasts and comedy roasts are means of expressing genuine affection—setting aside televised roasts where comedians insult a genuinely disliked figure because the disliked figure is being paid to be there—but they're coming at that goal from different angles.

Like a speech at a wedding, a roast's tone relies on its context. Comedy critic Jesse David Fox describes it well: "Everyone at a roast has consented to participate, knowing the rules. . . . There is an understanding that what is said would not be said otherwise." Both the subject and the audience know that people are supposed to say mean things at a roast, so they aren't offended when someone at a roast says you're a depraved monster. At a wedding, such remarks could end a friendship. At a bachelor party? That's more of a gray area. Roast jokes use a deliberately exaggerated level of hostility to achieve an ironic level of insult. Fox continues:

> It is incumbent on the roasters to understand the vocabulary of the medium, because if a joke is too cruel or not cruel enough or not clearly structured as a joke, the tenuous comedy frame could rupture. It is why roast jokes are the most jokey sounding of any jokes you hear in contemporary comedy.

This is all to make clear that in this context, the teller's intention is "I don't really mean this, but I must love you a lot to be able to write such specifically mean jokes about you." In *An Anatomy of Laughter*, Richard Boston notes that relationship is key here: "Comic insults are often playful, a kind of verbal tickling in which remarks that would be insulting delivered to a stranger are accepted by close friends as laughable."

Still, I've seen both wedding toasts and comedy roasts go horribly wrong when the joke teller has failed to take tone into account. With wedding speeches, it's usually when someone becomes more overtly hostile than they intend to be toward the married couple. What the speaker sees as playful ribbing looks to the audience like an attack. And on their wedding day, no less! With roasts it comes when the meanness of the jokes carries the tonal charge of a real attack, often because the joke teller has overestimated their closeness to the subject—or, as in the notorious 2002 *Comedy Central Roast of Chevy Chase*, because the joke teller has no relationship with the subject at all. The story goes that very few people who knew actor Chevy Chase wanted to roast him on-screen, and, as a result, the network hired comics to tell mean jokes about someone they had barely met. A false, playful roasting had become a real, insulting one, without the roastee being aware of it.

Years later, one of those comics, Marc Maron, would half-jokingly tell Chase, "I think we shared one of the worst nights of our lives together." For Maron, it was a terrible night because his performance died onstage. Looking back on the experience from his later status as an elder statesman of stand-up, Maron would reflect, "I'm not great with roasting. . . . Because [in my voice] when you're angry, if you're insulting somebody, it's to hurt them," but with roasts "there has to be a warm-heartedness to it." And so, ultimately, his tone didn't fit the bill.

Chase, for his part, recalls, "I just sat there and I thought, 'Jesus Christ, they don't like me.'" I don't think he felt disliked because the jokes told about him were mean, or even inaccurate, but because they were *impersonal.* It felt like an outsider's harsh criticism rather than an insider's faux-hostile teasing. As a result the roasters came off as needlessly cruel. Even now I feel uncomfortable watching it, and I'm not really a fan of Chevy Chase. Not that I feel close enough to him to ever tell him that.

Wedding speeches and comedy roasts are contexts where tone holds a heightened level of importance because they're situations with real emotional stakes. The stakes with other kinds of comedy are lower, but it can't hurt to approach your work as if they were just as high. Treat tone like radioactive material—a source of enormous power that, if mishandled, could lose you a few family members.

I would say you should also apply these guidelines to funeral eulogies, but the subject's already dead for those and therefore can't complain. Feel free to go nuts and let 'er rip.

A Little Help from Your Friends, If You Haven't Roasted Them Away

Fine-tuning tone in a vacuum can be hard. It's difficult to estimate how your tone is coming across to someone who isn't already aware of your intention. Luckily, you don't have to do it on your own. Tone calibration is a great reason to test your work on people who know you well enough that if you accidentally say something off-putting, they won't assume you're a monster. Pay close attention to their reactions. See where you lose them and whether an adjustment in tone will better establish your relationship with the audience or accommodate their larger context. I once saw a friend perform an early version of a joke about their confusion with proper trans terminology that, tonally, came off as hostile, belittling, and offensive. Several months later, I saw them deliver a version of the joke that was substantively the same but reworded to communicate a tone that came off as earnest, curious, and self-denigrating. By tweaking the tone of the joke, they'd managed to clarify its point—their difficulty adjusting to new understandings—and, as a result, they received a much warmer response from the audience.

Adjusting the tone of a joke is like adjusting the temperature of a greenhouse. Too cold, and the jokes will die. Too hot, and the jokes will die. But get it just right, and the audience will feel like your joke is a funny attack and not a threatening attack, ultimately making you the perfect closing act for a forty-five-minute wedding toast ramble.

See how I just did the "introducing a thing at the top and then bringing it back at the end" trick? It. Never. Fails. Take it.

Use it. Wow your family and astonish your friends. Just do it carefully. Tone is a sensitive thing, and small changes can have large effects. Small changes like, for instance, a joke's wording, which by an astounding coincidence happens to be the subject of the next chapter.

6
Wording

WORDS ARE MAGIC. Use them in exactly the right way and they cast a spell that debilitates your victim with laughter. But words are also delicate. Use them the wrong way and they inspire the world's biggest movie star to slap you on live television. Actually, words are less like real magic than stage magic, in that it takes hard work to give the audience the impression that what you're doing is easy. Joke writers are also like stage *magicians* in that many of them are kind of weird and off-putting and spent a lot of time alone as children. What I'm getting at here is that a lot of joke writing comes down to what Nell Scovell is able to say much more succinctly than me: "Specific words in specific order matter." Finding those specific words and putting them in that specific order can be the difference between a joke landing and flopping. Because when I say "**wording**," what I'm really talking about is "precision." Don't believe me? Then prepare yourself for a spine-tingling tale of humor gone wrong!

Tense Tension: A Cautionary Tale

Years ago, when I was a writer on *The Daily Show* and still carried the implied impressiveness of being a writer on *The Daily Show*, I was approached by *Discover* magazine to write a one-page humor piece for them. (Pro tip: Win an Emmy and all the mainstream science and technology magazines will want a piece of you.) I happily sent them an article entitled "20 Things You Didn't Know About the Future," which took the form of a timeline filled with nonsense jokes like "2107: Artificial intelligence aces the Turing test by becoming so uninteresting that it can't be distinguished from human intelligence. Lame dinner party conversation can now be conducted 300 percent more efficiently." Or, on the subject of replacing now-melted glaciers with plastic substitutes: "Fortunately, polar bears can't tell the difference because they have been extinct for 150 years."

Like I said, nonsense.

I was writing for a magazine that dealt in "sense," though, and the magazine's editors felt that I was using the wrong verb tense for *serious* nonfiction predictive writing. So they adjusted the tense of all the jokes from present to future, with each seemingly insignificant change making the jokes clunkier and less effective. The polar bears line above became "Fortunately, polar bears will not feel the difference because they will have been extinct for 150 years." It may take you a moment to really notice it, but for me reading that sentence is like walking with a piece of gravel in my shoe: I may get to the same place, but the trip is noticeably less pleasant.

The other joke quoted above became "Artificial intelligence will ace the Turing test by becoming so uninteresting that it can't be distinguished from human intelligence. Lame dinner party conversation will then be conducted 300 percent more efficiently." That "will then be" in the second line makes my stomach hurt. The first version ("can now be") keeps a joke set in the future existing in a sort of comedic present. You're there in the same tense and time as the joke. The revision, on the other hand, sets the joke up as a future thing happening an arm's length away from you. It forces the reader to take a few more milliseconds of mental processing time to decode, undermining the smooth premise leap the joke requires.

Over the course of the page, the added repetitious parade of "will then"s and "will have been"s took something that should have been light and fluffy—fast enough on its feet that the reader won't notice how dumb it is—and made it clumpy and heavy. Luckily, a more highly ranked editor noticed the changes, recognized the problem, and reverted everything back to my original tense before publication. They saw that this simple change in tense had thrown off the entire piece's rhythm.

Rhythm and Comedy: A Mostly Relevant Interjection

If the structure of your joke is where you establish its overall flow, then the wording of your joke is where you fine-tune its rhythm. **Rhythm** is a big deal in comedy, much as it is in music, and it's often described in musical terms. Mel Brooks wrote that rhythm "is the ability to know where the top of the vocality, the vocal message, happens. It's a rim shot, it's a whack, depending on what kind of comedy you're into." This is a statement that's as wise as it is not entirely clear to me what he's talking about. I think he's saying rhythm is a matter of tempo and duration. You may have heard of the importance of "comedic timing," something we can see easily in comedic performance, wherein the rhythm of spoken delivery is crucial to giving the audience the pieces of information they need at the right pace to process them. But we can also see that same kind of rhythm—a category which I see as including the concept of "timing"—in writing for the page. Take a look at how Brooks, in his memoir, describes a truck he crashed: "The front of the truck is fine. The back of the truck—not so fine." Much of the humor in the line comes from the rhythm we feel as a result of that skip-pause in time caused by the dash replacing the word "is," which slightly quickens the pace and adds extra emphasis to "not so fine." Sing the line, and you'll see what I mean even more. Come on, do it. I won't tell anybody.

But I'd caution you against taking the music/comedy connection too far. Both arts are built on patterns and rhythm, but for the most part, music is about the fulfilling of patterns, and comedy is about their disruption. Obviously there are a lot of exceptions to such a blanket statement (like jazz), but most music isn't in the business of surprising the audience. Even Joseph Haydn's Symphony No. 94, known in classical music circles as the *Surprise* Symphony, is only called that because the music suddenly gets really loud in the middle. To classical music audiences, this is hilarious. In comedy terms—not so much.

To my mind, the rhythms of comedy are less like those of music and more like those of horror movies. Horror, like comedy, is built on the tension that comes between a setup and a payoff. And the enjoyment of both crafts depends on the audience receiving just enough information to expect, but not predict the specific execution of, a sudden revelation. The structure of music is the reliable verse-chorus cycle of repetitions fulfilled, while the structure of comedy and horror is the abrupt sudden shock of disruption. This is something worth keeping in mind when you word your jokes—building your rhythm so that it leads smoothly to an abrupt and sudden rhythm change at the punchline. And then your joke will be so funny it's scary! (I apologize for that; let's move on.)

Wording: Not Just for Words Anymore

Before we look at some examples of how to work wording, I'd like to provide one of those authority-undercutting adjustments to the terminology I'm using. When I say "wording," I'm not just talking about jokes tied to language. I'm really talking about the precision involved in any sort of detail work necessary to put your joke across to the audience as effectively as possible. In this way "wording" could also mean the visual aspects of a sight gag—and in fact, in chapter 13, we'll talk about how the principles I'm about to go into also apply to visual humor. But until then, I want you to keep in mind that any joke, in any format or medium, can be made stronger when you pay attention to the intricate details of its construction and appearance. Of course, that being said, unless you were assigned this book by your mime professor (unlikely), most of your jokes will be made of words. So let's look at how to apply our comedic principles to them.

Putting Principles into Practice: Specifically Specificity

In earlier chapters, I introduced you (or reintroduced you, I don't know what your life's been like up until now) to three principles of comedy writing: brevity, clarity, and specificity. Now I'd like to apply those semiabstract concepts specifically to the wording of a joke, only I'm going to talk about them in reverse order. Try not to be confused!

Specificity in wording is an umbrella that covers a few different concepts. It could mean considering the cultural zeitgeist so that your language carries the proper subtext. It could mean paying close attention to the tenses of your verbs to preserve rhythm and clarity (I'm not still bitter about this, I swear). It could also mean choosing a word that adds detail rather than a vague one: something precise like "slimy" instead of a more general word like "gross." Or something evocative like "loathsome" instead of a less meaningful term like "gross." Or an easier-to-visualize phrase like "twelve dozen" instead of a more technical term like "gross." And then there are times when it's helpful to recognize the blunt force of a short, accessible term like, say, "gross." What specific word best serves your joke's purpose depends on what the purpose of that joke is and the sensibility of the joke teller's voice.

Overall, I find that specificity in joke wording falls into two categories: "saying something exactly right in a funny way" and "saying something exactly wrong in a funny way." In the "exactly right" category, some jokes rely on specific language conventions for their success. In a *New Yorker* cartoon by Jason Adam Katzenstein, a boxer sits in his corner of the ring as an older woman with glasses says to him, "He's got a weak left hook, but what do I know, I'm only your mother." Since this joke comes from the incongruous combination of two different kinds of specific wording—the stereotypical wording of boxing coaches and the stereotypical wording of passive-aggressive moms—it depends on Katzenstein sticking to those stereotypes as specifically as he can. If he'd phrased it as "Hit him in the face if you feel like listening to your mother," the joke wouldn't work.

Cliché language isn't always a bad thing in jokes, as long as that cliché language is the specific language you need to express the joke's premise.

Another example of a joke built on a very specific wording that brings with it a very specific meaning for the audience can be found in Jena Friedman's stand-up routine in which she pretends to sympathize with men who claim it's hard to be a man: "One of my best friends is a man. I'm actually half man. On my dad's side." Since this joke takes a common phrase ("on my dad's side") and applies its meaning in a nonsensical way to make a point about the idiocy of having to claim an identity to share sympathy with it, it needs to replicate that specific phrase exactly right.

My larger point here isn't about making sure your joke copies a preexisting template but about being aware that if you are intending to evoke a specific association in the audience's mind, then you should hew as closely as you can to the wording of that original thing you want to associate with. In both Katzenstein's and Friedman's jokes, the writer is doing the work of making sure their language conventions are recognizable so that the audience will have to do less work to recognize them.

Even jokes that aren't mimicking a preexisting phrase or speaking style can gain power from the use of the right specific word. For example, in the movie *The Royal Tenenbaums*, Owen Wilson's character, a posturing author of westerns, describes his newest novel thus: "Everyone knows that Custer died at Little Bighorn. What my book presupposes is . . . maybe he didn't?" The joke here lives on the word "presupposes," which is just awkwardly pretentious enough to set us up for the uninspiring anticlimax of "maybe he didn't?" "Presupposes" is just the right word to get across this character's precarious relationship with intellectualism.

Try out that line with "considers" or "proposes" or "hypothesizes" or "says," or any one of a thousand words that means "suggests," and it won't be as funny as it is with "presupposes."

What I'd suggest (presuppose?) you take from these examples is that when writing a joke, really pay attention to each word that carries meaning. Is there a synonym (or almost-synonym) that will carry even more potential meaning for the audience? Is there a modifier that might also add a deeper or greater meaning to what's being said? Think of each word as an investment, where you want to put in the least amount of words for the maximum amount of payoff.

Another way to use specific wording for humor is the surprise of hearing (or reading) a thought expressed in uncanny words that feel wrong but still get the point across. When Josh Gondelman writes "Even the Zodiac Killer was polite enough to remember to leave a note after he did a murder," he helps sell his premise (the Zodiac Killer's taunting letters were signs of good manners) by casually downgrading the act of killing to "did a murder." We don't expect to see the Zodiac Killer's brutal actions phrased so curiously, and we get a funny charge from the disruption of that expectation, adding to the effect of the joke.

The internet is full of humor like this, based on unlikely, even grammatically incorrect wording. Elderly elder millennials like me will remember the popular online photo of a curious cat with the caption "I can has cheezburger?" The joke wasn't the idea that a cat could talk—or even that a cat, given the option, would want to eat cheeseburgers—but that a talking cat would have a terrible grasp of English grammar. Deliberately wrong language isn't an invention of the digital age, though. The nineteenth century saw a vogue for humorously unwieldy new words ("discombobulate" is one of the few surviving terms from the craze), and, for better or worse, people have been making fun of foreigners' trouble with language probably since the first time a *Homo sapiens* did a devastating impression of a Neanderthal who said "Unk" when he meant "Onk." As historian Mary Beard writes about ancient humor, "Greeks were known to have made wicked fun of the terrible Roman accent," while on the Roman side, she notes, "One comedy of Plautus brings a Carthaginian onto the stage, who babbles some possibly accurate, but still incomprehensible, Punic." This is the dark side of wrong-word humor, which can slide pretty quickly into xenophobia or racism. This is why "funny" foreign accents are a form of humor I'll just go ahead and say you shouldn't spend much time dabbling in.

There is, of course, another specific kind of word that carries a specific comedic charge, the best friend of all fledgling comedy writers: swearing. Let's not lie to each other, swear words are hilarious. They add intensity to whatever's being said; they inspire taboo-breaking giddiness; and, since they can be used as nouns, verbs, or adjectives, they work as all-purpose rhythmic joke filler. For those reasons, I would never discourage writing jokes with swear words. But I would advise you to use them judiciously so they don't lose their special force. Something shocking—like the *f*-word, or violent threats against civil servants—becomes, through repetition, normalized and even banal. Speaking an unspeakable word makes it speakable, no longer taboo, and not necessarily funny in the way it once was.

So if you *do* use swear words in your comedy writing, learn to use them for a specific reason. A great example of this is a parody headline from *The Onion*'s book *Our Dumb Century*, "Holy Shit: Man Walks on the Fucking Moon" (with the subheading "Neil Armstrong's Historic First

Words on Moon: 'Holy Living Fuck'"). The joke here is in the overwhelming excitement of the moon landing, which is only expressible by injecting swear words into the stilted language of newspapers and official statements. What I find particularly beautiful about this joke is that what seems like a subversive act is actually a celebratory one, using this forbidden language to remind us of the wonder of something we've come to take for granted. The ensuing article, which essentially repeats the joke that *everybody* is swearing now, never quite reaches the heights of the headline, which is not merely using swear words but saying something *with* the swear words that couldn't be said without those particular words. Ideally, when you use swear words in a joke it's because they are the best tool to do the job, because the act of swearing in the context of that joke *means* something. That's what I mean by fucking specificity.

Clearly These Are Words About Clarity

Clarity in wording is all about making your words as easy to understand as possible. It's hard to achieve a successful synaptic leap if the audience has to puzzle out what's just been said to them. Jacques Barzun puts it in slightly less clear, albeit prettier, terms when he writes, "Writing is embodied thought, and the thought is clear or muddy, graspable or fugitive, according to the purity of the medium. Communication means one thought held in common. What could be more practical than to try making that thought unmistakable?" Or, as stand-up Norm Macdonald once put it, "Don't be afraid of saying things simply." If the content of your joke is funny, then you shouldn't feel the need to use complicated language to tell it.

One way to achieve this kind of clarity is through the specificity we've already talked about. Think about the Katzenstein and Friedman jokes that I mentioned above. They save time making their meanings clear by taking advantage of phrases or stereotypes that the audience can be reasonably assumed to already understand and that don't need any further information. But another, simpler way is to rework your material until its words are as transparent as possible.

Clarity doesn't always come right away. In the 1939 film *Ninotchka*, a die-hard Soviet Communist refers to the well-known "show trials" under Stalin, in which disfavored members of the Soviet Communist Party were coerced into publicly confessing to crimes they didn't commit, before being executed. She says, "The last mass trials were a great success. There are going to be fewer but better Russians." The phrase "fewer but better" is funny in how it's putting a dehumanizingly positive spin on mass executions. But a previous draft of the script had the line written as "The last mass trials were a great success. We are going to be fewer but better Russians!" This original phrasing is slightly less funny because it's slightly less clear, introducing a "we" that the viewer would need to identify and place within the context of the relationship between the speaker and the mass trials. In addition, "We are going to be fewer" also hits the ear in a strange way that isn't strange enough to be funny for sounding wrong. The clearer version, "There are going to be," sidesteps all this confusion by delivering the punchline more directly. Clear wording asks for as little effort from the audience as possible, even if that effort differential is a matter of tiny degrees. When you're talking about the milliseconds it takes an audience to get a joke, every tiny fraction of a fraction of a second you can shave off helps.

I'll give you an example of an unclear joke from my own work. Of course, you may say that I've already written plenty of unclearly worded jokes in this book. Well, hardy har har, smart guy. But I'll own up to a joke I wrote for an episode of the animated sitcom *HouseBroken* in which a poodle visits a psychic beaver to contact another dog's ghost (because, yes, joke writing *is* the greatest job in the world). I had a written a deliberately purple-prosy joke in which the beaver said, "So you wish to pierce the veil twixt our world and the great farm upstate." I thought this was funny because it sounded pretentious and also referred to the animal afterlife as a farm upstate, the old cliché told to children when their pets die.

Unfortunately, our first audience (the network executives) couldn't wrap their minds around those words. And as much as it pains me to ever say this, the executives were right. The wording hid the meaning of the sentence instead of clarifying it. I was writing with an eye toward mimicking overwrought gothic prose—already not the easiest writing to understand—and then confusing it even further by using a semicommon reference in an unusual way. Compare that with the simplicity of that Jena Friedman joke.

In the end, we replaced that line with "Ah! A soul wishes to speak to you!" This isn't even a joke. But it more clearly communicated what was actually happening in the scene so that the jokes coming after it would make more sense and, by extension, be funnier. This was the right thing to do. After all, a dog consulting a psychic beaver is already a funny situation. I didn't need to gussy it up.

The takeaway here is that for all that I said about specificity earlier, often the best wording is the clearest wording. Don't fall in love with a clever phrase or a funny-sounding word if it's getting in the way of just plain telling the audience what they need to know to laugh at your joke. When you write a joke, look at it and say, "Could this be said more simply or clearly?" After all, what you want the audience to laugh at is the premise of your joke. Your wording should support your premise—not the other way around.

Too Many Words About Brevity

It's easier to achieve clarity in your joke wording if you also practice brevity (and it's easier to be brief if you practice specificity). We've already talked about the purpose of brevity: getting the joke to the audience quicker so they can laugh at it harder. The trick to applying brevity to wording is so ultrasecret and super-hidden that I shouldn't even be telling you this:

> Use fewer words.
> That's the trick.

Ask yourself, as Barzun puts it, "What effect are you producing and at what cost of words? The fewer the words, and the more transparent they are, the easier they will be to understand." Or, as screenwriter Andrew Bergman more succinctly puts it, "One word too many in a thing and a joke becomes a sentence. . . . You just knocked all the air out of it." The leaner the wording, the defter and funnier the joke. See which words you can get rid of without losing clarity, and which phrases can be replaced by a specific word. If a word isn't necessary for the architecture of a sentence or the comprehension of the joke, then cut it out.

Should I really spend more time on this? I'd be a hypocrite!

Case Studies: Jokes That Do Words Good

Let's round out this chapter by taking a look at two jokes that bring brevity, clarity, and specificity together. A short example is a classic one-liner from stand-up comedian and Academy Award for Best Live Action Short Film–winner Steven Wright: "I went to a restaurant that serves breakfast any time. So I ordered French toast during the Renaissance." Every word here is a simple one (except for "Renaissance," which is the crux of the punchline), assembled in a straightforward way with no extraneous phrases or thoughts. When I think about this joke, I often inadvertently remember the wording as "where the *menu* said 'breakfast any time,'" but the actual joke doesn't mention a menu. What Wright has written is so clear that my memory adds details Wright trusts the audience to understand. By leaving out those details, Wright ensures the joke's brevity. The specific wording of "breakfast any time" is crucial for the later payoff, giving us exactly the right words to discern a pattern we recognize from life (restaurants serving breakfast food at any time of the day) that he can disrupt in the punchline.

That disruption—he assumes they mean "any time in history"—is a big conceptual leap for the audience to make, but there are no wasted details in the joke to distract them from landing the jump. Even the choice of "the Renaissance" is great because it's specific in as few words as possible. Think about how much rhythmically clunkier "in medieval times" would be, or how less well-known or potentially confusing "during the Mesozoic" might have been. At the same time, it might have been shorter to say "*in* the Renaissance," but it's not as specific as saying "*during* the Renaissance," which makes it extra clear he is expecting to travel through time for this breakfast. "During" versus "in" is the kind of small, subconsciously noticed calibration in joke wording that pays off in a larger response from the audience.

A more unexpected example of brevity, clarity, and specificity is a joke I stumbled upon at a produce stand in Maui: an empty box marked "Hawaiian Invisible Fruit! Super rare! 99 cents each!" This is possibly the most conceptually complex joke I've ever seen at a produce stand. The immediate joke is about the gullibility of shoppers looking for exotic or trendy ingredients—the farmer's-market version of the emperor having no clothes. The premise of the joke isn't what I find so impressive about it, though. What gets me is the specific, brief, clear wording used in telling the joke. If the box had just said "Hawaiian Invisible Fruit," it would be a clever joke, but not an especially funny one. But whoever farmed this joke (LITERALLY) did three things with wording that made my entire trip to Maui worthwhile (and not just because by including it in this book I've turned it into a tax write-off). First, they added "Super rare!" to the description. Now they're not just naming a nonexistent thing, they're pushing its nonexistent scarcity in a transparently untrue way. There's a little bit of con-man flop sweat in describing the contents of an empty box as "super rare." (There's also a second level of truth in the idea of something so rare it actually doesn't exist.) Second, they picked a specific price: "99 cents." It's not a funny number but a specifically recognizable one we've seen before and pick up quickly—*and* an incredibly low number for a supposedly rare fruit. Third, exclamation points after every single phrase, including the price, signal an over-the-top excitement: "Hawaiian Invisible Fruit! Super rare! 99 cents each!" Sure, that's technically a punctuation mark, not a word, but remember that by "wording" I really mean precision detail work. This is the power of clear, brief, specific wording: Eight words and three exclamation points can turn an empty box into a joke. The lesson I take from this is that every detail of a joke, from the punctuation to a specific number, carries the potential to build humor. Every detail is an opportunity to make your joke funnier—and if a detail doesn't make your joke funnier, you don't need it.

A Word of Warning About Wording

Wording is where you apply the final polish before a joke goes from your exclusive private property to something shared with as much of the world as is willing to subscribe to your newsletter. With that pressure in mind, it's easy to fall into the trap of wanting to make your joke so *perfect* that you never stop fiddling with it. At a certain point, working on the wording of a joke becomes procrastinating. Rather than an act of creative professionalism, it becomes an expression of personal neurosis, like being so worried about underarm sweat stains that you apply too much deodorant, and your shirt then becomes the exact kind of sopping mess you were afraid of.

Usually, the best wording for a joke is the one closest to your first way of phrasing it—only slightly clearer, slightly shorter, and slightly more specific. Beyond that, you risk reaching a point of diminishing returns. All of this is to say: Do your best with your wording, but don't waste your energy trying to do better than your best.

And now, having forced yourself to let go of your joke, the writing is done, right? Ha! You wish! You're not releasing the joke into the wild like a rehabilitated condor flying free forevermore—you're actually handing it over to your most vital, somewhat uninvited collaborator. Who is this mystery figure who will either make your joke a success or swat it to the floor in disgust? And how is it possible that the most important step in joke writing is the one you have the least control over? We'll explore that paradox in the next chapter.

7
Audience

YOU'VE DONE IT. After all the blood, sweat, tears, and Dorito dust, you've written a joke. You're looking at it right now and couldn't be prouder. Time to kick back and bask in its total completion.

Not So Fast!

You still haven't put that joke through the final stage of the writing process: telling it to an **audience** so they can have their say. It's harvest time on the joke farm! As Nell Scovell writes, "Writing is not what you start. It's not even what you finish. It's what you start, finish, and put out there for the world to see." Humor is ultimately a collaborative effort between you and your audience. Improv legend Elaine May said of her work with performing partner Mike Nichols, "Everything we've done has happened with the three of us. We two and the audience." But it's not an equal collaboration. You're going to do most of the work, but they get more say than you do. Steven Wright, writer of last chapter's brilliant breakfast joke, puts it well: "Sometimes I think a joke is really funny and they don't laugh at it at all and I have to throw it away. Happens all the time. They're in charge of what stays in the act by their response." As much as we all wish it were otherwise, the audience is the final arbiter of whether or not your joke actually works.

This isn't unique to comedy. In his 1957 lecture "The Creative Act," Marcel Duchamp—the pioneering modern artist who, as we'll see in chapter 13, was also one of the great art comedians—argues that a spectator's reaction to a work of art is a vital aspect of that work. He describes the creative act as a "struggle" in which "the artist goes from intention to realization": "The result of this struggle is a difference between the intention and its realization, a difference which the artist is not aware of. Consequently, in the chain of reactions accompanying the creative act, a link is missing . . . [a gap] representing the inability of the artist to express fully his intention." He calls this gap the "art coefficient," but to me it sounds a bit like the audience comprehension gap we've been building into our premises.

Much as an audience has to "get" a joke, that "art coefficient" leaves artistic expression in "a raw state, which must be 'refined' as pure sugar from molasses by the spectator." (In other words: *art* farming.) As a result, "the creative act is not performed by the artist alone; the spectator brings the work in contact with the external world by deciphering and interpreting its inner qualification and thus adds his contribution to the creative act." To Duchamp, it's the spectator, and not the artist, who has the final say on the worth and meaning of art. Applied to comedy, this means that the audience decides—through their laughter—whether your joke is funny, how funny it is, and what point it's making. The poetic way to say this is that the audience's laughter is the music to the joke's lyrics. The crass way to say it is that a joke can't fart without an audience to smell it.

I know, I should have stopped with the poetic way.

Anatomy of an Audience

What do you see when you picture an "audience"? Probably a bunch of people sitting in a theater, right? And you're on the stage? And when you look down at your notes you can't read them? And you're naked?! Yeah, we've all been there.

But forget about your own issues for a moment so we can expand the idea of **audience** to mean whoever you are trying to get a reaction from with your joke. That reaction could be a personal one, like laughter that cheers up a sick grandparent or impresses the date who lied about finding a "sense of humor" sexy on their online profile. Or it could be the professional reaction of "Here is money for writing this joke for my TV show/viral ad/wedding toast that I'm too lazy to write myself." In both situations, your audience is your boss. For all the authority and control that a comedian can exert, the audience truly has the power in the relationship. It's no wonder that success in comedy is often described in violent terms—that you "destroyed" or really "killed" out there—because everyone, at some level, wants to kill their boss. And to kill them (entirely metaphorically, of course), you're going to have to know at least a little bit about them.

What to Expect When You're Expecting a Laugh

We can hold this truth to be pretty self-evident: that not all audiences are created equal. Or, in the words of Steve Allen, "Do not make the mistake of assuming that just because a particular joke or funny story got a laugh down at the pool hall, or from your sorority sisters or fraternity brothers, it will automatically be appropriate at a Kiwanis luncheon, a Communion breakfast or a family reunion." His point is as true as his references are hilariously antiquated. Unless you stumble into a time machine on your way to the open mic night, it's unlikely you'll be telling jokes at a Kiwanis luncheon. But insert more twenty-first-century-appropriate contrasting locales (like a gun club meeting vs. drag story time at the public library), and you'll get the gist of it.

As we discussed in the chapter on tone, context matters. Who you are will have a massive effect on how an audience understands your joke. But who *they* are is part of that context, too. So the first questions to ask yourself are, in no particular order:

- Who is the recipient of this joke?
- What's their sensibility, frame of reference, and all the other keywords Kalan keeps repeating over and over again?
- How do I deliver my joke so that it fits as many of those parameters as it can?
- Who is likely to encounter my work?
- Where will they encounter it, and how?
- Will it be by choice or unsolicited?
- How might they expect to react to jokes they experience in that way?

The reader of a *New Yorker* cartoon expects to get a chuckle of wry amusement, not to be gleefully grossed out à la *MAD* magazine. The recipient of a funny birthday card expects a cute tease about their age, not a scathing attack on their complicity in institutional racism. The audience at a live performance of my podcast expects to see a PowerPoint presentation about which monsters would be good at sports, not to be the target of brutal, insult-based crowd work.

Moving between audiences can involve a certain amount of comedic code-switching. I know when I come home from work (or, more accurately, when I walk out of my bedroom office to the rest of the house where my family is), I have to dial back the aggression and crudeness of my humor. The hostility and boundary-pushing that's acceptable, and even desirable, among comedy writers is entirely unwelcome around my wife and children. When I forget this, I receive the sort of disapproving look my wife gave me when I told her the long brunch line we were waiting in was "worth it because they put real heroin in the pancakes." That comedic code-switching doesn't mean trying to become your audience or depersonalizing your material into universal mush. It means either working to help your audience understand the personal joke you're telling (as Wanda Sykes did with her "coming out as Black" routine) or considering what things your audience finds relevant and applying your voice to them.

When I performed stand-up on a tour of American military bases in Afghanistan in 2013, I was excited to write material that was relevant to the military's frame of reference (a world very different from my own) but that still came from *my* sensibility and perspective. I didn't try selling the idea that I was one of them (which probably would have made them mad), but I did try to make them feel like I was paying attention to them. I told jokes about how impressed I was by the trash-talking rivalries between the different service branches, in addition to my experience being fitted for the smallest available set of body armor. (John Oliver gave me the final punchline for that bit: me requesting the "child-soldier size.") Rather than sticking only to jokes that

I knew worked for comedy-nerd audiences, I tried to consider what my audience would want to hear about and then engaged with that from my point of view. If you're writing jokes for a college audience, think about college stuff. If you're writing jokes for the White House Correspondents' Dinner, think about scathing attacks on the political media they can enjoy pretending to be scandalized by. If you're writing jokes for a pharmaceutical sales rep convention, think about their role in the opioid epidemic. And so forth.

On second thought, maybe you don't want to tell them that opioid epidemic joke. Why? That's going to take a new subheading.

Avoiding the Two "Too"s (Tutus Are OK, Though)

Every audience has a point where they stop finding a joke funny and start finding that joke infuriating. In our chapter on tone, I mentioned how a joke can go too far, jumping the fence between playful and upsetting. A related concept is the idea of a joke being "too soon" because it deals with a sensitive subject that's still too raw for the audience to laugh at. Jesse David Fox describes this as an aspect of "comedy timing" (as opposed to the pacing- and rhythm-based "*comedic* timing"), which he defines as the time "when the audience is ready to receive a joke. . . . 'Too soon' does not mean too soon to tell a joke, but too soon to get the audience to be on board with it." I'd like to expand that idea of "too soon" into a broader concept: "too close." The closer the audience feels emotionally to the subject of a joke, the harder it can be to show them the humor in it. Or, as Richard Boston puts it, "Clothes are funny when they are either ahead of or a long way behind fashion. While they are in fashion, they are familiar and therefore not funny."

This means that in addition to being too close, jokes can also be too *distant* from an audience's experience for the audience to understand what's funny about them. Sticking with clothing as an innocent enough example that's unlikely to trigger anyone while reading this, today we may laugh at the silliness of old-fashioned neck ruffs, but we won't laugh at how small sixteenth-century neck ruffs are compared to seventeenth-century neck ruffs, although that is something I assume seventeenth-century audiences would find hilarious. Similarly, today we may laugh at the difference between baggy and skinny jeans, but to the silver-jumpsuited audiences of the far future, it'll all just look like "pants."

If a joke is too distant from an audience, it will bore them. But if a joke strikes too close to the audience's sensitive spots, it can turn them against you. For example, performing before an audience of prisoners in her special *I Coulda Been Your Cellmate!*, the comedian Mo'Nique makes jokes about how to skirt the prison's rules (taking something from their experience and applying her own voice to it), and the audience appreciates it. But when she takes a moment to talk about how cool the prison's guards are, she briefly loses the audience's goodwill. The guards' adversarial relationship with the joke's primary audience is too immediate and too visceral—too close—for Mo'Nique to make her point easily.

But here's the thing. I think that Mo'Nique could have found a way to make that audience laugh at that subject. Because even though audiences don't want you to go too far or too close, they still want you to go farther and closer than they *think* they want you to go. Consider your audience and you can probably identify the outer parameters of what they'll enjoy. As Mel Brooks says about his time entertaining vacationing Jewish families in the Catskill Mountains, "You learned what the audience expects, what they want. And then you have to learn a bigger lesson: Don't give them what they expect! Give them what they don't know and what they don't expect and maybe you'll get an even bigger explosion of laughter." When the writing is good, an audience can find humor in a joke that not only surprises but challenges them.

The secret, often, is in finding a way to challenge them while still giving them an escape hatch. In the next chapter, I'll mention how stand-up Don Rickles could perform extremely offensive material by using the escape hatch of revealing it's all a put-on, that he's really a nice guy. This is one way to safely build comedic tension in your audience, by letting them know that comedic tension will eventually be released in a safe way.

Stand-up Ronny Chieng does something similar in a routine that begins with him telling the audience, "Let's figure out which is the worst race. . . . On three I want you to shout out which race you think is the worst." The audience laughs at the audacity of the request, but Chieng refuses to let them off the hook, alternately cajoling ("Don't worry, we'll all do it together. I'll join in, of course I'll join in") and hectoring them ("This is happening! Whether you join in or not"). He's challenging the audience's understanding of their own expectations. What do they want to have happen? Will another audience member be revealed as a racist? Will *they* be revealed as a racist? Are they afraid of taking part, or afraid that part of them *wants* to take part? Chieng is taking the trope of the comedian who "says what everyone is thinking" and reversing it, forcing everyone else to do the saying and inducing a sort of giddy anxiety about a sensitive issue the audience may have balked at if Chieng had handled it in a more straightforward way (by, for instance, starting the joke by telling the audience, "You know you're all secretly racists, right? You think you aren't, but I know you are").

Chieng knows that the audience doesn't *really* want to reveal themselves as racists. They want to go to the edge but not fall over it. So after counting to three, he jumps on the audience before they have a chance to talk: "If you said anything, you're the worst 10 percent of your race." He provides them with an escape hatch by punishing them before they actually commit the crime, but not until after challenging their desires.

All humor is, in essence, a challenge to the audience. The act of listening to a joke necessitates accepting the challenge of whether you will "get" the joke. But not every audience wants to be challenged in the same way or to the same degree. Thinking about your audience ahead of time and all the factors we mentioned—context, identity, delivery method—will help you to gauge how far they may be willing to go.

Once you've estimated in your mind how far you can push the audience, plan on pushing them slightly farther than that. If you know your audience, and even more importantly, if you're *funny*, you can push them surprisingly far. Perhaps the most challenging joke I've ever seen pulled off was when my younger son, standing next to a pool in which my older son was swimming, shouted "Pee attack!" and proceeded to urinate on his brother. This is perhaps the most legitimately offensive piece of comedy I've ever seen. When a comedian tells insulting jokes about the city where they're performing, we say they're "shitting on" that place—but they're not actually releasing their bodily waste onto the audience. Rather than getting angry, however, my older son laughed and told his brother, "I like your work!" My boy had accurately gauged how far he could push his audience for a joke—which was much farther than I would have expected.

That's the kind of risky comedy you can get away with if you're familiar with the level of challenge your audience will tolerate, the kind of risky comedy your audience may not realize how desperately it wants. Mike Nichols said Elaine May's motto was "The only safe thing is to take a chance. If you keep trying to do the thing that worked last time, the encrustations of mannerisms begin to take you over. And pretty soon you're no good at all—and therefore not safe at all." By challenging your audience, you're also challenging yourself in the way all artists need to.

Still, I'd advise you not to literally pee on anyone. Without their consent, at least.

Anti-humor: Going Too Far on Purpose

There *is* a form of humor that tries to make an audience feel as if they've been peed on: **anti-humor**. Anti-humor is comedy intended to evoke confusion, annoyance, or knowing laughter by challenging the audience's understanding of how jokes work. This might involve purposefully breaking the mechanics of humor, telling deliberately bad or hacky jokes, or explicitly going after uncomfortable topics to *create* tension rather than *releasing* it. In my experience, professional comedy writers can find themselves drawn to these kinds of "wrong" jokes in the same way the host of a food travel show, inured to Michelin-starred restaurants, will seek out fermented innards or potentially fatal algae to bring a thrill to their bored palate. But anti-humor can be pushed far enough to make even hardened comedy professionals angrily sputter, "That's not even a joke!" And the reaction to anti-humor *is* often a sort of anger. After all, it's one thing to challenge someone's political views, moral values, or personal sense of worth—those get tested every day. To challenge someone's sense of humor is to attack their understanding of our shared reality.

A canonical example of anti-humor is the work of performer Andy Kaufman, who often went out of his way to confuse his audiences not just about what was or wasn't a joke but about what was or wasn't *real*. As a comedy-loving kid, I was baffled by Kaufman's "Inter-gender Wrestling Champion of the World" routine, in which he taunted women in the audience until they'd wrestle him for a cash prize. It's easier, in retrospect, to see the put-on, faux-masculine joke performance of this bit, but to contemporary audiences it was very hard to tell that he wasn't just a mean creep. That confusion wasn't a pitfall of Kaufman's work but exactly what he was aiming for. Similarly, in *The Eric Andre Show*, host Eric Andre mines humor from consistently refusing to fulfill the audience's expectation of what a talk show is supposed to be. Rather than stepping through a curtain to deliver a polished monologue, Andre begins each show by angrily destroying the set for a surprisingly long time, occasionally interrupted by a salsa dance sequence or an elaborate grenade battle with Nazi soldiers. From there, the show lives in the gap between what it's doing and what is traditionally considered entertainment.

Anti-humor functions less like traditional performance and more like a practical joke, making a fool out of a targeted person (or group of people) by putting them into a surprising, confusing, or embarrassing situation for the enjoyment of the joke teller. In some cases, the victim of the practical joke, once the joke is revealed, sees the humor in it and also laughs. But not always. Practical jokes inject comedy principles into the real world in a genuinely threatening way, testing what happens when the things we allow on the special space of a stage begin occurring in the wild. In a practical joke, you aren't telling a joke to someone but telling it *on* them and *through* them. It's why I don't really like them myself: Their humor relies on making someone feel bad, usually without that person's consent. There's a thin tonal line between practical joking and bullying, the latter of which I've been on the wrong end of plenty of times.

But even though I'm not a fan of practical jokes, I *am* a fan of anti-humor. Yes, there's certainly something snobbish and exclusionary about it, even a whiff of bullyishness, but there can also be something exciting for an audience in experiencing humor that feels truly different. After all, even the edgiest, intended-to-offend, bad-boy humor relies on the same basic joke principles that Plautus used when he roasted the Carthaginians for talking weird. To realize other principles are possible can be revelatory. I remember vividly the first time I saw comedian and musician Reggie Watts perform using a keyboard and a looping machine to create a surreal series of silly sounds that abruptly transformed into an English-accented account of wandering through a dream dungeon before dissolving back into nonverbal sounds again. I wasn't quite sure exactly *how* what he was doing was funny, but I laughed at how exciting it would be to find out. It's a worthwhile goal to shock an audience not just with taboo content but with new forms they aren't equipped to understand—yet.

Anti-humor's challenge to the audience contains an interesting contradiction. Since it depends on inciting annoyance and confusion, it can feel even more cruelly dismissive than the most savage, insulting audience roasting. But the reaction of the audience is also so fundamental to the working of anti-humor that, in a way, anti-humor is actually the most collaborative of all comedy forms. The audience isn't just there to consume the material but to be a true part of it. Of course, how enjoyable that is depends on the audience. Most people want to be in on a joke without being *in* the joke. In the case of anti-humor, it's not just enough to know your audience; you also need to know how willing you are to be disliked by them.

Your Audience Has Some Notes

It's a cliché for a writing instructional manual to say that all writing is rewriting, and this particular writing instructional manual is in no way above using that cliché! Comedy is rarely a one-time thing. Jokes are reworded and retold, shows create new episodes, and movies and prose pieces are followed by more movies and prose pieces. Each new or renewed work of comedy you create should benefit from the "notes" your audience gives you through their approval, their lack of approval, or literally verbal or written criticism of what they feel you didn't do well. As a sensitive creative person, you will at first feel the instinct to discard those notes. But as a professional who wants to constantly improve your abilities, you need to take those notes.

Tig Notaro once described this process in regard to her "Taylor Dane" routine that we talked about in chapter 3: "It's just a process of editing. . . . You notice that nobody's responding to this line or this chunk ever. This never gets a response. . . . You go back and think, OK, even if they're not laughing at it, is it part of setting up the story and it's necessary? And if it is, then you keep it, and if it's not, then . . . you just get rid of it." The highlight of that routine was a direct result of the feedback from the audience. "It was when I first said, 'And guess, you'll never believe who it was.' That was the big turning point for the story, because I feel like that line was in response to an audience being bored." Notaro understood where her audience was at that moment and reworked the routine so that she was implicitly telling them, as she describes it, "I'm with you, and we're together and here we go."

I had a similar experience while working on *Mystery Science Theater 3000: The Return*. I first ran the writers' room with a philosophy I called "MaxJokes"—literally, I wanted the maximum number of jokes that could be packed into the running time of the show. And guess, you'll never believe what the audience's biggest criticism was: too many jokes. Rather than arguing with their critique, I watched the show again and found that the audience was right. The jokes were too tightly packed, making it hard to digest one before another was shoved at them. On the next season, *Mystery Science Theater 3000: The Gauntlet*, I made a point of putting in fewer jokes and clearing out episodes that felt too full—to the point that Joel Hodgson, the show's creator, dubbed me the "Joke Killer." But each time I killed a joke, I felt like I was showing respect for the audience, our most important collaborator.

It's easy to dismiss an audience's negative reaction as "They just don't get it" or "They're not ready for this" or "They're idiots." But don't fall into the "You're wrong, I'm a genius" trap. Occasionally, sure, there are comedy writers who are ahead of their time. But, no offense, you're probably not. And even if you are, it takes a later audience to validate that the earlier audience was wrong. As Marcel Duchamp put it, "The artist may shout from all the rooftops that he is a genius: he will have to wait for the verdict of the spectator in order that his declarations take a social value."

When I find myself falling into this trap, I think about brussels sprouts. For generations, brussels sprouts were *the* standard comedy reference for bad-tasting food, universally considered a punishment to eat. Now, brussels sprouts are served all over the place. And I personally love them. Did tastes change? No! Brussels sprouts farmers and brussels sprouts scientists literally worked for years to breed sprouts that tasted better. And it worked! There's nothing wrong with taking criticism and improving your work. Or are you telling me you're better than an entire species of sprout?

Your Audience Has Some Dumb Notes

All that being said, beware of taking your audience's notes *too* close to heart and falling into the "You're right, I suck at this" trap. There are times when your audience's notes aren't helpful critiques about your wording, structure, or premise development. Sometimes their negative response cuts into the core of who you are and what constitutes your personal voice. You should resist taking those notes. Better to express your authentic voice, however it manifests, than to distort yourself to fit the expectations of an audience who, at some level, actually does want to be surprised and challenged. Especially since it's possible to win an audience back from the realm of disapproval. I've seen stand-up comedians who are literally being booed by an audience stay the course with their work and reclaim the audience's humor and applause. I've watched movies or TV shows make a joke I find disgusting, off-putting, or just plain poorly constructed and then regain their footing not by changing but by continuing what they're doing with greater confidence, style, and professionalism.

The notes you want to take are about whether you're communicating your ideas effectively and humorously, not necessarily about *what* ideas you're choosing to communicate. Remember that a specific note may be wrong in its particulars, but not in pinpointing the existence of a problem. Novelist Haruki Murakami argues the same point quite well: "When a reader has a problem, there is usually *something* that needs fixing, whether or not it corresponds to their suggestions. . . . How to do that is up to me."

At the same time, keep in mind that your voice won't connect with every potential audience member out there. As Nell Scovell puts it, "Subjectivity works both ways. Just because you allow yourself to be judged doesn't mean you have to accept that judgement." There are no "one size fits all" jokes. During that same joke-heavy season of *Mystery Science Theater*, I fought hard with my coworkers over a joke I insisted stay in, one that referenced the jingle from a commercial for a Poconos resort that was constantly on TV when I was growing up. Their argument? "Nobody will get this." And, true, most people probably didn't get it. But of the hundreds of jokes I wrote for the show, that is *the* joke that people mention to me the most—because it was so funny to them that someone *else* remembered this song from a dumb regional advertisement. All humor has a target audience, and it's this target audience's response that should matter to you. If an audience never laughs at the joke, you should listen to them. Always feel free to throw a joke away. As writer and performer Larry Wilmore says, "These are just jokes. You can always come up with more later." But don't be so quick to throw away the thought or feeling that made you want to *write* the joke.

Still, you will sometimes have to take a bad note for practical reasons. While writing a weekly newspaper column, I joked in one article that newspapers were obsolete, deeming them "the horse and buggy of media." I thought it was hilarious, but one particular reader did *not* find that column funny: the owner of the company. I didn't have a choice about taking that note, because I got fired. Chalk it up to really, *really* not understanding my audience.

Comedy and the Unknown

The audience is your boss, but they're not your enemy. They want the exact same thing you want: for them to laugh at your jokes. It can be frustrating that such a huge element of joke writing is out of the hands of the writer. But that's also where the excitement of creating humor comes from. I compared comedy to magic in chapter 6, and this is another way they're alike. For the magician, the enjoyment of magic isn't in the execution of the trick but in provoking the audience's response. Likewise, the real thrill of a joke isn't in writing it but in sharing it and seeing what happens. It's why we tell jokes about heroin pancakes to our wives, even when we think they probably won't like them. What if they surprise you and laugh?

That risk is what drives us to grow as artists, and it gives us license to try new things. Steve Martin describes a world in which he's never surprised by an audience's reaction as "a dull comedy heaven." If you're 100 percent sure how the audience is going to react, why bother telling the joke at all? Why play a game where there's no chance of losing? Our dependence on the audience's reaction is scary because their disapproval can feel so debilitating. But it's worth risking because their approval is meaningful. It is literally the most valuable part of joke writing: goal, reward, and final step all in one. It is, for lack of a funnier or less syrupy word, beautiful.

Part 3

Several, but Not by Any Means All, Uses of Comedy

ALL JOKES ARE BUILT OUT OF the same parts and principles, but that doesn't mean all jokes are used in the same way. There are a number of different forms, intentions, and audiences—let's call them "reasons"—for which you might want to write a joke, and those reasons should be taken into account when you work through your farming process. In this section, we'll look at some particular uses of joke writing that I've had experience with and can speak about with at least a little authority. I hope that by the end of these chapters you'll see the different ways jokes interact with the forms, intentions, or audiences they're written for, as well as the similarities that underpin all humor writing and what that may mean for you in practical working terms.

8
Stand-Up

I THOUGHT I WAS GROWING UP in the golden age of stand-up comedy. As a child of the 1990s, I was lucky enough to experience the consequence of the 1980s stand-up comedy club boom—namely, that there were a lot of people performing stand-up comedy. It seemed like every cable channel had its own stand-up comedy show, as if the government had ordered them to provide outlets for the nation's unsustainable overproduction of observational humor. There was such a thick slurry of stand-up comedy oozing out of my TV screen that it seemed like anyone could become a stand-up comic. Even me.

Turns out, I had no idea how much stand-up comedy it was possible for the world to contain. Looking back, years later—from a world of YouTube and social media, where a stand-up can self-produce and self-distribute the kind of one-hour special you used to need a pay cable channel's permission to bring into the world—the stand-up climate of my early years seems quaint. If we're talking about ready audience access to high-quality comedy, and ready access *to* audiences for comics outside of big cities and establishment television networks, then *now* is the golden age of stand-up. Because now, in theory, all you need in order to be a stand-up is the jokes.

CHAPTER EIGHT

What Is Stand-Up Comedy?

Stand-up comedy is when a person stands up on stage (hence the name) and tells jokes to an audience, presenting their thoughts uninterrupted, ideally, except by laughter and occasional applause. Seems pretty simple on the face of it. And yet, before we go further, I should mention the raging multiyear debate among comedy people about what is or isn't stand-up. Is Hannah Gadsby's special *Nanette* stand-up, since it takes an abrupt hard turn into dramatic anger as it critiques the basic premises of stand-up? Was Bob Newhart doing stand-up when he performed sketch comedy dialogues with imaginary characters? What if the comedian uses visual images or a guitar, like Demetri Martin? What if it's two people, like when Kate Berlant and John Early perform together? Is it stand-up if the comic is *sitting down*?

This argument over what is or isn't stand-up isn't entirely a bad thing. When artists argue about the proper definition of their art, it implies that they accept what they do *is* art and that the technical demands of the form and the creativity required to work within those formal demands are worth taking seriously. After all, nobody argues about what is or isn't coal mining. On the other hand, nobody on the outside of this argument—that is, the audience—really cares at all what technically is or isn't stand-up, as long as they're laughing. It's healthy to recognize that.

It's also healthy to recognize the artificiality of stand-up. You aren't talking *with* an audience but *to* them, holding the spotlight in a way otherwise reserved for teachers, elected officials, and the warden announcing the rules on the first day of prison. You're not interacting or conversing but performing, and this gives you license to say things you wouldn't, couldn't, or shouldn't say in a conversation. Occasionally someone in the audience tries to make it a conversation, and that generally goes badly for them. Audience, don't be confused: It's not a real conversation. That stand-up comedian isn't even a real person! Well, kind of. I'll explain.

Stand-Up, Voice, and Persona

When an audience watches a stand-up performing onstage, they buy into the illusion that there isn't anything between them and the thoughts and feelings of the person telling the jokes. But this isn't actually the case. Remember in chapter 4 I said that when you write a joke for your own voice you're really writing it for "you," the character version of yourself. In stand-up, that difference between you and "you" creates a sort of thin, protective membrane around the performer: the joke teller's persona. And that persona is where a stand-up's voice lives.

Persona is what I call "personality plus." It's an exaggeration of the teller's natural personality into a bigger, simpler, and more clearly defined comic self that expresses itself through specific kinds of jokes. You can boil down most successful stand-ups to the persona that they've carefully crafted for themselves. Not literally, I mean. Please don't boil stand-ups. What I mean is something like this:

Ali Wong: aggressive taboo-breaker
Aparna Nancherla: anxious introvert
Kate Berlant: overconfident eccentric
Katt Williams: cartoon super-pimp

JB Smoove: your uncle who is always doling out advice but doesn't have a job and still lives with your grandmother (credit for this description goes to the great comedy writer Devon Coleman)

Describing their styles and personalities this way may sound reductive, but part of being a stand-up is exercising that reduction on *yourself*. You are not merely your stand-up persona—your life offstage is much more complicated and nuanced—but your stand-up persona is the part of your life and your voice that gets used for laughs, a crystallization of the funniest specific aspects of who you are. Why? Because as we mentioned in our chapter on tone, the context of a performer's identity can make a joke funnier. Audiences will laugh more when they feel they have a sense of who the joke teller is and why these jokes are special to them. As veteran comedy writer Alan Zweibel writes of the less distinctive, more traditional comedians he wrote for at the start of his career: "Yes, they were funny, but they were also interchangeable. . . . Without specific voices or individual points of view . . . they were effective, but they were not memorable." Without a persona, a stand-up is just a bag of jokes with little for the audience to invest in. With a persona, those jokes take on a greater, and funnier, significance—not unlike how a banal inspirational maxim will get more attention when it's falsely attributed to Abraham Lincoln or Maya Angelou or whoever else brings more gravitas than "anonymous inspirational maxim writer."

Ideally, your persona, like your voice, develops from a place of reality. As Steve Allen once said, "Your stage self, for stand-up comedy, should be very close to your actual social self. . . . First of all, you'll be more comfortable, and second, if you try to adopt a persona foreign to you, audiences might detect the falsity of it." Of course there are some stand-ups who adopt invented comic personas—the blue-collar yokelness of Larry the Cable Guy, the over-the-top hacky depression of Neil Hamburger, the parodistic showbiz bombast of Steve Martin—but in these cases the inventedness of the persona is (a) part of the joke and (b) still a reflection of what the comedian thinks and wishes to communicate about the world. Ralph Waldo Emerson was probably thinking about stand-up comedy when he wrote, "As I am, so I see; use what language we will, we can never say anything but what we are." Try as you might, there is no escaping yourself. Which is the saddest thing you can tell a stand-up.

In some cases, a stand-up's persona becomes nearly the entire justification for why their jokes are funny. Don Rickles was probably the most beloved insult comic there's ever been, likely because his persona wasn't just "insult comic" but "nice guy who performs as an insult comic." Baked into his persona is the overarching joke premise that he doesn't really mean anything that he's saying (let that be a counterexample whenever someone tells you stand-up is entirely about speaking truths). It's OK to laugh at him, or to be attacked by him, because it's all a put-on. This gave him the license to tell jokes that would otherwise be unacceptable, particularly jokes about racial and ethnic stereotypes that have aged poorly but are told with such cartoonish spite that they end up feeling far less offensive than if we thought he might have actually meant them. Through his persona, Don Rickles is essentially roasting all of humanity, with all the underlying love that a comic roast is meant to communicate.

In other words, a stand-up's persona can legitimize their material for an audience by providing necessary context.

When a joke doesn't fit a stand-up's persona (when it lies outside that persona's sensibility), it can trigger the wrong reaction in an audience. Let's say you're going to see a comedian who has a "maniac" persona and is famous for doing crazy and messy things. Her most famous bit ends with her throwing baloney sandwiches at the audience. So when she starts throwing baloney sandwiches at you, you start laughing because that's what you expected from a comic whose persona is "She's liable to do anything, even throw baloney sandwiches!"

Now imagine you go see a stand-up known for her droll, deadpan tone, but halfway through a story about being romantically attracted to her therapist, she starts throwing baloney sandwiches at you. I suspect you wouldn't start laughing but would instead freeze up in some way. This isn't the person, or the persona, you thought you were seeing. You'd be confused. And confusion is the enemy of comedy. Well, confusion and people who won't stop talking during your set.

Building Your Persona

Identifying the part of yourself that can be exaggerated into a foundation for jokes isn't always a fun process. You know what, just take "always" out of that last sentence. During my years performing stand-up, I completely failed to figure out a distinctive persona that felt natural for me. This was partly because I bailed on stand-up after I realized I have little tolerance for hanging around comedy clubs in case a five-minute slot during the 1:30 a.m. show might open up. But it was also because at that point in my life I was attempting to avoid the parts of myself that would be funny if exaggerated. Like many young people interested in comedy, I got made fun of a lot growing up. I wasn't eager to do that kind of thing to *myself*. So rather than taking a look at what's funny about me, I ended up writing stand-up jokes that weren't specific to myself, and therefore I failed to reach the level of personal meaning that could make my jokes universal to an audience. I now see my mistake, as well as my mistaken belief about that mistake. A persona isn't a mechanism for insulting or teasing yourself but, rather, a way of accepting and embodying the things that make you special or different—and then using those things as a source for humor. Ideally building a persona shouldn't be a negative "what sucks about me" experience but a positive "what makes me uniquely myself" experience.

In some ways this work of excavating what's uniquely funny about yourself isn't so different from the joke-farming work we saw back in chapter 1: looking at a piece of reality, identifying the absurdity in it, and then trying out—and fine-tuning—funny ways to express that absurdity. Only in this case, the piece of absurdity is in *you*. Chuck Jones wrote, "Good comedy arises from the ability to bring to the surface, without shame, parts of yourself you would rather keep hidden." It's something we can see clearly in the work of the contemporary comedian who is perhaps the most beloved among other comedians: Maria Bamford. Bamford isn't just a brilliant joke writer ("I need to find a way to show people how much I love them despite all my words and actions") but is also rigorous in finding funny ways to honestly investigate her problems with her own existence.

Bamford's persona could be described as "adorably troubled depressive" or "confidently vulnerable oversharing neighbor." Her voice is built out of a genuine discomfort with life, but she expresses her persona's anxiety, overenthusiasm, and slippery sense of identity with a frequently cheerful tone. Her frame of reference encompasses genuinely dark thoughts and places, but her precisely calibrated tone reassures us that she's not out to hurt us. So when she criticizes the knee-jerk appending of numbers for suicide-prevention hotlines to obituaries for suicide victims, it's less harsh than one might expect: "As a person who's tried to kill themself, it always feels a little condescending. Like, I know what the fucking number is. I'm depressed, I'm not a moron!" Her persona embodies a casual acceptance of the emotions others might be embarrassed by. This signals to the audience that it's OK to laugh despite the potential for tragedy embedded in the premise. She's not insulting herself to get laughs but revealing herself.

Constructing a persona as coherent, complete, revelatory, and funny as Maria Bamford's isn't something you can do quickly (if you can do it at all, and if you can't, that's OK too: she's a genius). It develops through a process of creating material and testing it with an audience. Just as they'll tell you, through their reactions, if your jokes are funny, they'll also tell you whether your persona is funny or believable. Rarely does a stand-up emerge fully formed as who they are. As writer Marshall Brickman once said, "It takes years for the audience to help a comedian shape a comic persona." The hardest part of stand-up isn't writing the jokes, necessarily, but putting in the time it takes to listen to an audience again and again and not giving up as your persona discovers who it's supposed to be.

Writing Routines for Stand-Up

One joke-delivery method that's fairly unique to stand-up comedy is the **routine**, a collection of linked jokes. It can be a humorous story, or a multijoke examination of a topic, or a forceful but funny persuasive argument. Whatever the actual content, all routines end up being a series of jokes that build on each other as individually funny links in a larger comedy chain.

An example of this is a routine performed by comedian Wyatt Cenac on the subject (mostly) of Black History Month, which I will summarize here so dryly that he'll probably be annoyed with me when he reads this. The routine starts with Cenac acknowledging his mixed feelings about Black History Month because "nobody actually learns any Black history during Black History Month. And when I say nobody, I mean white people." He then suggests having the police pull over white people for lack of historical knowledge, which segues into the surprising number of Black history movies produced by Brad Pitt, leading to Cenac's suspicion that the actor/producer "went on one of those genealogy websites and just found out something disturbing." From there Cenac segues into talking about the after-credits teasers for Marvel movies and how Captain America, after his decades in suspended animation, almost certainly harbors the racial prejudices of the 1940s despite having a young man's face.

Each step of this act is its own discrete joke that stands on its own but also functions as the next car in a longer train of thought on the theme of how Black history is held as separate, and less important, than "American" history (meaning white history). If you like book analogies more than train analogies, then each joke is a chapter in the routine's story. But unlike a book, a stand-up routine is rarely written as one complete unit, start to finish, before being performed. Cenac described his creative process in an interview, saying, "I tend to write jokes as independent little things and then at some point I'll start to notice threads between them. . . . 'Oh, okay there's a thread here, there's a thread here,' and now maybe I can add a little connective tissue so it all feels like a complete kind of essay." His routines are therefore assembled from individual, preexisting jokes, like available rolling stock being pulled together into a freight train. (Sorry, I went back to the train analogy.)

I approve of this joke-by-joke method of routine writing. For one, it means that you're treating each joke as its own work of art—an individual idea worthy of a unique premise, which is worthy of precise wording—rather than as one small piece of the "real" work, the routine. A routine, like a chain, is really only as strong as its weakest joke. Better to take a series of strong jokes and find the connections between them than to visualize a grand routine and then load it up with mediocre jokes you only created to fill space between larger points.

When you try writing an entire routine from scratch—bedazzled by visions of a brilliant comedic epic that wrings every ounce of humor from a topic and astounds your audience with the totality of beautiful long-form work—you can easily be tempted to stretch ideas out longer than they can actually sustain laughter. I experienced this firsthand with my repeated failed attempts to write a long routine about Santa Claus. I tried very, very hard to put together a grand statement about parents trying to explain to their children that just because they lied about one magic bearded man (Santa), there's no reason to assume they're lying about the other magic bearded man (Jesus). It never really worked, though, because I was so focused on the goal of "a big routine" that I lost sight of the goal of "funny jokes." I eventually chopped the whole thing down to the only joke in the routine that audiences repeatedly laughed at: "I don't approve of Santa Claus. Why are we telling the people who kidnap kids exactly how to dress if they want to get kids to go with them?" It was far better for me to say one joke, get a laugh, and then move on to the next one than to stick with a routine that aspired to greatness but died onstage.

The opposite was the case with one of my more successful routines, "Baby Magic," in which (as I described several chapters ago) I dramatically revealed how magicians pulled off such tricks as "peekaboo" ("For centuries it has mystified history's greatest babies. A man seems to disappear before your very eyes!") and "got your nose" ("The magician merely slips his thumb between his pointer and middle fingers. A slight wiggle of the thumb completes the illusion"). This was one that I built organically: starting with the peekaboo joke and seeing that the audience enjoyed it, then eventually adding "got your nose," and so forth. I never developed a strong ending punchline for "Baby Magic," something that tied it all up in a neat, hilarious bow, but it didn't ultimately matter. Even if the joke didn't really go anywhere, the audience enjoyed each step on the way.

Why Stand-Up?

I originally thought I'd end this chapter with an argument for why you should perform stand-up. Then I realized there are already way too many stand-ups out there (for more on that, see the beginning of the chapter), and if anyone's even remotely interested in the form then they don't need my tiny nudge to get them onstage. With that said, I'll still argue that stand-up can be a great tool for the shy comedy writer who doesn't necessarily want to be a performer. Why? Immediacy. Few other forms of comedy involve such a short pipeline between the joke-writing neurons in your brain and the joke-enjoying neurons in the brains of the audience. When you perform stand-up, you get a real sense for what specific audiences feel is funny and how to mold jokes to fit that feel. It's also enjoyable to get that immediate laughter response. It shows you why all the lonely work of coming up with jokes is worthwhile. And if the audience doesn't laugh, the stakes for the beginning comedian are incredibly low. The worst thing that happens is the audience forgets you ever existed—which is no different than if you hadn't bothered trying in the first place.

9
Narrative Comedy

IT'S TIME TO TALK ABOUT writing narrative comedy—comedy expressed through stories and characters—which means it's time to talk about improv. "Whoa, whoa, whoa!" you shout as you nearly drop this book in shock: "Isn't improv *unwritten*?" Well . . . yes and no.

When I was a student at New York University's Dramatic Writing Program (they didn't have a Comedic Writing Program, or I would have been at that), I spent every Sunday night at the Upright Citizens Brigade Theater for their weekly improvisational show *Asssscat*, where the best improvisers in the city would create hilarious scenes out of nothing. After a few dozen shows, it hit me. I was watching performing, but I was also watching writing! Writing in real time! Because improv comedy is the most stripped-down example of what all narrative comedy writing is about: interaction. Interaction between voices, and interaction between voice and premise.

Narrative Comedy and Interaction

In a sense, all comedy is about interaction: the interaction between a joke teller and their audience. But **narrative comedy**—found in movies, sketches, novels, and the like—involves the specific interaction between multiple comedic voices in states of opposition, collaboration, or indifference to each other over a set length of time. Whatever the dynamic or relationship between those voices is, that's what should be the source of your comedy. In saying this, I'm knowingly stretching the definition of "voice" as far as possible—like a small piece of Saran Wrap straining to adequately cover a bowl of cookie batter—to include "the world" of a narrative: the environment outside of the character(s) that contributes to the tone or voice of the overall work. Stephen Merchant, cocreator of the faux-documentary sitcom *The Office*, once said that in the show, "all the jokes were dependent on the way that the character David Brent wanted to portray himself versus the way he was being portrayed by the documentary crew." David Brent's voice attempts to convince the audience he's cool and respected. The world voice of the documentary crew shows us he's actually pathetic, arrogant, and unlikable. The humor of the show lives in that conflict.

A lot of narrative humor lives in conflict, from Laurel pissing off Hardy to Steve Urkel pissing off everyone else on *Family Matters*. This is because comedy comes from characters being placed in situations or relationships that push them to extreme behavior. Why extreme? Because, let's face it, reality is pretty boring. We're used to it because we get reality every damn second of the day. To get an emotional rise out of an audience, comedy has to have some element of the unordinary—whether that's a crazy idea or just a normally hidden feeling being brought to the surface. In narrative comedy, characters or events should act in ways either bigger or smaller than reality. The cartoon cat that has an outsized reaction to a mouse slamming a hammer on its toe, literally changing shape from the pain, is funny. The cartoon cat that displays a bizarrely *under*sized reaction, refusing to display emotion even as red lightning bolts of pain radiate from its toe, is funny. A cartoon cat that says "Ow!" and then walks away isn't particularly funny. If you're writing something and it isn't coming out as funny as you feel it should, the issue might be that you aren't exaggerating the humorous aspect of it enough.

But conflict isn't the only kind of dynamic that pushes characters to a place of extremes. Actress Holly Hunter describes narrative interaction well when she says, "You have your own set of rules, as a character. And all these other characters have their own sets of rules, too. . . . Part of comedy is a collision of my rules with your rules." That collision can be hostile, but it can also be cooperative. When I performed as half of a sketch duo, The Hypocrites, one of our most popular sketches was about two New Jersey guys egging each other on to deliver increasingly elaborate and deluded speeches about what a lady-killing superstud they imagined Queen singer Freddie Mercury to be. There was an inherent conflict here between their beliefs and actual reality, but the joke came from the way the characters *agreed*, pushing each other to extremes of misunderstanding expressed through cartoonish Garden State accents.

Weren't We Talking About Improv?

Yes, I was just getting back to it! This kind of interaction between voices is what improv comedy is all about. But is improv really "writing"? Well, we've already stretched the definition of "voice," so why not pull on all of these definitions like taffy? I propose that *writing* is any act of conceiving and developing a joke or story. Improv is writing through the act of performance—spontaneously and without preawareness of the narrative you're telling. There are perhaps three key differences that set improv apart from traditional narrative comedy writing. First, you can't spend as much time working on it. All improv comedy is writing without the luxury of infinite time to think (not that any writer has infinite time, since we'll all die eventually). Second, you can't go back and rewrite improv, because it lacks the permanence of form that comes from being recorded (although, again, no recording is truly permanent because the sun will eventually go nova and obliterate the earth and everything on it). So if we can set aside depressing thoughts of cosmic futility, maybe we can see improvisation as the *purest* form of writing.

The other difference between improv and traditional writing is the primacy of creative collaboration between performers. Improvisers often talk with near-crazed excitement about the "group mind" through which performers discover a scene's premise and narrative arc together. In essence, they bring together their separate individual voices to create a new, shared voice which none of the individuals could have reached on their own. But to be honest, even *this* isn't that different from other forms of narrative comedy writing. All films, TV shows, and plays take multiple people to bring into existence, and all are examples of creation-through-collaboration. Even single-author books have editors (like this one! Hi, David! And yes, Tamara, I see you copyediting there as well . . .). The open non-secret of human culture is that it takes way more people to write something than the few names that get the official credit or blame.

So if improv is writing, how do you use it to write jokes? Well, an improviser would tell you that you *don't* write jokes. Rather, you should be reaching for truthful character interactions that feel funny rather than generic, interchangeable one-liners. But this is also good advice for any work of narrative comedy. Not that I don't enjoy a strong one-liner, but narrative comedy functions best when it springs organically from who the characters are and what situations they find themselves in. Quoting Chuck Jones again: "Humorous dialogue, we discovered, is not what is said; it is *where* it is said, *how* it is said, *who* is doing the saying, and who are the characters involved and/or physically or verbally responsive to that dialogue." In other words, the building blocks of narrative comedy aren't gags and jokes but voice, premise, and the ways in which they interact.

One thing this means for the non-improv writer is that you can write really wonderful narrative jokes by mimicking the process of improvisation, not unlike how I built my joke-farming process by breaking down the steps I assumed my unconscious brain was going through when it thought of a joke. One way that I've done this, though it sounds silly, is by pretending that I am more than one person when I'm writing something. Rather than sitting in one spot and just thinking, I will physically move to different spaces in a room and talk through the work out loud in conversation with myself, as if I'm more than one person working on the script. I find that these different personal voices begin to meld with the voices of specific characters until, rather than one writer pretending to be two or three writers collaborating, I become one writer pretending to be each of the different characters in the scene—which is what a writer should be doing anyway.

Improv also often takes, as its starting point, a random suggested work or phrase from an audience member. Similarly, if I find myself blocked and my fox trick from chapter 1 isn't working, I will throw a new element into a scene or an unrelated thought into a character's head. This forces the work, and my thinking, into a new and often more productive direction, if only because it's surprising to me.

These improv-inspired techniques can be useful because whether narrative comedy is prewritten or not, it always comes down to interactions involving characters with something funny about them, a situation with something funny about it, or both. Let's look at an example from sketch comedy: the "Dead Parrot" sketch, written and performed by members of the pioneering British group Monty Python in 1969. In the sketch a man wants to return a pet parrot after discovering it was actually dead when he bought it and had been nailed to its perch to make it look alive. The customer (who speaks in a very pretentious way) argues with the pet store owner (a slimy con man who refuses to admit the bird is obviously dead). All of the jokes in the scene come from the interaction of these elements and the conflict dynamic that results. The customer pushes the store owner to make increasingly exaggerated statements about the health of the dead parrot ("Of course it was nailed there. Otherwise it would have muscled up to those bars and VOOM!"), The store owner pushes the customer to make increasingly exaggerated attempts to persuade him that the parrot *is* dead, culminating in a speech by the customer made up of roughly a dozen different ways of saying "dead." There are almost no jokes in the scene unrelated to the "dead parrot" premise, and there are no jokes that could be said by anyone other than these characters in this situation. What this means, as with a lot of the best narrative comedy, is that in context the jokes are very funny, but out of context they don't really mean anything. Which, of course, you know if you've ever heard a nerdy teen quote Monty Python in conversation.

This "Dead Parrot" sketch is also an example of heightening in a narrative comedy form. The disagreement between the characters pushes them to greater extremes of behavior, but it happens at a believable (for this ridiculous premise, at least) pace. Often, first-time sketch writers will jump too quickly from their characters encountering a situation to their characters screaming at each other in anger because they mistakenly think the screaming is the funny part. What's really funny, however, is seeing the steps a character passes through as they progress toward the screaming in anger (like obliviousness, confusion, attempted patience, irritation, and doing their best not to scream in anger). As with life, so with narrative comedy: Screaming about something is only effective when other people understand *why* you're screaming about it.

Jokes and Their Relation to the Types of Narrative Comedy

I should make it clear that in talking about narrative comedy, I'm not necessarily talking about the ways a writer crafts the larger category of *narrative*. Though any narrative, humorous or not, also relies on interactions among characters and between characters and their world, my focus here is really on writing jokes for works that take a narrative form. There are any number of books out there about how to write stories for novels, film, TV, theater, and so forth in greater detail than I can do justice to here. But I do want to touch briefly on the ways that jokes function within different kinds of narratives before going into further depth about the comedy sketch, which is a joke-centered narrative medium that it's harder to find published guidance on. It's also a form that holds a special place in my heart because it's the first type of comedy I ever wrote seriously. Just as a bar tapes its first dollar to the wall, I still have the bent piece of wire hanger I used to make my necktie "float" in an early-career sketch where I played an astronaut with a foreign accent that I now understand was incredibly offensive.

For most narrative comedy, how jokes are used is a direct consequence of how long the work is. Shorter works tend to be more joke-centered, while longer works are more plot-centered, using jokes along the way. Good comedy plots aren't often funny in themselves, but, rather, they create opportunities for funny things to happen. If you don't believe me, just think about the number of times you've laughed at a summary of a funny movie. Take the movie *Everything Everywhere All at Once*, whose plot could be described as "A depressed mom has to save an infinite number of parallel universes from her daughter while getting audited by the IRS." Or look at the plot of the madcap live-action cartoon *Barb and Star Go to Vista Del Mar*: "Two unassuming single women on a beach vacation get caught up in a supervillain's diabolical plan." Did you laugh when you read either of those descriptions? Probably not. But you can see how they would create the circumstances for funny things to happen and a structure to support the delivery of jokes.

This isn't to say that movie jokes are just irrelevant filigrees garlanding the plot; they can also express and reinforce the sensibility of a film. A film like *Blazing Saddles* can have its characters literally leave the movie, helping to establish a ridiculous and parodic sensibility. Meanwhile, a movie like *Booksmart*, which operates in the real world but has the slightly exaggerated tone of a teenager's perspective, can't break the fourth wall but *can* include a stop-motion animated drug hallucination scene. However, a movie like *The Big Sick*, which wants the audience to genuinely worry one of its characters will be trapped in a coma, needs to tell jokes that accord entirely with a world we recognize as real. That's three different specific joke sensibilities, and that's just from comedies starting with "B."

On the shorter end of the narrative-joke spectrum is sketch comedy, in which the plot-joke relationship is reversed. A sketch can be anything from a thirty-second web video to a ten-minute movie parody. I would argue that anything much longer than that starts to feel like it wishes it were sitcom or a movie but isn't. Since sketches don't demand the same investment of time and emotion as longer narratives, plot isn't as important in them, and delivering jokes becomes the primary goal. Still, the jokes should build from a premise consistent enough that it doesn't dissolve into a string of random gags.

You can almost think of a comedy sketch as a series of jokes that are also components of one large, overarching joke, much like the fractal structure concept we talked about in chapter 2. A sketch, just like an individual joke, requires a clearly communicated premise that contains an idea or point, organized through a structure that tells the audience where the funny beats are in the sketch, and it speaks, in the end, with a coherent and specific voice. How do you craft a comedy sketch in that way? Well, it helps to know what type of sketch you're writing.

Robin Thede, creator of the TV show *A Black Lady Sketch Show*, helpfully breaks down the "three types of sketches: character driven, concept driven, and situation driven." In **character-driven sketches**, the jokes emerge from a character who's funny in a specific way. In the sketch "Dylan's Burger" from the show *I Think You Should*

Leave, a professor having dinner with his former students creates an awkward situation when he becomes obsessed with tasting the cheeseburger that one of the students ordered, proceeds to eat the whole thing, and then becomes increasingly aggressive in keeping his burger theft a secret, to the point of trying to record the others threatening the president so he'll have blackmail material to use against them. The premise of the sketch is built around this one strange character, his bizarre personal goal, and the effect it has on the other characters. Nothing else about the situation, setting, or the other characters is presented as skewed in any way.

Situation-driven sketches find their humor in the reactions of characters to a situation in which they find themselves. In the *Black Lady Sketch Show* sketch "Courtroom Kiki," a judge, bailiff, and lawyers are so overcome with delight when they realize they're all Black women that they can't focus on the actual proceedings. They've never experienced an all–Black lady courtroom and can't stop celebrating and remarking on it. The characters in the sketch aren't really silly, and they come off as more or less "real" people. It's the (unfortunate) rarity of the situation they find themselves in that generates the jokes.

Finally, **concept-driven sketches** are sketches built around a funny idea that may have only a minimal amount of actual narrative to it. Two *Saturday Night Live* commercial parodies showcase the spectrum of concept-driven sketches. In the 1991 sketch "Happy Fun Ball," a chipper advertisement for a red rubber ball becomes a series of increasingly extreme warnings ("If Happy Fun Ball begins to smoke, get away immediately. Seek shelter and cover head") that hint at a surprisingly bizarre backstory for the ball ("Ingredients of Happy Fun Ball include an unknown glowing green substance which fell to Earth, presumably from outer space"). The point here is how little corporations care about their customers, but it's expressed without any real characters or story. A different type of conceptual sketch is 2016's "Wells for Boys," an ad for a life-size well "for sensitive boys to wish upon, confide in, and reflect by" because "some boys live unexamined lives. But this one's heart is full of questions." As it unfolds, the ad becomes about the supportive, defensive-against-the-world relationship between a mother and her young son who will "grow up to have a wildly passionate and successful creative life, but not just yet." Though the characters aren't named and there's no story beyond brief interactions, a much larger narrative is implied—albeit through the format of a fake toy commercial. "Happy Fun Ball" shows how minimal a concept you need in order for a sketch to be funny; conversely, "Wells for Boys" shows just how much emotional depth a concept can contain.

"Character," "situation," and "concept" are not dogmatically delineated categories, however, and sketches often straddle the lines between them. Writer/performer Natalie Walker's "Female Role Audition" web videos are an example of combination character/concept sketches. In each, she portrays a cliché type of female character (with titles like "lady with a British accent who so fiercely supports the difficult man she loves" or "lady we hate because she is temporarily keepin the people w the symmetrical faces from bein together" [*sic*]) acting out dialogue that articulates the cliché or demeaning aspects of these well-worn stock characters. The humor comes from both the individual character and the larger concept that the character is illustrating.

Character, situation, *and* concept sketch ideas are all combined in "Porcupine Racetrack," a sketch from the show *The State* that takes the form of an elaborately produced musical set at a racetrack for enormous porcupines. Through their brief songs, we see the wealthy enjoying the track, a priest gambling to save his orphanage, and a slow porcupine who won't lose faith in himself. All of the jokes in "Porcupine Racetrack" emerge from characters in situations emanating from the core concept "What if *Guys and Dolls* were about a racetrack for porcupines?"

Way back in chapter 3, I flipped through a selection of joke formats to decide which one best got across my feelings about the fact that humans are destroying the planet. The earliest stage of sketch writing involves doing the exact same thing: finding the best means to express your ideas to the audience, perhaps after trying out multiple options. What type of sketch is right for the context in which you're writing? If you come up with an idea for a funny character, think about what kind of situation, setting, or interaction will best highlight what it is that makes your character funny. If you imagine a funny situation in which someone might find themself, think about how that situation can be heightened to push a normal person to an extreme reaction. And if you conceive of a funny concept that doesn't necessarily lend itself to a dramatized scene or passage of dialogue, then think about what format would allow you to communicate the concept as clearly as possible to the audience. Not all conceptual sketches have to be commercial parodies, of course, but it's a popular format precisely because it's such an easily identifiable one. Since the audience is already aware of the structure and intent of a commercial, it's easier for them to find the funny or unique conceptual idea that emerges from the sketch's various interactions—as well as the point that the sketch will invariably be making. But there are plenty of other structures that lend themselves to a similar sense of familiarity.

Straight Men: Who Needs 'Em?

That subheading came out more inflammatory than I intended, so let's define what I mean by **straight man**. Much narrative comedy has been built around the dynamic between a funny character and a so-called straight man who provides setups for, and reactions to, the jokes. A classic example is the "2,000 Year Old Man" routines of Mel Brooks and Carl Reiner, in which Reiner's serious interviewer sets up Mel Brooks's jokes about life as a caveman. Some comedy writers will tell you that you need a straight man character to ground your work in a recognizable reality. After all, as comedy caveman Brooks puts it (albeit in a non-caveman context), "Everything surrounding the comedy has to be real." I once took a sketch-writing class from a brilliant comedy writer I respect greatly, who literally said, "You need a character who points out what the game of the sketch is." But is that really true? Do audiences have trouble recognizing where the joke is? I say no. So let's get controversial! (Though maybe not as controversial as my subheading might have led you to expect.)

Let's set aside the obvious issue with using a gendered term that divides characters into the opposing categories of "straight" and "funny," which . . . look, I don't really need to explain the problematic aspect of that, right? But attempts to substitute terms like "active character" and "reactive character" or "voice-of-reason character" only highlight my real, nonsemantic issue with this kind of comedy foil. When a character is explicitly set up as the voice of reason, their role becomes explaining the joke to the audience. And if a joke has to be explained, then it's being told wrong. (Although if jokes are being *analyzed*, on the other hand, the audience is getting really valuable insight and should leave a positive review of the book that's providing that analysis on the retail website of their choice.)

If narrative comedy is written well, then the audience's foreknowledge of *reality* should function as the voice of reason. Perhaps I'm giving the audience too much credit, but in my experience if a premise is communicated clearly, then they will pick up on whatever aspect of the character, situation, or concept is purposefully off-kilter. In my aforementioned Freddie Mercury sketch, the audience didn't need a third character to point out these guys were wrong about Freddie being a ladies' man. The audience did it in their heads, leaping the gap in the premise and comprehending the joke. If your work needs a character to point out what aspect of behavior is being exaggerated, then it probably hasn't been exaggerated enough. If your sketch is about someone trying to bring their "service elephant" onto a plane, the flight attendant shouldn't have to say, "That's a wacky animal to bring onto a plane!"

There's a counterargument to be made, though, that the reactive character can operate as a vehicle for the audience's natural curiosity when faced with something out of the ordinary. For instance, the flight attendant could ask the elephant's owner how he even got an elephant through the airport, and the passenger could answer, "I put him in a separate bin at security." But if a character just points out "That's not how that's supposed to work!" as the active character goes about their business, then they aren't being a surrogate for the audience but the surrogate for a writer who didn't figure out how to set up their premise clearly.

Perhaps, then, my unintentionally inflammatory subheading may have overstated the case, and reactive characters *are* useful as long as they don't react by merely stating the premise of the active character's actions. And perhaps my problem with these "straight man" characters is that often they aren't treated as "characters" at all but as dramatic crutches. A reactive character who truly takes part in a scene, who changes through their reactions to the joking character, and whose reactions (and interactions) lead the joking character to further action, can be a valuable part of a piece of narrative comedy. Although Carl Reiner's interviewer is technically necessary to get jokes from the 2,000-year-old man, the funniest parts of their routine are when Reiner, rather than clarifying the old man's jokes, adds to them, responds to them, or interrogates them, spurring the old man to heighten or develop his jokes. The best way to look at a straight man is to see them as someone helping the funny character to be funny, rather than helping the audience to get the joke.

Of course, there is one qualified exception to what I'm saying: a specific audience that needs more help understanding jokes, perhaps even to the point of requiring a reactive character who explains what element of reality has been skewed for humorous purposes. This special audience simply hasn't had the time to accumulate a full experience of reality or of how jokes work. The technical term for this audience is "children," and we'll talk about writing comedy for them in the next chapter.

10
Children's Comedy

LAUGHTER IS A PART OF LIFE from infancy. Children love to laugh, and it often comes more easily to them than to adults. As my four-year-old son said to me while I was writing this book, "It's nice to laugh at the end of a joke. Especially if it's a funny one." The qualification is useful, though, because the reality is that kids will also laugh at jokes that *aren't* funny. Or at least jokes that aren't funny to adults. And then if they really like a joke, they'll repeat it over and over and say "Get it?" even if they don't fully get it themselves.

When we're babies, all it takes to make us laugh is the element of surprise. When an adult covers their face and then uncovers their face, they perform a little three-act joke for the baby: I exist! I don't exist! I exist again! Until the baby develops object permanence, this existential back-and-forth is pretty much all you need. Once they figure out that you don't vanish forever when you cover your face, though, children begin providing the determined joke writer with a challenge: The gap in comprehension between you and your audience has to be shorter, because children, with their tiny little mental legs, aren't capable of making the same logical leaps as adults. Or, to put it another way, kids don't know shit.

CHAPTER TEN

Writing for Kids: Like Writing for Adults, But Less So

Kids lack an adult frame of reference when it comes to jokes. This isn't just because they don't have experience with jobs, dating, and those clowns in Congress but because they don't have much experience with *jokes*. They haven't had time to absorb the ritual forms of joke telling or hear the most oft-repeated jokes. In some ways, this can be a huge boon for writers. Because kids don't know what's been done before, you don't have to be as original when you craft jokes for them. To children, even the oldest, corniest jokes are cutting-edge. I cherish the memory of when my older son read a book in which a character said, "What am I, chopped liver?" He found this expression so hilarious that he literally called me into his room to read it aloud to me. I didn't have the heart to tell him that it was a hacky thing to say even before his grandfather was born.

Am I telling you to take comedy that already exists, slap a new coat of paint on it, and serve it up to kids who don't know any better? Not exactly, and not just because you shouldn't serve paint to kids. If you're a comedy writer, I'm sure you want to write jokes that are *your* jokes and not just someone else's retold. But you can wear your influences more openly without worrying that your audience members will kidsplain back to you that your joke's been done before. No kid is going to call out the slow-talking sloth DMV workers in *Zootopia* for being basically the same joke as sketch duo Bob & Ray's classic "Slow Talkers of America" routine. And no kid who's ever read my picture book *Sharko & Hippo*—in which a shark gets frustrated because every time he asks his hippo friend for a specific item, the hippo hands him a different item that sounds like the thing he asked for—has recognized that it was heavily inspired by a scene in the Marx Brothers movie *Animal Crackers*.

But a child's lack of exposure to the vast annals of comedy isn't always helpful, because it also means children have a narrower frame of reference for humor. I find that deadpan jokes don't work as well with kids, sarcasm can go totally unnoticed, and meta jokes that call attention to their own mechanisms are much harder to pull off successfully. Kids simply don't take the same things for granted that adults do—they haven't yet developed the same internal patterns—so it's harder to make jokes that take advantage of those assumptions. This applies to a child's cultural frame of reference, as well. It's hard to write a successful parody, for instance, for a child who may not be aware of the original work being parodied.

That being said, a child's lack of experience with the world and the comedy therein is hardly an insurmountable barrier for the grown-up comedy writer. There are two very powerful weapons in your arsenal for overcoming these odds. One of them we've already talked about, and the other one involves remembering what it's like to be a child in the first place. These weapons are structure and silliness.

Structure: It's What Kids Crave

I know, I know, we had a whole chapter about structure earlier in the book. "Whew, that was a lot of talk about structure!" you thought as you flipped through the book. "I'm sure the latter half of the book is mercifully structure-free." And then BAM! More structure! I'm bringing it back because in some ways, structure is even more important for children's humor than it is for adult humor. In writing for adults, a joke's structure helps the audience to understand the joke. In writing for kids, a joke's structure doesn't just signal how to understand this *particular* joke, but *all* jokes like this one, and even the *concept* of jokes in general. If structuring a joke is like giving someone directions on how to drive to Funnytown, then imagine what it's like when the person you're directing doesn't even know how to drive in the first place.

The key to structuring jokes for kids, then, is to rely even more heavily on the fundamental basics: clear setups and payoffs, quickly graspable and repetitive patterns, and a minimal amount of twisting. A great example of this at its simplest is the picture book *Blue Hat, Green Hat* by Sandra Boynton. On each page, four animals wear the same item of clothing in different colors. The elephant, moose, and bear cub (or possibly a tailless dog, I've never been able to tell) wear the item correctly, while the turkey just can't seem to get his act together and wear his clothes right, all of which leads to the narrator's repeated punchline: "Oops." This happens six times in a row—hats, shirts, pants, coats, socks, and shoes—and each time ends with the turkey screwing up by wearing the item wrong. Finally, the turkey gets dressed properly . . . and jumps into a swimming pool for the final "Oops."

This is a particularly simple book, and kids pick up the joke right away. The pattern is set early: three correct animals and one foul-up turkey doing something so obviously incorrect, like standing in a hat, that kids understand the disruption. The book is sheer structure, built on the simplest building blocks of a repeating pattern whose disruption, in turn, becomes a repeating pattern to disrupt one last time. By building her patterns so clearly, and walking the reader through it step by step, Boynton is essentially saying, "This is how a joke works."

A similar comedic-structure-that-also-teaches-that-structure can be found in David Ezra Stein's picture book *Interrupting Chicken*, where a father chicken is repeatedly exasperated by his daughter interrupting the stories he reads her so that she can warn the main characters about the danger they're about to face. The pattern here is another simple one: The father chicken starts reading a traditional fairy tale, the daughter chicken jumps in and interrupts the story, he gets annoyed, and she promises not to do it again. And then she does it again. The father chicken states aloud what the little chicken is doing incorrectly, explaining the joke to the audience so that they can understand it and be ready for it the next time. It's a classic active character/reactive character construction, because, regardless of everything I said last chapter, a character who clarifies the situation can be helpful for younger audience members.

Often in writing we try to cover up the internal scaffolding of our work so that it comes across as an effortlessly perfect miracle. Don't do this with kids' comedy. You want them to see how it's constructed, and, unlike with adult audiences, the joke can be successful even if the kid audience sees the punchline coming ahead of time. Children have very little in life that they feel control over, so they enjoy and are empowered by being slightly ahead of the material they're seeing. You may have seen the classic children's theater bit where one character pretends to look for another character, somehow totally oblivious to that character being right behind them. The kids in the audience shout, "Behind you! Behind you!" and the adult performer pretends not to understand or responds so glacially slowly that the hidden character has time to go hide somewhere else. Kids enjoy being the ones who know the secrets of the universe for once.

I chase that feeling in my picture book *Horse Meets Dog*, in which a dog assumes a horse is a big dog, and the horse assumes the dog is a baby horse. The joke comes from both the characters' confusion and the opportunity for the kids to know more than the characters in the book. In an early draft of the book, the characters were much more assertive at the beginning—the dog saying he's a dog and the horse saying she's a horse, but neither taking each other at their word. It was my editor, Donna Bray, who suggested the characters not actually state what kind of animal they are until close to the end. This had the benefit of not only making the book less repetitive but also giving the kid readers that extra little edge over the characters. It provided them with a wider—but not too wide—premise comprehension gap for them to cross on their own and feel smart about. No matter how much about the adult world seems incomprehensible to kids, at the very least they can tell a dog from a horse.

Just as you might feel the impulse to cleverly complicate your joke's structure, you might also shy away from the kind of very blatant repetition that I'm describing in this chapter. But again, that repetition is something that children enjoy. Children want the same stories read to them over and over, and the same movies shown to them over and over, and the same songs played for them over and over, until their parents are driven mad! Mad, I tell you!! The familiarity of that repetition is comforting to them, and in writing for them it makes sense to steer into that comfort. I don't mean that you need to write them the same kinds of stories they've seen before but instead that you should build a sense of repetitive familiarity into your jokes. You might say, "But my comedy isn't about comfort, it's about shocking the audience." That's totally cool, but why do you want to shock kids? They're not the problem. It's adults that are screwing the world up.

Silliness: Kids Ask for It by Name

If you were going to ask my children what they think is funny, they almost certainly would *not* say "Daddy." They'd say "Minions." The jabbering, destructive, idiotic, irritating henchmen characters from the *Despicable Me* universe of films. Why do my kids think the Minions are funny? Well, they're jabbering, destructive, idiotic, and irritating. To put it in one word, they're silly, and kids love silly things. I could craft a brilliantly effective, structurally fine-tuned, uniquely personal joke, and it will never make my children laugh as much as one image of a Minion's butt. Because what's even sillier than a Minion? Its butt.

Goodnight Moon author Margaret Wise Brown once said, "To be a writer for the young, one has to love not children but what children love." I take this to mean that when writing for children, don't make the mistake of being too far above your audience. Remember, as we discussed in our chapter on audience, you want to write jokes that *they* think are funny. Your work may be teaching kids how jokes work, but you're not trying to teach them which jokes are funny. They know what things are funny to them, and if you want to make them laugh, you have to meet them where their funny bones are. Writing comedy for kids isn't for the easily ashamed or preciously dignified. They love all the dumb things you're afraid they love: toilets, characters screaming and hitting each other, pants falling down, and so forth.

You know what they don't always love? Wordplay. My kids enjoy when I read *Alice's Adventures in Wonderland* to them, but Lewis Carroll's elegantly mathematical wit doesn't get them guffawing as much as when the characters in Dav Pilkey's *Dog Man* books sing a parody of "Take Me Out to the Ball Game" about poop.

This isn't to say that all toilety silliness is merely crass and vulgar. The *Dog Man* series uses its toilet humor to tell an increasingly nuanced story about forgiveness and the redemptive power of love—a message my kids are only receptive to after they get their dose of poop jokes. It's worth repeating the Joe Flaherty quote from chapter 3, "It was always most important to make the audience laugh. After that you could make social comments, or make a point, anything, but first and most important make sure it's funny." For kids, as with adults, silliness opens the door to easier acceptance of the serious.

For me the core elements of silliness are exaggeration, the unexpected, and logical illogic. **Exaggeration** is, of course, taking something about the world and stretching it in scale or intensity to a ludicrous degree. Successful exaggeration for kids should exist in their relatively limited frame of reference, but within that frame of reference there's a lot of fun to be had. Not having been disillusioned by life, kids have a very firm sense of how the world is supposed to work, and those elements can be exaggerated into jokes they find hilarious. There's a scene in the first issue of Jeff Smith's comic book *Bone* in which the main character, Fone Bone, is told that winter "hits fast" in the valley he's just traveled to . . . right before an entire season's worth of snow is suddenly dumped on his head. Even though my younger son has lived his entire life in Southern California, he knows snow doesn't just plop down all at once like that. So he laughs every time we get to that part.

My next element of silliness is **the unexpected**. I don't just mean random surprises but rather a sense of seeing things acting at odds with the way a child expects them to (i.e., the snowfall in *Bone*). B. J. Novak's *The Book with No Pictures* has a very clever conceit—it's a "picture book" that instead of pictures contains text meant to be read aloud by an adult, which forces them to say silly things like "I am a monkey who taught myself to read" and "BluuRF." Each of these things is an unexpected, and therefore silly, thing for an adult to say. Beyond being silly, though, they're also unexpectedly embarrassing, reversing the power dynamic between the child and the grown-up in a way that children revel in.

Even as you're exaggerating and being unexpected, you should also be thinking somewhat logically. Silliness isn't just a matter of nonsensical gibberish. It helps if there's a sort of **logical illogic** to the silliness, a twisted rationality to the joke being presented. In a sketch I wrote for *The Who Was? Show*, Isaac Newton sits under a series of fruit trees, each time getting bonked on the head. Only after he sits under an apple tree is he inspired to think of gravity. But before that he's hit on the head by a banana and a coconut, and he narrowly misses being crushed by a piano from a "piano tree." This is a silly, unexpected, illogical thing, because pianos don't fall from trees. At the same time, however, it's presented as part of the same logical pattern of "increasingly large things that are not apples falling from trees." If a piano had fallen from a moving company's crane instead of a tree, it would have been more logical in its relationship to reality, but less logical as the third step in a sketch about increasingly big things falling from trees. Not to mention it would also be less funny.

Perhaps another way of describing logical illogic is that the silliness must remain true to itself—that each kind of silliness has a consistent sensibility. Even the Minions, for all their random acts of nonsensical destruction and incomprehensible jabbering, follow logically illogically from the established rules of their own personalities. When they impersonate the crew of an airplane and decide, on a whim, to nearly crash the plane into the ground, it's silly and irrational. But it's a silliness that makes rational sense coming from the Minions. Even silliness must follow the rules laid down by its own silliness—they're just silly rules.

Premise Building, Kid-Style

Discovering or developing a joke's premise can already be a challenge. How do you find a premise that will resonate with this bizarre, half-formed creature we call a "child"? The best advice I can give you is to free yourself from your adult perspective and ground your humor in things kids will recognize from their own frame of reference. Charles Schulz's *Peanuts*, a comic with a mature, often melancholy tone, is beloved by children in part because, as Bruce Handey writes, "the strip's surface concerns are children's: friendships, pets, baseball, kite flying, thumb sucking, schoolyard crushes." In other words, when creating the strip, Schulz put himself in a kid's world. I mentioned that my book *Sharko & Hippo* is inspired by a Marx Brothers routine, but it also resonates with the common kid feeling of frustration when a friend doesn't want to play the way that you want to.

Premises for children should aspire to the same condition that Ariel in *The Little Mermaid* desires for herself, to be "part of their world," only here we mean the world of kids and not the world of princes who don't seem to care if their girlfriends have opinions on anything. Look under the hood of successful kid comedy, and more often than not you'll find that it's connected to some real kid-world feeling or experience. The book *Crazy Clothes* by Niki Yektai is a very literal example of this: A child gets too silly while getting dressed and annoys their mother but blames it all on their clothes acting up instead. The book *Secret Pizza Party* by Adam Rubin and Daniel Salmieri is a less literal example of this: It's the story of a pizza-loving raccoon who has trouble getting the pizza he craves because he's a raccoon. Most kids have not been raccoons, but they *have* felt what it's like to be denied the thing they want. The story is silly, but the emotional basis of the premise is relatable. Kid humor is often built on these kinds of universal feelings, such as

- being misunderstood or ignored
- wanting something and not getting it
- fear or suspicion of new things
- conflict with friends, siblings, parents, or pets
- something not happening the way you expected or hoped

These aren't particularly funny feelings. But as I said in the chapter on premise, the point of a joke isn't necessarily funny in and of itself. Good kid jokes, like good adult jokes, use humor to say something. They are expressing a perspective on the world that is informed by a specific frame of reference. Start with something real, then make it silly.

And yeah, I hate to keep bringing up the goddamn Minions, but they're a good example of that, too. What are the Minions but exaggerated, nightmarish extrapolations of a child's perspective and frame of reference? They have the same immature whims and gluttonous or violent desires as kids—but they also have the power to act on those whims and desires by stuffing their bodies with junk food, blowing things up with rockets, and dancing whenever and wherever they want. That's what draws children into their world so strongly, even more than the fact that they have butts.

When you've built your joke premises on relatable feelings, structured them clearly, and coated them liberally with silliness, you can make kids laugh. Even more than that, you can make kids laugh at surprisingly meaningful ideas. As we talked about at the top of this chapter, the first thing a baby laughs at is the very fact of existence. That's pretty deep for a baby.

11
Satire

ALTHOUGH I BELIEVE, as I said in chapter 3, that every comedic premise has a point behind it, I don't believe every joke has to communicate a serious message. It's perfectly acceptable for a joke to play off our understanding of reality in the form of silly nonsense that merely distracts us from the horrors of being alive—in fact, it's essential. Humanity cannot live by raw emotional honesty alone! Let the people laugh at dumb stuff! That being said, there's one form of comedy this belief doesn't apply to, one form of comedy that not only needs to communicate a serious point but also succeeds or fails based on how well that point is absorbed by the audience—even if they don't end up finding it particularly funny. What makes that mission difficult is that it's a form which often delivers its message by pretending to tell us the opposite of what it means. As a result, it's a form inordinately reliant on capturing the proper tone. This form is satire—where multiple intersecting levels of facetious statements and sincere feelings regarding touchy subjects are presented to an audience that may not expect it, may disagree, or may be looking at their phones and not completely paying attention.

CHAPTER ELEVEN

What Is Satire?

Satire is a tricky thing to define, partly because the word is often used pretty loosely to mean "jokes that are critical of something." I think this is because satire, unlike other joke uses we talk about in this book, isn't defined by its shape (like stand-up or narrative) or its audience (like children's comedy) but by its *intent*. Literary critic Northrop Frye defines it as "militant irony," which feels like a pretty good start.

Satire is humor that targets a point of view, concept, or situation and inflates it to a grotesque degree in order to identify and attack that target. To put it in the simplest possible terms: *Satire exaggerates to reveal.* It takes a problematic aspect of life that has become so generally accepted that the audience doesn't see it as a problem anymore and then pushes it down a slippery slope of embellishment until the problem has become so ludicrous or shocking it can no longer be ignored. As US Air Force Academy English professors Lt. Col. Frederick Kiley and Maj. J. M. Shuttleworth write (I know, I'm also surprised to be quoting ranking military officials in this book), "Satire must break through the crust of familiarity which obscures our judgment of matters we are too closely involved in to judge objectively." This is why the movie *Dr. Strangelove* has been the standard-bearer for satire for the past sixty years (even though—hot take!—I've never found it all that funny). Through its story of an insane Air Force colonel and an impotent president bumbling their way into humanity-extincting nuclear war (probably not a favorite of two Air Force officer English professors), the film takes a thought that has been living secretly in the back the audience's minds and forces that idea to the front of their minds, where they can't pretend they don't see it: that world-destroying weapons are being handled by ludicrously incompetent fools and maniacs.

Satire can't arise in a vacuum. Even more than nonsatirical comedy, it must react to something that already exists: a system, a person, a fashion trend, a particularly goofy animal. . . . Satire's reactivity often takes the form of explicitly mimicking the thing being satirized so that its flaws can be exaggerated, as Charles Yu does in his novel *Interior Chinatown*, which tackles Asian American stereotypes in American media by telling its story in screenplay format and forcing its characters to live out stereotypical roles in their private lives. In this way, satire can make its point by play-acting the opposite of its true beliefs to a ridiculous degree. When Sacha Baron Cohen, in the guise of his racist foreign TV personality Borat, gets an audience of Americans to sing along with his song "Throw the Jew Down the Well," he adopts the veneer of an anti-Semite in order to expose how quickly and easily an audience will accept and repeat anti-Semitism. He's not actually advocating throwing Jews in wells. But as I'll get into later, satire can be as tricky to understand as it is to execute. At least one member of his audience might have walked away excited about the idea of filling their well with Jews. Which, I must make clear, as a Jew myself, is not a great thing to do with Jews.

We talked earlier about how in comedy writing you have a certain understanding of your audience—what frame of reference they bring to a joke, what they expect from a joke, and, very important for satire, how far they're capable of being challenged. Add to that list an estimate of what implied cues they will be capable of processing. And then on top of that, you also need an understanding of the people who are *not* your intended audience who may also encounter this work. It takes a lot of understanding your potential audience to make sure that your satirical intent is understood.

What Isn't Satire?

Not everything that makes fun of a thing is satire. Satire often gets mixed up with **parody**, another reactive comedy form based on something the audience already recognizes. The distinction I make between satire and parody is that parody makes fun of a target's style or surface but not necessarily its underlying ideologies. Satire, on the other hand, makes fun of a target's underlying ideologies, which may mean making jokes about its style. Above all, as literary critic David Worcester pithily puts it, "The content of satire is criticism."

To put it in comedy-song terms—the best terms to use when explaining things—Weird Al Yankovic's songs "Like a Surgeon" (a parody of Madonna's "Like a Virgin") and "Amish Paradise" (a parody of Coolio's "Gangsta's Paradise") are parodies, not satires. The former is a play on words, and the latter is an incongruity joke about treating peaceful Amish people like violent gangsta rappers. Weird Al is not making a pointed message about virgins, surgeons, rappers, or the Amish. You *could* make the case that he is going after the tragic romantic self-glorification of hip-hop by applying the same tropes to the peaceful, rural Amish. Actually, that's a pretty good case you made, but really I think he just thought, "Wouldn't it be funny to rap about the opposite of rappers?" Conversely, I'd argue that Weird Al's song "Perform This Way" (a parody of Lady Gaga's "Born This Way") *is* satire, because it's explicitly calling out the artificial, commercial quality of Lady Gaga's early attention-getting shock tactics—targeting the subtext of the style, not just the style.

Because satire is often about big important political stuff, political humor usually gets called satire regardless of its form. *The Daily Show with Jon Stewart*—where, as you already know, I spent my formative years—was a topical comedy show that addressed political topics, so it often gets called satire. But since Jon Stewart spoke to the audience as himself, without playing ironic games of meaning, it doesn't truly fit my definition of satire. However, on our sister late-night comedy show, *The Colbert Report*, host Stephen Colbert addressed political topics through the filter of an exaggerated, ironic persona who outwardly stated the opposite of the show's true intentions. That's satire.

Occasionally, *The Daily Show did* use actual satire. One of my favorite segments that I worked on was an epic, eighteen-minute satirical parody in which Jon burlesqued the ranting of a then current, now mostly forgotten melodramatic, conspiracy-mongering broadcaster. By adopting and exaggerating the form of the thing Jon was criticizing, he dipped his toe briefly into the kind of satire Stephen Colbert swam in on a nightly basis.

Writing Satire: Step One

Northrop Frye noted two essential components of satire: "One is wit or humor founded on fantasy or a sense of the grotesque or absurd, the other is an object of attack." Grotesque humor's the easy part. The harder part is getting an object of attack worth joking about.

In other words, there has to be grit in the satirical oyster so it can poop out a comedy pearl. The first step in writing satire is recognizing what your grit is.

Let me take you through an example of getting to the grit. And I say "let me" purely as a formality since I don't need your permission. This example is one I've seen oft attempted but rarely accomplished, involving a subject that I hope someday dates this book rather than damning it to eternal relevancy: the seemingly unsatirizable President Donald Trump. For those reading this in virtual space libraries three millennia from now, Donald Trump was a man of such transparent greed, deceit, spite, arrogance, narcissism, corruption, and ignorance that we had no choice but to elect him to high office—twice. He was the living embodiment of everything fairy tales say is bad, and also a third of American citizens thought he was sent by God as their personal beast-warrior revenge-messiah.

Many have tried, and as of this writing I believe nearly all have failed, to satirize this man. Most satirical attacks on Trump have engaged with his exterior traits—his bombast, his vulgarity, his conceitedness, his style. All the stuff that was obvious to anyone who watched him on TV for a few minutes. These attempts may have been fine parodies, but they failed to engage with him on a deeper level and reveal something unsaid. This is partly because of the nature of this particular satirical subject. Cartoonist Ruben Bolling said that Trump "changed the way that I do satire. . . . I used to take what a politician that I disagreed with would say, or what their policy was, and I would exaggerate it. But Trump is better at it than I am, than I think all satirists are." Bolling means that Trump is so outlandishly outrageous, selfish, and ignorant that any attempt to exaggerate him cannot match up to his actual reality. Bolling's solution (a good one) is to take what Trump said and "take it literally, and then I put it in a new context" that highlights the absurdity of his words and actions.

The other reason that Trump is hard to satirize is the same reason many other subjects are difficult to satirize: Crafting satire requires you to become intimately familiar with the inner workings of something you hate. Which is a really unpleasant thing to do.

Satire is the opposite of medicine: You must first do some harm. To inflict damage on a problem—and hopefully inspire people to solve that problem—you've got to really understand the thing you're satirizing. This means taking the time and energy to really study something you already know you don't like. Pulling off that *Daily Show* satire of the hyperbolic conspiracy broadcaster meant watching many hours of that hyperbolic conspiracy broadcaster's hyperbolic conspiracy broadcasting, until I began to forget there was anything else to watch *but* hyperbolic conspiracy broadcasting. After all those hours my cowriter and I understood the target inside and out, inside being the key part. For satire it's not enough to see the surface of a thing and replicate it. You need to know *why* the thing manifests that surface. To once again quote comedy legend Ralph Waldo Emerson, "The power depends on the depth of the artist's insight of that object he contemplates."

Regarding our Trump example, this would mean watching his speeches and interviews and reading about his life without getting distracted by his objectively hilarious/troubling manner of nonstop, over-the-top lying. What hides beneath the surface? To me the only kind of man who constantly talks about his own greatness is a man who knows deep down that everybody thinks he's a fool and must constantly, nakedly demand validation from the same people whose opinions he pretends he doesn't care about. Parodies of Trump may have recognized his narcissism, but few have dived far enough into the Marianas Trench–low self-esteem at the root of it. So I've found my Trump-grit: the pathetic vulnerability that drives him. Now what do I do with it?

Writing Satire: The Other Steps

Step two is taking that insight from step one and figuring out how to exaggerate it in a way that reveals it. Here I need to develop a premise that allows me to exaggerate the neediness that I'd noticed until it's undeniable to the audience. Since this is a hypothetical project, let's say I can use any kind of joke delivery method. Do I write a sketch where an actor playing Trump runs around the White House demanding hugs? Or is it a biopic presenting his life as if it really happened the way he *says* it does, with himself as the only strong man surrounded by soldiers and police officers crying on his shoulder (something he claimed was *always* happening to him)?

In judging which way to write this joke, I want to keep my eye on the three guidelines of brevity, clarity, and specificity. Which premise will most clearly and quickly communicate my specific message to the audience? Which premise provides the least possibility of the audience misinterpreting what I'm saying (a clear and present danger of something like the ironic biopic option)? All forms being equal, I think I'd take the option "none of the above" and instead take real footage of a Donald Trump rally and dub in new dialogue that applies his stylistic tics to the feelings that really underlie his personality: "Everyone agrees I'm desperate for attention. Nobody's more desperate for attention than me. Little babies crying for their mothers, they wish they were as desperate as I am. And I cry way better than them. 'Waah! Waah! Waah!' Maybe I shouldn't say this, but I'm a better baby than babies." This, unfortunately, is pretty on the nose. I might get just as much mileage from playing real footage of a Trump speech and then at the end dub in the seeming non sequitur, "Of course, my father never hugged me."

The examples above could be funnier, sure, but the point is that I'd take his speech and turn it into a therapy session, exaggerating the content to reveal that his speeches already are therapy sessions. Now I just need to write the jokes and rewrite them and rewrite them again. That's the fun part.

Satire's Expiration Date: Soon

One of the strengths of satire is that it can feel vital, shocking, and relevant. One of the weaknesses of satire, though, is that what's shocking and relevant today feels tame and irrelevant tomorrow. Steve Allen puts it well when he says that "full appreciation of satire can take place only as long as the satirized subject is still considered to be of some social importance." Considered by whom, you may ask? By the audience, that's whom. This is another case where having a sense of your audience's feelings about a subject will help you decide what is worth satirizing and how to satirize it. The worst mistake in writing satire for an audience isn't touching a subject that's too sensitive, but the opposite: touching a subject that no one cares enough about to stay mad at anymore. Unfortunately, this is the ultimate fate of nearly all satire.

The Smothers Brothers Comedy Hour was one of the pioneering shows of American satire, performing pointed jokes addressing the Vietnam War, political hypocrisy, and drug use from 1967 until it was canceled midseason by CBS in 1969. From taking on politics by sending cast member Pat Paulsen on a long-running, cynical campaign for president to taking on organized religion through jokey sermons from comic David Steinberg, Dick and Tommy Smothers were unafraid to go after hot-button issues through ironic comedy that was as controversial then as it is surprisingly tame now. Not that the work isn't still funny, but when you watch it today, it doesn't feel particularly biting. And why would it? It's not 1969 anymore. Similarly, Stephen Colbert's audacious to-his-face roasting through ironic praise of then-President George W. Bush at the 2006 White House Correspondents' Dinner is a shining memory (comedy filmmaker Adam McKay said at the time that it was "one of the most heroic acts of the last fifteen years"), but watching the actual footage today no longer carries the same charge, now that the powerful man being targeted is no longer in power.

Once we accept this as a limitation, however, it can become a part of our creative process. If satire inevitably has a short shelf life, then it frees you to write to the moment without worrying about how well it will work in the future. Perhaps the most powerful satirical work of my lifetime is the legendary 9/11 issue of *The Onion* published on September 26, 2001. Fifteen days earlier, the United States had suffered a terrorist attack of such shocking ferocity that it became a prominent cultural opinion that comedy was no longer possible. The writers of *The Onion* proved that wrong by putting out an issue that felt, at the time, like a humorous thunderbolt—funny, trenchant, and at times emotionally powerful.

Headlines like "American Life Turns into Bad Jerry Bruckheimer Movie," "U.S. Vows to Defeat Whoever It Is We're at War With," and a point-counterpoint editorial,

"We Must Retaliate with Blind Rage / We Must Retaliate with Measured, Focused Rage" did an amazing job of capturing the confusion, grief, and anger of the time. The issue's best article is the heartfelt Carol Kolb–written "Not Knowing What Else to Do, Woman Bakes American-Flag Cake," a stunning vignette sympathizing with a character while poking fun at the pointlessness of her response. *This* was satire that found a funny way to say out loud the things that felt like they needed to be said at that moment.

And I mean literally "at that moment." Because the writers deliberately dialed back the potential ferocity of their satire, and avoided certain targets, because of the tenor of the time. Articles like "Hijackers Surprised to Find Themselves in Hell" and "God Angrily Clarifies 'Don't Kill' Rule" feel more cathartic than satirical. This was by design. As one of the editors said years later, "I suppose you could argue that it's not particularly edgy or irreverent at all, it's just kind of maudlin. But I mean, that was the time for maudlin, you know. If there ever was one, in humor, anyway." Kolb, too, has explained, "There were a lot of jokes that got thrown out because they were shocking in the wrong way. . . . We also wanted to avoid any headline like 'Thing Everyone Knew Was Going to Happen, Finally Happens.' Or a headline like 'We Told You So, America!'" Whether every article from that issue works as satire now or not, it was the right way to address that particular moment when America didn't need a humorous lesson in its past crimes but a humorous lesson in the necessity of humor.

This is all to say that when you write satire, remember that it likely won't hold up for future audiences. Also remember that it really shouldn't. Don't aim for timelessness; aim for now. If the hoped-for result of satire is to push us to address a problem, then truly powerful satire *should* lose its power. It's OK that I don't find *The Smothers Brothers* radical or edgy anymore because it means we're no longer at war in Vietnam. And that's an objectively good thing.

Satire and Tone

Satire is sensitive stuff, operating within a delicate space of mischievous duplicity, often wearing the borrowed clothes of its enemy. Claude Rawson and Ian Higgins, discussing the work of Jonathan Swift (whose pro-eating-Irish-children essay "A Modest Proposal" is textbook satire, in that textbooks often use it as their example of satire), write that "it flirts dangerously with its own literal content, thus entertaining a shocking thought by simultaneously meaning it, not meaning it, and, as it were, not not meaning it." This means tone is vital in satire. Only by striking the right tone can you show how uncomfortable those borrowed clothes are and that you don't not not not mean the thing you kind of but aren't really saying. I think that came out pretty clearly.

Satire, above all, needs to carry a tone of irony, and as we saw when we talked about all things deadpan, irony is best communicated by a lack of emotion. Satire must speak dispassionately, creating an emotional space between what it says and what it feels. This can be hard to do when you despise something enough to write a satire of it, but Shuttleworth and Kiley note that when satire fails, "it fails because it loses control," becoming something akin to "invective or diatribe." No less than the legendary satirist Mark Twain once said, "A man can't write successful satire unless he be in a calm judicial good humor." Lose your cool, and you may disgust your audience with your rage—or even worse, you'll drop the irony that signals to your audience what you're actually trying to say.

Still, it's possible to be too cool for school, and by "school" I mean "satire." Satire depends so heavily on achieving a controlled, ironic tone that, ironically, if it's *too* controlled it overshoots the tone and can become mistaken for the thing it's satirizing. In other words, the borrowed clothes start to fit. Take the infamous July 21, 2008, *New Yorker* magazine cover by Barry Blitt, who sought to satirize unfounded rumors about then–presidential candidate Barack Obama—that he was secretly a Muslim and/or a terrorist—by portraying Obama, in traditional Muslim attire, fist-bumping his wife Michelle, who is dressed and armed as a '60s revolutionary. Context, such an important factor in received tone, tells us Blitt was trying to satirize the false rumors by exaggerating them. But if the same image had appeared on the cover not of the liberal-leaning *New Yorker* but of the conservative-leaning *National Review*—or as a contextless image posted online, where art is routinely stripped of its identifying characteristics and repurposed—would the irony and the intent have been clear?

Satire is the form of comedy most vulnerable to the internet rule known as Poe's Law, which Wikipedia describes thus: "Without a clear indicator of the author's intent, any parody of extreme views can be mistaken by some readers for a sincere expression of the views being parodied." Just take the case of author Norman Spinrad, whose satirical novel *The Iron Dream* presented a "lost" science fiction novel by Adolf Hitler in order to expose the latent fascist tendencies of the sci-fi genre—only to pull off its conceit so well that, according to Spinrad, his book appeared on the American Nazi Party's recommended reading list. It sometimes seems like no satire is too outrageous to be mistaken

The Politics of Fear, Barry Blitt's *New Yorker* cover of July 21, 2008, sought to satirize unfounded rumors circulating about then-presidential candidate Barack Obama. The context already set by the liberal-leaning magazine was crucial to the interpretation of the joke's tone.

for fact. In 2018, Twitter user @pixelatedboat wrote a satirical excerpt from a fake Donald Trump tell-all book. The excerpt claimed the president had demanded that his TV be tuned to "the gorilla channel," with an anonymous insider saying, "He'll watch the gorilla channel for 17 hours straight. . . . I think he thinks the gorillas can hear him." Though seemingly clearly a joke, it was presented so realistically and reinforced so many people's assumptions that many took it as real. Which shows us it's important to carry that ironic tone in your satire not just because people *can* be fooled but because sometimes they *want* to be.

For satire to work, its intent must be clear. Unfortunately, when the author's intent is too clear, it can wreck the ironic illusion, which spoils the joke and defuses the satire. If jokes are about sudden comprehension, and satire is about making you think, then a satire that explains itself to you is worse than merely lacking power—it's not funny. The key is to maintain the proper amount of ironic tonal distance from your target: close enough that it's clear what you're criticizing, while far enough that it's clear you *are* criticizing it.

Why Not to Write Satire

The difficulty of writing satire is baked into the form. Its goal isn't just to make the audience laugh but also to make the audience *change*. This means satire's highest purpose is to reach those who either don't agree with you or don't want to listen to you. It's offensive comedy, both in that it's on the offense and that it says things people may be offended by. It's not fully working if it doesn't challenge the audience, and as we talked about earlier, audiences only like to be challenged *so* much—that "much" usually being "less than the satirist is challenging them." The fate of most satire is to make its point before either being dismissed or attacked. As poet Peter Steele says about Jonathan Swift, "Every one of Swift's rhetorical victories as a satirist is a pyrrhic victory." Satire rarely effects the actual change it desires. It can even have the opposite effect. I'd argue that the surface-level satires of Trump have had the countereffect of turning him into a cartoon character that audiences could more easily ignore or perversely enjoy. And even worse, in the parts of the world where government oppression makes acts of satire particularly powerful and important, creating it can mean imprisonment or death.

In sum, satire is difficult, easily misinterpreted, alternately ineffective or dangerous, and often not that funny.

So Why Get Involved with Satire at All?

Because when it works, satire can be *amazing*. I'll let writer and semipro wizard Alan Moore tell you why:

> If a magician puts a curse upon you, then your hens are probably going to lay a bit funny. Your child might be born with a squint. These are things that are survivable. They're not that terrible. Whereas, when a bard puts a satire upon you, then that will destroy you in the eyes of your friends. In the eyes of your family. Potentially in your own eyes. And if it's good enough satire, if it is finely worded enough, then even two or three hundred years after you're dead, people might still be laughing at you and your absurdity. That was why satires were feared.

If you can pull it off, satire is very powerful magic.

When Satire Works

Satire *can* work. Satire *can* be both funny and eye-opening. But satire only has that impact when reacting to something unsaid, an uncomfortable truth. This is the grit in the oyster—the silence surrounding the unsaid. Satire must deliver a genuinely surprising revelation or break a genuinely foundational taboo. Unfortunately, audiences typically gravitate to work that reinforces their existing beliefs. How do you get over that resistance to being truly challenged?

Is the answer to trick the audience? To lull them into what seems to be a straightforward work of comedy and then, when they least expect it, hit them with something shocking? I don't think so. Rather, it means doing the very hard work of identifying something the audience understands but is afraid to admit until the satire gives them permission to do so. In discussing the *Onion* 9/11 issue, writer Todd Hansen said, "We were just trying to reflect what everybody was going through. . . . We were trying to be honest about how we felt." I believe the true route to successful satire is to be honest about what you feel, even when that feeling feels like a weird feeling to feel.

Take Joseph Heller's 1961 novel *Catch-22*, a brilliant satire of military chaos and incompetence in a World War II bomber squadron that concerns the arbitrary cruelty of modern, dehumanized society and the illogic of human institutions. *Catch-22* would eventually become a very successful book, and you may have even read it in high school, the place where dangerous literature is safely defanged by injecting it into minds too hormonally distracted to pay attention to what it's saying. But reading it now, the book still hits hard, because I think Heller is telling us something we may only dimly accept in the back of our minds, and which had lain especially hidden in the years after World War II: That for all the rah-rah mythmaking about "the good war" against Hitler's iron dream, even a "good" war is horrible. That the experience of fighting in that war, even for freedom, even after victory, was frightening, irrational, painful, and often shameful. Heller was daring to name the "good" war as bad, for the winners as well as for the losers. This was the grit that he turned into his pearl.

Mid-twentieth-century America, when Heller was writing, was a particularly fertile time for satire because unsaid truths were lying around all over the place. A dominant, unironic mainstream monoculture gives would-be satirists a lot to push back against. In today's more fractured culture it can seem harder to find the thing that must be said. But mid-twentieth-century America doesn't have a monopoly on self-deceit. Just look at Boots Riley's 2018 film *Sorry to Bother You*, in which a Black man becomes a successful telemarketer by affecting a white-sounding voice . . . and then gets drawn into a world of voluntary indentured slavery and pharmaceutical research that turns Black men into mutant horse-human hybrids. The film's success isn't just in how funny it is but also in how it exaggerates two things that we all kind of know but that are hard to face because of our complicity in them: (1) the general acceptance of whiteness as the default standard for "person," and (2) the fact that the convenience-filled technological wonderland we inhabit is built on the suffering of others, both the workers who build it and the future generations who will pay for our wastefulness. Riley understands that foreign lithium miners dying so we can have cell phones are easy to ignore, but you can't miss a mutant man-horse's huge on-screen genitalia. That's an exaggeration that really reveals.

If you're looking to write satire, first look for the thing that goes unsaid. Not the thing that's already being argued about, but the thing everyone at some deep level is afraid to say. And not only afraid to say out loud but afraid to say *to themselves*. The thing we're all afraid to admit.

Then admit it to yourself. I know, it's a hard thing to do.

It hurts to poop out pearls.

12
Prose

OFTEN ON A QUIET EVENING, as I sit enjoying a book, I will come across a joke I find so funny that I simply have to share it with my wife. She's usually reading her own book, not wanting to be disturbed in order to hear an out-of-context joke from a book that, if she'd wanted to read it, she would already be reading. But even worse than bothering my wife (who knew being bothered by me was part of the deal when we got married), I'm bothering the delicate relationship that's supposed to exist between a reader and a joke that isn't meant to be heard but *read.*

Writing a joke purely to be read is, in some ways, the purest test of joke writing. A prose joke is meant to be experienced alone, without the emotional emphasis of a joke teller's vocal performance or visual cues to assist in communicating its meaning. It doesn't even have multiple audience members peer-pressuring each other into laughing. No, this laugh must be pulled from a lone, quiet reader.

But it *is* possible to genuinely laugh out loud while reading prose. Because the opposite dynamic between my wife and me happens when I literally laugh out loud at something I'm reading, such as when writer Hallie Haglund, in her online newsletter *That Hurts My Feelings*, described reading the news as "my way of feeling like I'm part of the world, instead of a ghost who spends her days creating things nobody asked for, with no legitimate reason to show my face in public beyond shepherding my children to and from school. Do I shower? Not particularly." Hearing me laugh at that "Not particularly," my wife asked, "What's so funny?" I read it to her, but really I should have just handed her the computer screen, because that joke doesn't need my help.

What I Mean by Prose

Everyone's favorite part of this book is when I define things, right? It's not? Well, I'm going to do it anyway. When you picture **prose** writing, I'm guessing that you imagine print. Books and newspapers—and maybe even magazines, the coelacanths of the media world (in that they're still around even though everyone thought they went extinct a long time ago). You're right, those things are prose. But prose can be much more than those things. The joke you saw on the back of an Old Spice deodorant stick, with its hyperbolic, absolutely unreal claims? That's prose humor. The "Chill Bitch, You'll Get There" novelty sign on the back windshield of the car in front of you? That's prose humor. And, most important of all, the funny social media post that was shared with you on your neighborhood group chat? That's also prose. If it is a joke delivered in text-to-be-looked-at (or felt, if read in braille), then it is prose humor.

As I write this, what was previously one of the foremost platforms for online prose humor—Twitter—is rapidly curdling and perhaps dying completely. But I think the humor forms and styles it helped bring into the world will outlast it, because they open the door for text jokes that are quick to deliver and understand, without needlessly extending

A stick of Old Spice High Endurance Deodorant, ca. 2012: Prose humor can be found everywhere.

them to a length that justifies being a whole book or article. Examples are jokes like this tweet by @anniew:

> Consider how many of your problems would go away if you were a watercolor illustration of a small hen in an apron.

Or this one by @iconawrites:

> "Hustle hard and become highly skilled!" Why, so the goddess Athena can grow jealous of my skills and turn me into a spider? No thanks.

I can imagine a world where each of these is expanded to essay length, with incredibly diminishing returns.

Take this tweet by @JNalv parodying one of Outkast's greatest hits:

> I'm sorry Ms. Jackson (Oooooo) / I am four eels / Never meant to make your daughter cry / I am several fish and not a guy

This is a joke that works, for me, because of the sudden combination of recognition and incongruity: It communicates a premise built on the idea that some words sound like other words, but their divergence in meaning entails further divergences if you continue juxtaposing them. I don't think it's a premise that can support an entire full-length song parody. And if it were delivered in a stand-up routine, @JNalv would need whole introduction ("I was thinking the other day about how there aren't many hip-hop songs about fish . . .") in order to justify the joke while also ruining it. The other option would be to just blurt this out, unannounced, which—let's face it—would be weird. The brief, tossed-off quality of online prose humor justifies these kinds of quick, stripped-down jokes. It feels like an unmediated flash of thought from the writer's brain to our own. It also justifies a lack of hewing to traditional grammar, punctuation, and spelling rules in a way that probably horrifies your average Air Force English professor but that excites me as a comedy writer.

Writing Prose for Pages, Screens, Billboards, Cookie Fortunes, and Anywhere Else Text Can Go

First let's establish what you should already be assuming by now. No matter what the form (essay, tweet, stick of deodorant), prose humor operates according to the same comic mechanisms as any other joke. An idea is communicated by a voice through a premise, supported by structure, marked by tone, for the enjoyment of an audience. As models, let's look at two examples of prose jokes, one from a traditional humor essayist, Jack Handey:

> Eventually, I believe, everything evens out. Long ago, an asteroid hit our planet and killed our dinosaurs. But, in the future, maybe we'll go to another planet and kill their dinosaurs.

And one from online prose humorist Paul Dochney, who tweets under the handle @dril:

> need someone in or around geigertown, philadelphia to help me dispose of approx 7500 live guinea pigs. i can not pay you, i will not pay you

Despite the differences in, say, paying attention to proper punctuation and grammar, both of these jokes are operating through a similar comedic voice that I'd call "oblivious sociopath." They're taking advantage of that vacuum caused by the absence of a live performer to create their own form of a stand-up's persona—but because they don't have to be there telling you the joke, they can push that voice to an extreme of ignorance or insanity.

As with the jokes we've talked about previously, both of these also use a premise to communicate an idea with a specific tone. With the help of a tone of unearned superiority, both Handey's premise (everything evens out through a series of interplanetary dinosaur murders) and Dochney's premise (someone demanding pro bono help disposing of guinea pigs) get at the idea of how ignorantly arrogant men feel they can speak their mind or demand assistance without expecting pushback or argument.

Both jokes also operate through three-act structures, and you know how much I love those. In Handey's, each sentence is an act. In Dochney's, act 1 takes us to the guinea pigs, act 2 is his inability to pay, and act 3 is his refusal to pay.

And finally, both jokes also shape their wording around the principles of brevity, clarity, and specificity. Handey's sentences are unaffectedly clear, completely lacking extra, unnecessary words. There's an unpretentious specificity of wording in the mirroring of "our dinosaurs" and "their dinosaurs" (rather than trying to come up with a clever new way to describe them like "prehistoric almost-dragons"). Setting aside the grammatical errors that I think are a strength and not a weakness of online prose humor, Dochney's joke is still communicated clearly and briefly. But he's also making particularly good use of specificity in phrases like "in or around geigertown, philadelphia" and "approx 7500 live guinea pigs," as opposed to, say, "can someone close by help me dispose of a lot of guinea pigs." He's also showing us the way small wording choices can make a joke funnier. The inclusion of "in or around" and "approx" add to the word count, but their lack of certainty helps make this unrealistic request feel slightly more real (do we really believe this guy would have an exact count of his guinea pigs?), which helps highlight how bizarre the situation is. And in the closing "i can not pay you, i will not pay you," the contrast between "can" and "will" makes the speaker simultaneously more hostile but also strangely principled.

So if prose humor works by the same rules as the other forms we've been discussing, why does it get its own chapter? For one thing, because there *is* something specifically special about prose humor, a factor unique to text structure: spacing. The visual, physical arrangement of words on a page—or bumper sticker or clothing label or whatever—can help to provide rhythm to a reading joke.

The prose-joke writer can arrange their text visually in a way that reinforces or creates a structural shape. Looking at another tweet from Dochney, we see such structure in action:

> Food $200
> Data $150
> Rent $800
> Candles $3,600
> Utility $150
> someone who is good at the economy please help me budget this. my family is dying

Here we have a pretty straightforward list joke: a pattern of reasonable costs disrupted by a ridiculous expense, with the placement of the comparatively low utility bill *after* the candle-price disruption making the joke less straightforwardly "setup/punchline." The same joke could have been told using a linear sentence structure ("Food $200. Data $150. Rent $800"), but it would lack the "family budget" specificity of seeing the items in actual list form. By spacing it out this way (spoiler alert for the section on prose rhythm), Dochney also forces us to focus and concentrate on each of those entries just a little bit longer. Finally, by arranging this joke as a list, he can disrupt the visual format with the two last lines written as traditional sentences (albeit without proper punctuation or capitalization). The change in visual structure reinforces the written structure of the joke by mimicking the disruption in the content.

This kind of creative text arrangement isn't just for online prose humor. After all, there are *rules* about grammar, but there aren't actual *laws* that could land you in jail. In her novel *White Teeth*, Zadie Smith communicates a character's feelings of unimportance partly through a similar vertical arrangement combined with nontraditional punctuation:

> He was a man whose significance in the Greater Scheme of Things could be figured along familiar ratios:
>
> Pebble: Beach.
> Raindrop: Ocean.
> Needle: Haystack.

This short pile of analogies reinforces the idea that this guy is nothing special. A nobody. Not even worth having full paragraphs or sentences used to describe him. I think it's very funny, and funnier than if the same thing had been said in a straightforward block of text. This is all to say that the seeming nakedness and plainness of written text on a page can impose limitations on the effects a joke writer can go for—but they also provide opportunities for achieving those effects by other means.

Rhythm & Prose

Another major challenge in writing prose comedy is renouncing your total control of the pace and delivery of a joke. Your nightmare is someone like me who reads very quickly and impatiently and does not absorb written text with the tempo of spoken words. Your goal, then, is to guide the reader's eye so that they see the words you want them to see when you want them to see them. Text arrangement can be used to achieve that goal, especially in your use of sentence length. Each period that a reader comes across acts like a speed bump, forcing them to slow down. Each long sentence without a period encourages the reader to speed up, and, like a speeding car finally hitting a speed bump, the eventual period provides a proportionally greater impact and damage to the reader's brakes and suspension.

Sarah Vowell's essay "Pop-A-Shot," about her devotion to a miniature basketball arcade game, gives us two nice examples of using sentence length to control pace and rhythm. First, a long sentence:

> Often, we have to stand behind some six-year-old girl who bogarts the game and whose father keeps dropping in quarters even though the kid makes only about 4 points if she's lucky and we are forced to glare at the back of her pigtailed head, waiting just long enough to start questioning our adulthood and how by the time our parents were our age they were beholden to mortgages and PTA meetings and here we are, stuck in an episode of *Friends*.

You'd expect that a long, run-on sentence would tire your reading eyes out and cause you to read slower the longer it went on. But the opposite is true. The length of the sentence means we have more runway to increase our reading momentum and correspondingly to increase the speed of our reading rhythm. We keep expecting a period, and keep not getting one, and almost instinctually we begin to move through the sentence faster and faster, looking for that period, building an intensity of rhythm just as the sentence itself is building an intensity of self-loathing over being an adult playing pop-a-shot basketball.

Now compare that to this example from the same essay:

> Unlike the game of basketball itself, Pop-A-Shot has no standard socially redeeming value whatsoever. Pop-A-Shot is not about teamwork or getting along or working together. Pop-A-Shot is not about getting exercise or fresh air. It takes place in fluorescent-lit bowling alleys or darkened bars. It costs money. At the end of a game, one does not swig Gatorade. One sips bourbon or margaritas or munches cupcakes.

In this example, we've got periods aplenty, and each time we hit one we pause just for the slightest little millisecond. But that millisecond is enough to create a staccato rhythm that fights our momentum and keeps us from speeding through what she's saying. As a result, instead of one big impact, we have a series of smaller impacts that accumulate in strength, each one adding power to the next.

The kinds of word placement we looked at earlier also affects an audiences' reading rhythm. This tweet by @DrakeGatsby uses list spacing to create a similar staccato effect to what Vowell achieved through her parade of punctuation:

> "I'm hungover"
> - Lame
> - Big deal
> - Get off the couch
>
> "The gods have punished me for my indulgences"
> - Oh damn
> - That sounds serious
> - Shall I prepare a healing poultice?

That empty space around each line acts similarly to Vowell's short sentences—it forces us to stop and reset, slowing our pace as we move through the joke. Though very different forms of prose humor (although ironically similar in addressing the subject of how we fill our lives with ill-used moments), they both find ways to put reins on the reader's pace. Even though a prose comedy writer doesn't have total control of how their audience experiences their work, they still have *some* control, and a smart joke worker makes the most of that control.

Tone Alone

We've talked about how tricky tone is in comedy, and it's doubly tricky in prose for the same reasons I keep mentioning: Namely, you're not there to read the room and clear things up if you make a mistake or are misperceived. Prose is similar to satire in how easily its level of irony is misunderstood by an audience. This isn't unique to comedy. I'm sure we've all had the experience of reading a text or email and immediately interpreting it as a passive-aggressive insult. In even my most innocuous, perfunctory emails I end every sentence with an exclamation mark because the period is the second-most-passive-aggressive piece of punctuation. The first? The *ellipsis*, duh . . .

So imagine someone misreading your comedy essay or online joke in the same way. What you intend to be delightful and facetious comes off as cloying, overbearing, condescending, or, worst of all, sincere. How do you avoid this? Remember the methods for modulating tone that we discussed in chapter 5: establishing your level of overt hostility or aggression and your closeness or distance to the audience. One way I like to think about that relationship in prose is by asking, "Am I in a conversation with the reader?" Here's an example where I think the answer is *no*, when magician Ricky Jay writes about his experiences with animals: "The sordid experience of sharing the stage with grouse, geese, and gerbils, I do not deem worthy of recollection." Reading that, I find his huffy dignity funny, but the formal wording and sentence structure used to communicate that huffy dignity also make it clear that he is writing *to* me and not inviting a response.

But a prose writer can also close the distance between themself and the reader by doing, well, the things I've been doing throughout this book: asking rhetorical questions, poking fun at myself, poking fun at the reader without being too insulting, and saying things like "we'll be discussing" when it's perfectly obvious that you'll be discussing nothing because I'm doing all the talking. Even a single tweet can express openness to conversation or a closed-off boundary between writer and reader.

In addition to these techniques that we've already discussed at greater length (see? I did it again!), I have a tool I use for testing the tone of my written work that is as effective as it is anticlimactic—I just read what I've written out loud. When I hear my words, I can usually identify places where they're not coming off the way I've intended them to. Inevitably, there's something that could be made emotionally or verbally clearer. I attempt to clarify it by adjusting my words, and then I read it out loud again. That's pretty much it. I wish I had a more interesting solution for you on this one. But sometimes the secrets to improving your craft are less "ancient occult mysteries" and more "otherwise obvious things nobody bothered to tell you." This will also help you make sure your joke still works if some nerd decides to read it out loud to their spouse.

Alone with the Rest of Us

At the top of this chapter, I said that prose humor is meant to be experienced alone. There's no teller, and there's no crowd of people reading each word over your shoulder at the exact same time you do. But in the brave new world of online prose, the interactivity of the internet allows everyone to be alone while also being together. The design of many of the platforms on which online prose appears deliberately breaks down the unilateral content transaction of traditional prose humor, replacing it with a leveling between "writer" and "audience." The audience can share their reaction publicly, with comments and additional jokes attaching themselves to the original work like an ever-spreading coral reef. Though if you're the person whose joke started the whole thing, it can feel more like a suffocating encrustation of barnacles.

If a joke in the nonwired world is successful in getting a laugh, it will probably be repeated—often, as I mentioned, by me to my wife. But in the online world, a successful prose joke invites contribution. Many online comedy writers have experienced the annoyance of tweeting a joke and then having many people reply with their own, usually not as good versions of the same joke. It's something like heckling, except the audience doesn't need to be drunk to have the courage to do it—and even worse, they think they're *helping*, whereas the heckler understands perfectly that they are wrecking the show. Writing prose comedy online means dealing with an audience that is alone but wants to connect with others. Disgusting, right?

Well . . . not entirely. If we can let go of our need to feel specific authorship for our work (something I'm still working on), then perhaps this collaborative aspect of online humor can open new doors for the innovative comedy writer. Rather than looking at the audience as crashing the party we're hosting, we can treat jokes the way they were treated in times past—as shared creative cultural objects to be retold and reshaped in interesting ways. One way that online prose humor accomplishes this is through jokes that become refillable forms. In 2022, Twitter user @doulbedoink posted the following:

> "Omg did you see what Vaush said to contra on twitch? Like he was streaming the whole ti-"
>
> You bolt awake in the mountains of Carthage. You are not online. It is 217 BC. You are the general Hannibal, and you have changed your mind. The future cannot come to pass. Rome must burn.

It was all a dream! Poking fun at the triviality of the things the internet obsesses over! Other Twitter users felt that such a useful joke format didn't need to be a one-time thing. They quickly took this joke as a template they could use by replacing the first line with a specific current topical reference (none of which are worth quoting here because they're all, by design, nearly incomprehensible only days after being posted) or replacing the Hannibal paragraph with a similar moment of grand historical importance. By taking possession of @doubledoink's joke, audience members remade it into a tool for expressing a particular concept and feeling.

To see something you wrote turned into a sort of public-domain joke format is assuredly frustrating. Your personal expression has been depersonalized, a piece of your property seized by the community in a comedic variant of the Soviet nationalization of industry. But only part of a joke's job is bringing glory to its creator. A joke is also engaged in creating interpersonal connections, not only between the teller and the audience but between the members of the audience as well. What fuller consummation of that work can there be than to write a joke that allows the audience to build those connections between each other and become, for a moment, the tellers, seeing the joke from both sides?

Perhaps I'm personally intrigued by this idea of writing a joke and letting it go because it runs counter to so much of what I find somewhat overdone in modern humor: an emphasis on one individual's personal truth about life or politics, the exaltation of a comedian's voice as something uniquely special in its contribution to the world. The idea of a joke that provides a premise and a structure while leaving space for voice *to be contributed to* feels like an interesting admission that professional comedy workers don't have a monopoly on what's funny. What if the conflict-riven boundary between joke teller and audience that I described earlier in the book were instead an open space of engagement and enjoyment? What if there were a way to write prose humor so that not only did the audience feel less alone but the writer felt less alone as well? Until the development of online humor, this sort of iterative humor writing was a cumbersome, slow process. Now it's quick and easy. Just as the internet has helped us learn to stop worrying and love bad grammar, maybe it can help us feel the same way about communal comedy cultivation. Traditional prose writing can pretend to be a conversation, but online prose is already in one. Writing jokes that provide structures to be reused and updated in order to facilitate that conversation is an intriguing new frontier for the twenty-first-century joke writer.

Unless, of course, you want to be paid a living wage for your work, in which case you'll probably prefer to do things the old-fashioned way.

13
Visual Humor

I'D FORGIVE YOU FOR GETTING THIS FAR in the book and assuming that the only way to write jokes is with words. After all, this book is made of words, most of my examples have been made of words, and there's a chapter called "Wording," for crying out loud. But there's a whole world of humor we've only occasionally touched on involving language's no-strings-attached booty-call frenemy: **images**. It's a world of comedy that doesn't deserve the short shrift it often gets, since visual humor is perhaps the most accessible form of all. As György Kepes puts it in his book *Language of Vision*, the image "knows no limits of tongue, vocabulary, or grammar, and it can be perceived by the illiterate as well as by the literate." Why, then, if this form of humor travels so far, does visual humor often get forgotten when we talk about writing comedy?

I think there's two reasons for this: First, it's hard to describe visual humor using words. (Just watch me struggle with it later!) Like trying to describe what's beautiful about a painting, trying to describe what's funny about a visual means losing some or all of the effectiveness of the original work. Because these jokes don't easily translate between verbal and visual languages, a person can assume those languages operate by different laws. In this chapter I'm going to do my best to show you that this isn't true. Writing visual humor follows the same basic principles as writing verbal humor.

The phrase “writing visual humor” might sound weird, which leads me to the second reason that it sometimes gets ignored: A lot of people don’t think of visual humor as a form of “writing” because it either doesn’t use words or uses them sparingly. As a member of the Writers Guild of America, I’ve often heard the old chestnut that animation writing isn’t traditionally covered by my union because in the old days cartoons weren’t written but drawn. This line of thinking is, to use a scientific term, very dumb. A work of visual humor is conceived and crafted; there is a skillful execution of a deliberate intent to communicate a narrative, idea, feeling, or joke. That’s what writing is. It doesn’t matter if you’re doing it through words or through pictures, pratfalls, or porcelain—all of which we’ll touch on in this chapter.

Looking Is Reading, Picturing Is Writing

There’s a wordless, single-panel cartoon by Amy Hwang in which a cow shopping for jewelry peruses a display of long necklaces that all end in cowbells. How did this joke come into being? We know she’s not drawing a portrait of something she saw in real life. We know that she didn’t just start idly doodling and end up with a finished cartoon. This visual humor has a narrative thought behind it, so obviously it was *written*. And although I don’t know Hwang’s creative process, I imagine she went through the same sort of creative process a verbal joke writer would follow. Perhaps she recognized the visual similarity between human necklaces and cows wearing bells, rejected the idea of showing a human wearing a cowbell for the more subtle approach of showing a cow with a necklace, and then created the opportunity for the reader to make that connection between human and animal for themself by showing us the premise of a cow *shopping* for a cowbell.

The lack of a caption or dialogue means Hwang's audience has to make a leap to decode the image and get the premise, just as they would for a verbal joke. And once they've done that, they have an opportunity to try understanding the point Hwang's joke is making. The way I read it, the cow in Hwang's drawing appears to be reaching for one particular necklace among a display of several nearly identical necklaces, with a slightly pleased, "Ah, *this* is the right one for me" expression on her face, and I suspect

This cartoon by Amy Hwang shows that a written comic narrative can be expressed without any words.

Amy Hwang / *The New Yorker* Collection / The Cartoon Bank.

that Hwang is saying something about the foolishness of humans trying to express their individuality through mass-produced consumer goods. Or perhaps she's making a point about how foolish it is for us humans to dress ourselves up in order to pretend we're not all animals. It's also possible she just thought, "Cowbells are like necklaces for cows," and I'm being a Duchampian observer by imposing meanings on the work. Whatever the case, I laughed at the cartoon when I saw it—just as Hwang intended when she wrote it—*and none of that happened by accident*! It happened because Hwang wrote this joke that way.

The Verbal and the Visual Can Be Friends

I worry that in trying to break down categorical barriers between verbal and visual humor I'm actually only calling attention to and reinforcing them, creating an opposition between the two. So let's end this nascent verbal/visual beef by looking at examples where both verbal and visual information are vital to the joke.

One way verbal and visual elements can be assembled is for the words to act as a setup and the visual as a payoff. An example of this is a comedy sketch from the web series *Dr. Brown* in which a woman asks the title character (played by comedian Phil Burgers) for directions to a nearby pub, which he replies is "a couple of hours away." She is surprised as she remembers it being pretty close to where they're standing, but he advises her, "Give yourself an hour and a half, two hours tops." Then, after the woman leaves, he begins walking away *unbelievably slowly*. Like he's walking through molasses instead of air. It's amazing how slowly he walks. The walk alone is a funny visual, but rather than present it on its own, Burgers has made it funnier by setting it up with a verbal situation that helps communicate a point about differing frames of reference.

There's a similar mechanism at work in many of Harpo Marx's jokes. As the Marx brother who never speaks, he integrates his physical and visual comedy into a sound-based/verbal world in a way that continually uses silent actions as the payoff to words and phrases. For instance, in *Horse Feathers* Harpo responds to a homeless man's request—"Hey buddy, would you help me out? I'd like to get a cup of coffee"—by silently retrieving from his pants pocket a full, steaming hot cup of coffee, complete with saucer, that he apparently just happened to be carrying around. On its own, the act of pulling a cup of coffee from a pocket is an unreal visual moment, but it only works as a joke in the context of the words that prompted it, which, in the frame of reference of the audience, should lead to Harpo giving or denying the guy money. But Harpo disrupts our expectations by taking the words of the request completely literally and hands the man coffee that's somehow been in his pants without spilling or cooling. The visual joke of the surprise coffee doesn't function without the verbal request including the words "cup of coffee."

Verbal/visual jokes can work the other way around, too, as visual/verbal jokes where the words pay off the imagery's setup. We can see that in the popular internet meme "This is fine," made out of the first two panels of cartoonist KC Green's "On Fire" installment of the comic strip *Gun Show*. In the first panel, a dog wearing a hat sits at a table, calmly drinking coffee as flames engulf the room. In the next panel, the dog responds, "This is fine." The comic goes on for another four panels as the dog continues reassuring himself while catching fire and melting, but the

In the "This is fine" meme, the words pay off the setup provided by the imagery. From KC Green's online comic "On Fire," *Gunshow*, January 9, 2013.
© KC Green.

way most people have seen this strip—the first two panels removed from a larger context—is a great example of a visual setup (this dog's in the middle of a fire) and a verbal punchline (his positive acceptance of the situation). So you see, there's no reason for words and pictures to be at odds. Like the protagonists of a rom-com, they may fight at first, but you know the whole time that they're going to end up together.

Visuals Are Doing It for Themselves

But enough with the tyranny of words! Let's talk about visual jokes that shove away the offered arm of the verbal, shouting, "Get back, I've got this!" (metaphorically, of course: the visuals don't shout anything because they don't use words). The basic mechanism of visual jokes is still the disruption of explicit or implicit patterns. Take another Harpo Marx moment from *Horse Feathers*, this one completely wordless, in which Harpo takes out a banana and then unzips the peel, disrupting our internalized pattern of "how bananas get opened." There's no verbal angle to this joke: It's not responding to a remark or a visual pun on a common phrase. But it's built out of the same joke elements, arranged in the same way.

Similarly, visual jokes also work best when they follow those famous, beloved principles (say it all together with me): *brevity*, *clarity*, and *specificity*. Visual jokes should take the same care with what they show and how they show it as verbal jokes take with their wording. Comics legend Will Eisner, applying this principle to creating comic books, said this in a way that I think works just as well for visual humor writ large: "Each panel should be regarded as a stage wherein an arrangement of elements takes place. They must be arranged with a clear purpose. Nothing in a panel or page should be accidental or placed there casually." Furthermore: "The success or failure of this method of communicating depends upon the ease with which the reader recognizes the meaning and emotional impact of the image." The work of a visual humorist (after coming up with a premise, of course) is in making sure a visual is easy to understand, stripping down the details so we aren't overloaded with information, and making those details specific to enhance the inherent humor and relatability of the joke.

All of this is beautifully executed in a sixteen-image, entirely wordless *Calvin & Hobbes* strip by Bill Watterson that unfolds as follows:

Panel 1: Calvin looks out a window, smiling, because it has snowed outside.

Panel 2: Calvin is gone from the window instantly, with the steam from his breath still visible on it.

Panels 3–7: Calvin puts on layers of winter clothes.

Panels 8–10: Calvin walks outside, realizes something, walks back inside.

Panels 11–15: Calvin hurriedly takes off all his winter clothes and runs through the house.

Panel 16: Calvin walks into the bathroom.

It's a pretty simple joke—all that work undone instantly because he has to pee—but Watterson sells the comedy of it through his use of brevity, clarity, and specificity. Since the whole joke is how much work goes into getting ready for playing in the snow, clarity is essential for depicting that process and only that process. Watterson purposefully composes the panels without backgrounds so there's no "dead inventory of optical facts" (as Kepes would say) to distract or confuse us from the main action of dressing and undressing. The only thing that isn't made clear is *why* Calvin is undoing his earlier work, which of course *is* the joke and has to be held back until the last possible moment. When we see Calvin walking into the bathroom, we suddenly understand the situation, but up until that moment Watterson's focus on clarity allowed the audience to wonder "Why is he undoing what he just did?" instead of "What's going on with him?"

Watterson uses brevity masterfully as well. Sixteen panels total, with five for putting on winter clothes and four for taking the clothes off. The joke relies on us feeling like putting on and taking off are complicated processes, but we don't see every step, and the steps we do see get only one image each. This keeps us moving quickly through the comic, guiding our pace and rhythm in a manner analogous to the sentence-length techniques we saw in the chapter on prose. Also, because the reveal of the bathroom doesn't happen until the last panel, we have fifteen images for the setup and only one for the punchline. Like all good jokes, this one tells itself and then ends itself as quickly as possible.

Despite its brevity, the important details for the strip's story never feel generic. Comics artist Scott McCloud writes, "Don't just rely on stock generic features; a dress, a car, a smile. . . . Get ready to get specific." This is exactly what Watterson does by making sure that we can clearly see what specific items of winter wear Calvin is dealing with, how specifically frantic he is when he struggles to get his boots off, and even that he still has snow on his boots from being outside briefly. His actions are specifically methodical during dressing, and then specifically sloppy as he undresses, just leaving his clothes on the floor. And the few backgrounds we do see have just enough detail that they feel like specific rooms and not lifeless signifiers for "bathroom" or "entryway." If you really want to be impressed by Bill Watterson, look through his work paying close attention to the reality he brings to set decoration like chairs and umbrella stands. He's put a lot of work into making this a clear, quick, engaging read. This shouldn't surprise you, though, because this wordless strip was, of course, written.

It Only Hurts When I Laugh, and Vice Versa

Although I've been attempting to keep the peace by stressing the equivalence of words and images, there *is* one kind of joke that works much, much better visually than verbally: slapstick, the comedy of physical violence and pain. Which, when you state it that plainly, sounds like something only a psychopath would love, but try to watch Daffy Duck getting shot in the face so that his bill spins around his head without laughing. Who's the psychopath now?

Just as we talked about how jokes can be too close to or too far from an audience to be funny, successful slapstick relies on causing just the right measure of pain: enough to mean something, but not enough to become tragic. I maintain that the best illustration of this is a *Muppet Babies* scene in which Fozzie Bear trips and falls and everyone laughs, so he then pretends to trip again on purpose as a joke and nobody laughs. The reality of pain (or illusion of real pain) is necessary for this kind of humor, and obviously falsified pain won't do the trick. It's a funny bit, and honestly a better demonstration of comedic schadenfreude than you'd expect from a kids' cartoon about animal toddlers.

Slapstick, while looking painful enough to be funny, can't be so painful that we genuinely worry for the performer or character it's happening to. The joke in silent-film star Buster Keaton failing to leap from one rooftop to another, just like the joke in Wile E. Coyote realizing too late that he's run off the edge of a cliff, only remains a joke as long as we know the next shot won't be the main character's broken and bloody body. The exception to this is when the point of the joke *is* the shock of seeing violence go farther than you expect it to. In the film *The Other Guys*, heroic action cops Samuel L. Jackson and Dwayne Johnson leap off a roof and fall—and then keep falling, and keep falling, and then hit the ground, dying instantly on impact. It works as a funny disruption of what we'd normally expect to happen when a movie hero jumps off something (they usually don't die), but it's also bloodless and unreal enough to remain palatable.

To put it another way, it's shocking/funny in *Django Unchained* when Django shoots the villain played by Laura

Cayouette and her body flies out of the frame with cartoonish force. It's shocking/not-funny in the drama *A Simple Plan* when a shotgun blast throws the suspicious wife played by Becky Ann Baker into the air before her body then slams against a wall and falls to the floor, where the camera lingers on the lifeless corpse. (Audiences may sometimes suddenly laugh at scenes like this, but it's the awkward laughter of "I don't know how to respond to this," not the satisfied laughter of good joke.) In slapstick, there's usually an inverse proportion between how funny something is and how realistically it damages a living body.

Amazingly enough (OK, it's not *that* amazing), slapstick also follows those same guidelines of brevity, clarity, and specificity. We need to clearly see what painful thing is happening; both the violence and the pain it results in should feel specific; and it should happen as quickly as possible (there are few things less funny to me than extended close-ups of comedy actors yelling as they slide down a banister or drive off a cliff, dragging out interminably what should have been a passing flash of humor). The moment in the superhero movie *The Avengers* when the Hulk picks up Loki and slams him repeatedly against the floor is a genuinely funny slapstick moment because the violence happens quickly, clearly, and to a specific character at the hands of a specific character (for what it's worth, we immediately thereafter see Loki groaning in pain, but not dead, as an actual person slammed against the floor by the Hulk would certainly be). Even extended slapstick sequences, when successful, are composed of a string of specific, clear, brief incidents. Sticks and stones may break characters' bones, but the principles of comedy are forever.

CHAPTER THIRTEEN

When Art Is Funny

All jokes have some kind of point to them, and just because a visual lacks words doesn't mean it has nothing to say—in fact, it might say something complex enough to require, oh, I don't know, a thousand words. Fine artists have long used visual humor to raise complex questions in the minds of their audience. That's right, not only can comedy be an art, but art can be funny. Take Marcel Duchamp's sculpture *Fountain*, a urinal laid on its side with the name "R. Mutt" signed to it. *Fountain* is a work that forces us to examine our assumptions about how, exactly, we define "art," as well as who gets to define it. It's also one of the great practical jokes in art history. And I know I said earlier that I don't like practical jokes, but this is a practical joke with an actual *point*.

To wit, friends of Duchamp's who owned an art gallery made the laudably open-minded pledge that they would display the work of any artist who paid an application fee. Duchamp decided to test the limits of that open-mindedness by pseudonymously submitting a urinal—which they then refused to show, revealing they weren't as open-minded as they thought they were. (I assume they also started rethinking their friendship with Duchamp.) But Duchamp's *Fountain* is more than just an artsy-fartsy *practical* joke, it's also an artsy-fartsy *incongruity* joke about how silly it is to see a urinal in an art gallery. What if somebody didn't get the joke and peed in it?! That's comedy liquid gold (at least according to my sons—see chapter 6)! *Fountain* also operates according to the joke principles we've been talking about, most particularly the importance of context. *Fountain* is only a joke because of where the viewer encounters it. In a restroom, a urinal is just a urinal. In the gallery setting

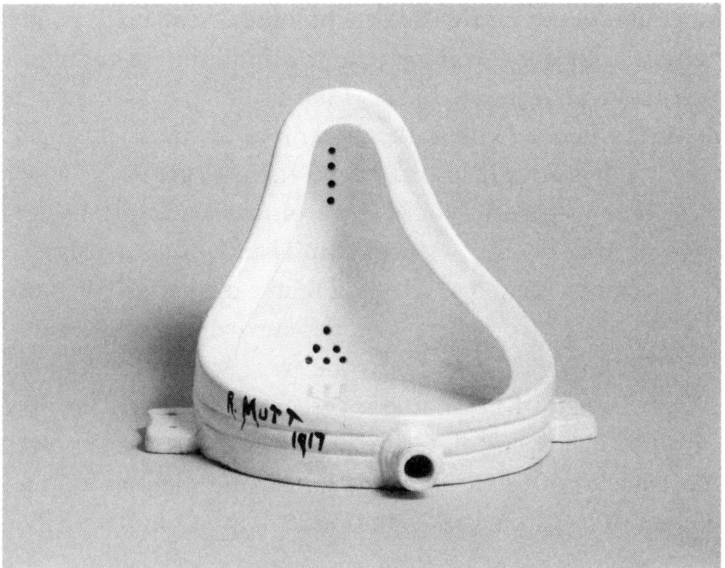

Marcel Duchamp's sculpture *Fountain*, 1917, serves as a practical joke that draws on incongruity for its humor.

it takes on a comedic dimension. As comedian Ed Wynn supposedly said, "Comedy is not opening a funny *door*, it is opening a door *funny*," which is to say that the subject of a joke isn't what makes it funny. The humor comes from the angle the joke writer finds to view that subject and execute the resulting joke.

In conceiving this work, I assume Duchamp went through the same thought process that a comedy writer goes through: "I want to make a point about my friend's principles. What's an offensive thing to see in a gallery? Now let me limit those offensive options to things that are shocking and funny without being disturbing." After all, he could have submitted a mess of roadkill, but that would be more gross than funny. A clean, pristine urinal, on the other hand, only becomes offensive in the minds of the audience, who know of its intended use. Like any joke, *Fountain* relies on the audience to fill in the final piece of information and take the cognitive leap that allows them to get it.

Fountain's point is about the arbitrary assumptions embedded in the concept of art. But visual jokes can also be more directly related to a feeling than a message. This is the case with my favorite art joke, the surrealist sculpture *Object (Le déjeuner en fourrure)* by the artist Meret Oppenheim, which consists of a teacup, saucer, and spoon lined entirely with fur, inside and out. The premise of this joke involves the vagaries of texture, taking something that should feel pleasant (soft fur) and changing its context in a way that

Meret Oppenheim's sculpture *Object*, 1936, harnesses the humor methods of incongruity, context, and shock.

makes it unpleasant. It's hard to look at the sculpture and not imagine how disgusting it would feel to drink something out of a cup lined with fur—I always imagine eating cereal in milk out of it, which is *so* gross.

I'm not reading too far into *Object* by calling it a joke. The idea came to Oppenheim when, wearing a fur-lined bracelet to lunch, she and her friends began laughing at the idea of covering everything in the restaurant with fur. Taking this concept, Oppenheim refined it to the clearest, briefest, and most specific thing that would be humorously disgusting to cover in fur—a cup—thereby harnessing the humor methods of incongruity, context, and shock. It even functions in my favorite three-act way in terms of the audience *seeing* the cup and spoon, *realizing* it's covered in fur, and then *imagining* how unpleasant it would be to use it.

They may be treated differently than a comic strip, slapstick fall, or stand-up joke, but ultimately both *Fountain* and *Object* operate on the same principles of successful humor. They disrupt an established pattern—our assumptions about urinal usage and dishware—for the purpose of laughter that communicates a point. It's good to remember that a comedy writer doesn't need to be restricted in how they create their comedy; there's such a wide variety of comic forms and such potential for humor in each of them that we shouldn't feel limited to working only one medium or style our whole lives. There's humor to be found everywhere. You don't need words to tell a joke.

14
Podcasting

AS OF THE WRITING OF THIS BOOK, I have been cohosting *The Flop House*, a comedy podcast about bad movies, with the same two friends for over a decade and a half. Longer than any individual job I've held. Longer than the lives of my children. Longer than my marriage. Depending on when you're reading this, it's possible I will have crossed the threshold past which the portion of my life in which I hosted this podcast will be larger than the portion of my life in which I did *not* host this podcast. Somehow, after spending my time working in sketch, stand-up, late night, sitcoms, animation, comic books, children's books, and prose, the defining comedic form for my career is something that didn't even exist when I first started writing comedy. It's very possible that comedy podcasting will turn out to be the reason God put me on this earth.

Isn't that disappointing?

Well, yes and no. Comedy, as we discussed, is ultimately about connecting with an audience, and podcasting is where I've felt that connection most closely. Our podcast is loose, silly, and almost entirely ad-libbed. But that doesn't mean it doesn't involve writing. In fact, it involves two kinds of writing: prewriting and writing in the moment, or what I like to call "writing on the fly."

What Do I Mean by Podcasting?

Podcasting contains multitudes. Technically it's a medium, not a genre, so you can find podcasts representing pretty much every form of comedy we've already talked about. (Except visual comedy—sight gags are wasted on ears.) But there's a particular kind of comedy that I find works particularly well as a podcast that shares elements of stand-up, sketch, improv, and late-night comedy but isn't exactly any of those things: unscripted comedy podcasts. Now, there are a lot of very good scripted podcasts—podcasts where performers act out a fully written script—but their writing isn't all that different from the narrative humor we talked about earlier. They're a return to old-time radio, which goes to show you there is no form of comedy that is ever uselessly obsolete. It's always worth studying the comedy of the past if only to see what's usable about it now. Or, if you just really like antique comedy, it means you shouldn't feel like too much of a dork.

Another way to describe unscripted comedy podcasting is as "long-form conversational comedy." This involves generating something humorous by alternately guiding and following the flow of a funny conversation. Steve Allen once said that "we laugh loudest over incidents we experience or observe directly," and this is the kind of experience you should aspire to create for your podcast audience: one that, like improv, is especially funny because it feels like the audience is witnessing the *moment of creation itself*, as opposed to merely the *product* of that creative moment. In practical terms, comedy podcasting thrives on quickly recognizing and taking advantage of unplanned funny moments. On one episode of *The Flop House*, my cohost Dan McCoy mispronounced the movie title *Beastmaster II: Through the Portal of Time* as "Porthole of Time," leading us to build an impromptu sketch around the idea of a cruise ship employee warning passengers, "You are the one cabin that has the Porthole of Time. *Please* don't go through it. 'Cause you'll end up *in Time*." After taking turns listing the amenities of the ship, we continued, "Don't mess with the portholes, in general. Time or not. . . . Don't open 'em, don't worry about it. Listen, we've got a whole mall on the ship. There's a pool. Why are you—why are you investigating the windows?"

This is the kind of conversational riffing, known as "bits," that comedy people do with each other in their spare time. This particular bit was never performed again, but it became a favorite reference point for us and our audience. Not just because we thought it was funny but because of the excitement of witnessing a comedic idea sprouting in real time and being harvested on the fly. Also like improv, comedy podcasting requires being open to sudden inspiration and to discarding plans you might have had for what you were going to say next. Podcasting is often an exercise in throwing away jokes, never to be delivered because the circumstances that birthed them have already changed. Which is a lesson that can be applied to comedy writing in general. If much of writing is rewriting, then much of writing is also discarding what has been rewritten. It also means internalizing that Duchamp audience-observation process, so that you can recognize what jokes will work and won't work. This is something you'll also do with all of your *written* comedy, of course; in that case, you'll just have more time to do it.

CHAPTER FOURTEEN

Thousands of Close Friends You've Never Met

It's easy to assume podcasting is analogous to other forms of passive entertainment like TV, movies, and staring glassy-eyed and drooling at an empty fish tank. But when conversational media is piped directly into your ears without any visual component, often during routine or unremarkable times of your life, it begins to feel less like entertainment and more like a relationship. If stand-up creates the feeling of a person talking to you (when it's really a performer performing a performance), then podcasting creates the feeling of a person talking *with* you. Podcast listeners don't usually sit down and concentrate on a podcast in the same way they'd watch a TV show or read a book. Instead, they listen while running errands, doing chores, or commuting—the same times when they might otherwise call a friend on the phone. As a result, podcasting gives the listener the illusion of being on a phone call where they never speak and only listen. And be honest, we've all been on phone calls like that.

Podcasts creep into the more intimate corners of listeners' brains, sparking a surprisingly direct connection closer to that of music than traditional comedy. I've had the eerie feeling of listening to someone else's podcast and then remembering the conversation later as if I had been in it. Friends who listen to my podcast often don't realize how long it's been since we've actually *talked* because they've been hearing my voice in this intimate way.

Over time, this connection between a podcaster and their audience can become strangely meaningful, and if your audience sticks with you long enough, they will hear you age in real time. My *Flop House* audience has heard me go from a callow young man in my midtwenties to a cranky middle-aged man in my early forties and has come to feel they really know me. It's something I wish I'd thought about ahead of time, because I really would have put in the kind of writing work that I'm about to tell you to do.

Prewriting Your Podcast: Voice

Comedy podcasting relies on the same elements of humor that all humor writing does. Voice? Premise? Sensibility? Tone? Oh yeah, the gang's all here, and each can benefit from some pre-conception (a.k.a. "writing") to prepare you for the in-the-moment writing of the episodes themselves. Here, I'll be talking about how *The Flop House* approaches these elements—it's my show, so I know it best—but of course this kind of thinking is applicable to comedy podcasts in general. As long as one of your goals is to be funny, then you'll be working with the same elements.

A podcast's voice is set by the personality of the host or hosts. As in stand-up, a podcast host is presenting a *persona* to the world. Find the aspects of your real personality that best lend themselves to being funny in the moment and come to you naturally enough that you can express them quickly. Do you possess an off-putting amount of enthusiasm? Or are you prone to meekly undercutting yourself? In normal conversation, either of these can be liabilities. As a podcast host, they're great. Instead of running from them, keep them in mind as comedy tools you can apply in real time to bring humor to a conversation.

You won't be doing this persona work in a vacuum. As with narrative writing, your persona will be interacting with other voices in the form of cohosts or guests. (It's hard for me to think of single-voice comedy podcasts that don't come off as audienceless stand-up or a lunatic ranting at the shadows in their hospital room.) Balancing these voices is key. I've seen several online memes that attach the caption "Every podcast is hosted by these three guys" to preexisting images of a nerdy guy, a handsome guy, and a glum guy. This is both incredibly reductive, considering the variety of podcasts out there, *and* also incredibly true in the case of my podcast: There's the chatty, annoying know-it-all (me); the sweet-hearted party dude (Stuart Wellington); and the sensible, glum, secretly weird normie (Dan McCoy). Obviously, these are simplified and exaggerated personas. But these are also personas that mesh well and create chemistry together.

By "chemistry," I mean a dynamic relationship that contains energy, enthusiasm, and a small amount of conflict that results in a kind of interaction-leading-to-exaggerated-reaction narrative. Every successful comedy podcast is the audio equivalent of a Venn diagram, with a shared passion or relationship that connects the voices, but also easily graspable differences in temperaments, backgrounds, or opinions. If the voices don't overlap at all, conversation will be stilted or awkward. If they overlap too much, the conversation will be boringly repetitive. Or, in either case, everyone will just argue with each other in a not-fun way.

You'll find this push-and-pull of similarity and difference in almost every successful multihost podcast. On *My Brother, My Brother & Me*, the McElroy brothers share a frame of reference and background—they're literally brothers—yet Justin, Travis, and Griffin have different enough personalities to sustain a consistently self-replenishing dynamic. On *Couples Therapy*, hosts Naomi Ekperigin and Andy Beckerman bring different backgrounds (outspoken Black woman and neurotic Jewish man, respectively) but also the shared frame of reference of being married to each other. Not that you have to share a family with your cohosts. On *Drink Champs*, host N.O.R.E. and his guests all come from the world of hip-hop, but their different perspectives reveal themselves as they drink together (or abstain) over the course of the episode. There's a reason that podcasts cohosted by friends are often pleasing to audiences: The similarity–difference ratio of a friendship that makes it fun to talk with each other *also* makes it fun to listen to.

Prewriting this balance of voices involves choosing your conversational partners and designing your personas, but it's also about setting the rules for how your podcasting personas will interact, and the sensibility and tone they're setting. Make it clear where the boundaries of comfort are in terms of ridicule or interruption: Are you and the other voices comfortable with a wild free-for-all, or would everyone feel like they had an equal chance to contribute if it were more orderly and respectful? Which of you is most comfortable taking the lead, and which of you would rather be the voice that chimes in with commentary? Are there any subjects that are *too* personally contentious and need to be avoided? By shaping this dynamic you won't only make it more comfortable to work together, you'll be shaping the show's consistent sensibility, which the audience will come to anticipate and look forward to.

Setting these rules is like building a work process for your podcast. And like a work process, anything you set now can be changed if it stops working. The only necessary feature in the design of this process is that it gets you to a mental place conducive to thinking of funny jokes quickly. As you release regular, consistent episodes, you will feel your dynamic evolve and adjust to the most natural fit. The great thing about podcasts is that it usually takes a long time to build an audience, so you'll have all that time to figure out your podcast's voice. Sure, starting a podcast can feel like you're shouting into an empty, uncaring void. But on the plus side, in space no one can hear you bomb.

Prewriting Your Podcast: Premise and Structure

Podcasts, like all conversations, need a launchpad to get them going. But unlike conversations, comedy podcasts also need their launchpad to double as a home base to return to after a long trip through tangents, misunderstandings, and inspired nonsense. To put this in the broadest, most existential terms: All a conversation has to do is start and end, but an unscripted comedy podcast needs a reason for being. A lot of your prewriting will go into figuring out what that reason is. What is your podcast's premise? The real question, though, is not "What is my podcast about?" but "What is my podcast *ostensibly* about?"

And that word "ostensibly" is going to be doing a lot of work.

Even though you'd be forced to admit to the enemy spy who injected you with truth serum that your podcast, deep down, is really just about you and your friends goofing off, your *audience* needs a reason to justify listening to you and your friends goofing off. Remember how a comedy movie needs at least the rudiments of a narrative to pull the audience through it, and that even the silliest joke has an idea behind it? Similarly, your podcast has to ostensibly be about something. So *The Flop House* is ostensibly about bad movies. *Dough Boys* is ostensibly about fast food. *Couples Therapy* is ostensibly about relationships. *Yo Is This Racist* is ostensibly about whether or not things are racist, yo. But no fan is listening to these shows *only* to hear about these things. These podcasts aren't really vehicles for delivering information but for delivering personality-based comedy.

Your ostensible purpose will also help you to figure out the format and structure you'll follow in each episode. And you'll remember (if you haven't taken a really long time to read this book) that structure is important because it tells an audience how to understand what makes a joke funny: where to find the setup and where to find the payoff. In a comedic podcast, structure also helps your audience keep their bearings. Honestly, the thing that keeps me from enjoying many comedy podcasts is the feeling of "I have no idea how far into this I am or how much is left to go," which often leads to the more visceral reaction "I do not want to hang out with these people." Something as small as starting every episode with an introductory "Let's talk about our day" and ending with a concluding "What are our final thoughts about this subject?" gives the audience the sense that you know what you're doing, even as everything you say in between those two segments tells the audience you're winging it while praying the whole thing doesn't fall apart.

Structure and format also create opportunities for humor. The podcast *Birthday Girls House Party* is ostensibly about the concept of parties. Each episode is built around the idea of a different kind of themed party (a Tupperware party, or a "New Year's Eve in New York" party, or an anthropology party). The cohosts play a "game" related to the episode's theme—really just a prompt question for which they've individually prepared answers—with the reactions to those prewritten answers acting as a springboard for unscripted comedy. In the "Hair Party" episode, for example, they play a game about ideas for using discarded hair, and cohost Rose Johnson is comically delighted that she and cohost Beattie Edmondson have both independently come up with the idea of sending discarded hair to their enemies. She is then comically appalled at Edmondson's *other* suggestion of weaving the hair into "winter tampons." The heart of the episode's comedy is less in the hair jokes and more in, as the episode's guest describes, "the trajectory of Rose being like, 'I can't believe we're on such a similar wavelength' to like 'I don't know you at all.'" A small amount of comedy writing has set up a narrative arc of interactions, and even some low-stakes conflict, that results in a huge unscripted payoff.

A consistent structure means you don't need to create your comedy conversations from scratch every episode. Your format or segment order becomes the reality voice you can push against to create opportunities for jokes. If you're taking the audience on a comedy podcasting journey, they don't need to know every bend in the road in advance. But it does help to have a map. And as with your joke-writing process, the more you travel with that map, the less often you'll have to consult it. You'll learn the lay of the land and know where you're headed.

But don't be afraid to ask your cohosts for directions, or even ask them to redraw parts of the map. Are they enjoying it in the moment? Are they inspired by what you're contributing to make contributions of their own? If the ideal of a comedy podcast is to create an entertaining conversation, then your cohosts or guests aren't just collaborators but also your podcast's first audience. If they're not having fun, then maybe your persona or premise needs to be rethought. But if they *are* having fun, then it's likely your listeners will pick up on that feeling and have fun as well. When this works, you may end up with an outlet for comedy that allows your jokes to reach a totally new audience. And even if you don't, you're still having fun with your friends. You're making a connection with another person through telling a joke. Isn't that the whole reason to do it?

Conclusion

WELL, FOLKS, THE SUN'S STARTING TO SINK behind the hills of my joke farm. The shadows of the comedy crops are growing longer. And frankly, I'm starting to get tired (of this farming metaphor).

But before we say *adios*, I want to go over the main ideas I've been trying to communicate in this book. Just in case you had the sheer, unmitigated gall to skip from the introduction to the conclusion, here's what you missed (along with a ton of hilarious jokes, and also I said some mean things about your family in chapter 4. Think I'm bluffing? Read the book or you'll never know for sure!). First among these ideas is that all jokes are built out of the same basic elements, each of which answers important questions:

Structure: What part of this joke is meant to be funny?
Premise: What is this joke saying? How is it communicating that?
Voice: Who is telling this joke? Where do they come from? What do they think?
Tone: How does the joke feel? How sincerely does it mean what it's saying?
Wording: What's the best way to use the formal tools at your disposal to make your joke as clear and funny as possible?

Audience: Who is the joke being told to, and how do *they* feel about it?

Those elements are best utilized to answer those questions by following three basic principles:

Brevity: Your joke should take as little time, verbiage, or imagery as possible to be told.
Clarity: Your joke should be clearly understandable to your audience, and the first step toward that is making it clearly understandable to yourself.
Specificity: Your joke gets closer to universality the farther it gets from generality.

These same elements and principles are the foundation of all quality joke writing, no matter the form in which you're working. Different crops may need different amounts of sunlight, water, or soil, but they all need *some* combination of those things to grow. Humor scientists have yet to invent the lab-grown, petri-dish clone meat of comedy.

Maybe this systematic way of looking at joke writing seems like the opposite of the chaotic, Dionysian ideal of humor. But just as *eating* candy is fun but *making* candy is not, writing jokes takes real work. And while it's possible to write humor by instinct, doing so puts you at the mercy of the specter of unreliability (by far the least popular horror movie monster) and limits what you can accomplish. Being really funny means taking humor seriously. Chuck Jones has written about "the two primary rules of all creativity. The first is that you must love what you are doing: the second is that you must be willing to do the often dull and tiring work necessary to bring each creative endeavor to completion, [so that] only the love should show." Joke farming means doing the hard work now of figuring out how your brain best writes a joke in order to make it easier for yourself later, when you actually need to get your brain to write those jokes.

I think you'll see that having a repeatable, reliable joke-farming process takes a lot of the anxiety out of writing jokes and sharing them with the world. The more reliable your writing is, the more reliable your audiences' responses will be, and the less you'll sweat and agonize over that moment when your joke needs to prove its worth to another person. A reliable process won't remove *all* the risk of creating humor, nor should it. The risk is part of what makes it exciting. But your process should remove enough of the risk to lessen the emotional angst of producing work for the only form of art that absolutely requires an immediate, involuntary emotional response from its audience. (For the purpose of this sentence I'm considering pornography not an art but more of a private utility.)

Laughter is a semiconscious reflex reaction to something funny. It can't be reasoned, explained, persuaded, begged, bribed, threatened, or seduced out of an audience. The truly great comedy writers never take their ability to trigger that reflex for granted, because everyone in comedy has a little fear inside of them that they might someday lose it. This is why we farm.

Specialized Advice

I hope this book has been helpful to all of you readers, whether you're a beginner, an experienced professional, or a civilian non-com (that means "non-comedian"). I've got some final short pieces of advice for each of you. If it's not your turn to get advice, maybe step out into the hall, but don't leave the building yet. The book is almost over, and I'd hate for this to take longer than it needs to.

For the beginners out there who want to be part of this beloved, undignified world of comedy but worry that they aren't yet ready to start writing jokes, I have three words: You *are* ready. When it comes to joke writing, as with all art, the only way to do it is to do it. No amount of prep work can substitute for doing the actual work. Just as you can't research your way into being a painter or plan your way into being a singer, you can't wait your way into being a comedy writer. It's easy to be nervous or scared and then procrastinate until the moment you're no longer nervous or scared. But if you don't force yourself past those nerves, then the moment without them will never come.

To the experienced professionals reading this book to help them develop the abilities they already have, I want to tell you that there's no upper limit to your potential, and there's also no such thing as perfection. It's on us to continue challenging ourselves to refine our skills, knowing that they will never be fully refined. This is the only way to open up new levels of fulfillment in our work. Quoting Chuck Jones again: "If you can look at anything you do and be satisfied with it, you are in the wrong trade. Frustration and anxiety are the handmaidens of creative work." It's frustrating when you try something new and it doesn't work. It's also frustrating to do the same thing over and over and over again. I know I prefer the first frustration. I apologize if I'm making professional comedy writing sound like a never-ending series of frustrations, but you're a professional comedy writer—you already knew that was the case.

Finally, to the civilians who needed help writing jokes for a specific moment in their life, or who were just curious how this humor thing they like so much works, I hope I've helped open your eyes to some new ways of looking at jokes and the bizarre clockwork behind their hilarious facade. It's always beneficial to understand how something works, even if you don't intend to make it a part of your professional or practical life. Knowledge allows for greater appreciation of anything. It's why I was glad I watched my son's bris, even as it horrified me. I hope reading this book gave you a similar experience.

Your Most Important Audience

Before we finish, I want you to think about one last thing. There's one audience you must always keep in mind while you're working. The most important audience there is, the one whose appraisal of your work carries the most weight, and who is always with you on your trek, even though when you look back you only see one set of footprints in the sand. Wait, that makes it sound like the audience is Jesus. Forget the footprints thing—the audience I'm talking about is *you*.

Only you will have to experience every one of your jokes, finished and unfinished, told and untold. Only you must stake your name, reputation, and self-esteem on the jokes you create. Only you know what jokes feel genuinely meaningful for you to tell. Only you know what you think is funny! It's not worth writing jokes that don't satisfy the audience that is you. The Jewish sage Rabbi Hillel supposedly said, "If I am not for myself, who will be for me?" Similarly, ask yourself, "If I don't think this is funny, why will anyone else?" Your own sense of humor should be your guiding star in your work. Comedian, entertain thyself. Have faith in your own sense of humor, until the audience tells you it stinks. And even if they do, at least you made yourself laugh.

Good luck and good farming!

Acknowledgments

IF YOU'RE READING THIS PAGE, then either you *really* loved this book, you're procrastinating doing some actual joke writing, or you're looking to see if I mentioned you. Whatever the reason, I should take advantage of you being here to thank some people.

First among them is my editor, David B. Olsen, without whom this book literally would not exist. It was David who contacted me out of the blue—a total stranger who claimed to work for a publisher—and asked if I'd be interested in pitching a book about joke writing. The very type of book that, for years, I'd been waiting to be asked to write by someone who claimed to work for a publisher! As it turned out, David *did* work for a publisher, and depending on how many decades from now you're reading this, he probably still does. David's guidance through every stage of the process—his shepherding of the book through the gauntlet that is academic publishing—was necessary and essential. He was great at nudging me to explain my nebulous comedy concepts in clearer and more tangible ways, and he always had a good reason for why I should remove a joke I found hilarious (usually because it was too gross). Blame or thank him for the loss of my multipage, incredibly self-indulgent analysis of Abbot & Costello's "Who's on First?" routine. Thank you so much, David, for helping me write this book.

Similarly, I'm indebted to my literary agent, Steven Malk, for his support and advice in all of my literary endeavors, including this one. I'm glad that he and I could finally work together on a project without talking animals in it (well, not many of them, anyway).

I'd be extremely remiss if I didn't also thank manuscript editor Tamara Ghattas for her thorough and probing copyediting and for creating the first-class index that comes at the very end of the book (stay tuned!). Whether reminding me not to use so many interrobangs or torturing herself for days on end about whether "whomever" or "whoever" was better for my voice, Tamara took a level of care with this book that it possibly didn't fully deserve. I'll leave it to her to tell me whether I used the word "remiss" properly. In addition, I know there are many other people at the University of Chicago Press who helped this book along its way, and though their names may not be mentioned here, I am extremely appreciative of having them in my corner.

Comedy seems to be proliferating at a nearly exponential rate, and there's far too much of it for any single person with children to keep track of. So I'm deeply grateful for my friends and colleagues Adam Lowitt, Sara Schaefer, and Dan McCoy, who generously shared their recommendations of what's been making them laugh in recent times. And I'm especially thankful for the in-depth research assistance and recommendations of Devon Coleman, one of America's most unjustly unsung comedy minds.

If the most horrifying sentence in the English language is "Would you come to my improv show?" then "Will you read the first draft of my book about comedy?" is pretty close behind. So I'm thankful to three of the most talented writers I know, my comedy brother Brock Mahan, my work wife Hallie Haglund, and my professional idol

Lauren Sarver, for reading an early draft and giving me their thoughts about reshaping and sharpening it. I'd also like to thank the peer-review peers who peer-reviewed a later draft of this book. Your thoughts were invaluable, but I don't actually know who you are. So I'll just say "Thank you" to the next few people I meet who look vaguely professorial. And a special sort of almost-thank-you goes to Zhubin Parang, who said he'd read a draft of the book but never quite got around to actually doing it.

This is a pretty short book, but it's the culmination of many years of loving, dreaming about, and working in comedy—work that wouldn't have been possible without many more people than I can reasonably thank here. I'll narrow it down to saying the podcasting chapter wouldn't exist if the aforementioned Dan McCoy hadn't asked me to join him and Stuart Wellington on *The Flop House* more than a decade and a half ago. My fundamental understanding of professional comedy writing rests almost entirely on what I learned working with the staff of *The Daily Show with Jon Stewart*, above all from Jen Flanz, Rory Albanese, and the titular Jon Stewart. My knowledge of most of the classic comedy mentioned in this book comes from being exposed to it by my grandmother, Barbara Preschel, who unfortunately passed before this book went to press, which is a pretty sad thing to drop into the end of a book about comedy.

I'd like to thank my parents, Marc and Abby Kalan, for allowing young me to indulge in the ridiculously impractical dream of studying writing and becoming a professional comedy writer. It came true somehow, and nearly twenty years later I still haven't had to get a respectable job! Fingers crossed the streak continues!

My biggest and most grateful thanks must go to the most important people in my life, and therefore in the entire world. First, thank you to my sons, Sammy and Gabriel, for constantly inspiring me, forcing me to find new ways to entertain you, and introducing me to new, innovative ways to get a laugh, such as peeing on your brother's head.

Finally, if you added up all the nice things I said about everyone else in these pages and multiplied it by a thousand, you might have some fraction of how grateful I am every day for my wife, Danielle, whose love has fueled my existence and pulled me back from numerous precipices. This book would not be here without her, and I might not be, either. No other laugh has ever been as beautiful as hers, nor meant as much to the joke teller.

Even if I still think she was a little harsh about that heroin pancakes bit.

Notes

Introduction

6 **"the humor inventions of comedy writers"**: William F. Fry and Melanie Allen, *Make 'Em Laugh: Life Studies of Comedy Writers* (Science and Behavior Books, 1975), 1.

Chapter 1

17–18 **"It takes a powerful generative force"**: Edward Steichen, *A Life in Photography* (Doubleday, 1963), n.p.

18 **"If they grow talons, we will grow a thick shell"**: This joke appeared on *The Daily Show with Jon Stewart*, episode aired January 6, 2010, on Comedy Central.

25 **"When you're in trouble with a script"**: Ruth Flippen, quoted in William F. Fry and Melanie Allen, *Make 'Em Laugh: Life Studies of Comedy Writers* (Science and Behavior Books, 1975), 90.

27 **Once that joke was finished**: The John Kerry joke described above appeared on *The Daily Show with Jon Stewart*, episode aired January 19, 2015, on Comedy Central.

32 **"a certain control over the spontaneous states"**: Ralph Waldo Emerson, "Intellect," in *The Essential Writings of Ralph Waldo Emerson*, ed. Brooks Atkinson (Modern Library, 2000), 268.

33 **"A lot of pure instinct"**: Scott McCloud, *Making Comics: Storytelling Secrets of Comics, Manga, and Graphic Novels* (HarperCollins, 2006), 55.

"Every technique we use": McCloud, *Making Comics*, 155.

Chapter 2

38 **"Seven Hundred Hobo Names"**: John Hodgman, *The Areas of My Expertise* (Dutton, 2006), 112–28.

39 **"Reentry Talking Points"**: Henry Alford, "Reentry Talking Points," *New Yorker*, March 14, 2022.

40 **"suppressed desire to logical ending"**: Ernie Kovacs, quoted in *The Vision of Ernie Kovacs* (Museum of Broadcasting, 1986), 52.

41 **"where does baby oil come from?"**: Jane Wagner, *The Search for Signs of Intelligent Life in the Universe* (HarperCollins, 1986), 25.

41–42 **"We have three brains"**: Del Close, quoted in Charna Halpern, Del Close, and Kim Howard Johnson, *Truth in Comedy: The Manual for Improvisation* (Meriwether, 1994), 54.

42 **Harpo Marx, the brother who doesn't talk, tries to play a pay phone**: *Horse Feathers*, directed by Norman Z. McLeod (Paramount, 1932).

43 **"in our daily lives we often commit closure"**: Scott McCloud, *Understanding Comics: The Invisible Art* (Harper Perennial, 1994), 63.

45 **"Without information, there is no joke"**: Mel Brooks, *All About Me! My Remarkable Life in Show Business* (Ballantine, 2021), 237.

"It's been a very interesting year": Michelle Buteau, *The Comedy Line Up*, episode "Michelle Buteau" (Netflix, 2018).

46 **"leaping outside what had appeared to be"**: Steve Allen with Jane Wollman, *How to Be Funny: Discovering the Comic in You*, 1987 (Prometheus, 1992), 13–14.

49 **"I broke up with my boyfriend"**: Rita Rudner, quoted in "Rita Rudner: One Funny Lady," interview by John Blackstone, *CBS Sunday Morning*, May 4, 2008.

50 **"It is a truth universally acknowledged"**: Jane Austen, *Pride and Prejudice* (1813; Penguin Classics, 2003), 1.

51 **"'Good' structure is not a fixed quality"**: Gerald Mast, *The Comic Mind: Comedy and the Movies* (University of Chicago Press, 1979), 65.

52 **"the basic law of his art"**: Richard Schickel, *Harold Lloyd: The Shape of Laughter* (New York Graphic Society, 1974), 90.

two hapless thugs attempt to bully a crowd: *Kung Fu Hustle*, directed by Stephen Chow (Columbia TriStar, 2004).

54 **"Strongest baby ever maybe"**: @peteyusa, "Strongest baby ever maybe," TikTok, September 17, 2021, https://www.tiktok.com/@peteyusa/video/7005726942020373766.

55 **"Zoom and Bored"**: *Looney Tunes*, episode "Zoom and Bored" from the *Merrie Melodies* series, directed by Chuck Jones (Warner Bros., 1957).

55 **"The Coyote has built a rickety construction"**: Chuck Jones, *Chuck Reducks: Drawing from the Fun Side of Life* (Grand Central, 1996), 198.

57 **"I lay eggs"**: @geemcgwee, "I lay eggs," TikTok, October 17, 2022, https://www.tiktok.com/@geemcgwee/video/7125979564433509678.

58 **"It's the same old story"**: *The Naked Gun: From the Files of Police Squad*, directed by David Zuker (Paramount, 1988).

"The social season in our city": Robert Benchley, *Benchley Beside Himself*, illustrated by Gluyas Williams (Harper & Brothers, 1943), 103.

60 **"God called to him"**: Isaac Asimov, *Isaac Asimov's Treasury of Humor*, 1971 (Houghton Mifflin, 1991), 329.

Chapter 3

65 **"If you say two and two"**: Billy Wilder, quoted in Cameron Crowe, *Conversations with Wilder* (Knopf, 1999), 18.

"I broke up with my boyfriend": Rudner, quoted in "Rita Rudner: One Funny Lady," interview by John Blackstone, *CBS Sunday Morning*, May 4, 2008.

66 **Tig Notaro's routine about repeatedly running into the singer Taylor Dane**: Tig Notaro, "Can You Believe It," track 11 on *Good One* (Secretly Canadian, 2011).

68 **"It was always most important to make the audience laugh"**: Joe Flaherty, quoted in Sam Wasson, *Improv Nation: How We Made a Great American Art* (Houghton Mifflin Harcourt, 2017), 188.

"We first of all locate the four children": Jean Kerr, *Please Don't Eat the Daisies* (Doubleday, 1957), 84.

69 **"the unexpected copulation of ideas"**: Samuel Johnson, quoted in Richard Boston, *An Anatomy of Laughter* (Collins, 1974), 63.

"You can leave in a taxi": *Duck Soup*, directed by Leo McCarey (Paramount, 1933).

Buster Keaton, running from the police: *The Goat*, directed by Buster Keaton and Michael St. Clair (Metro, 1921).

"the twist you never saw coming": Nell Scovell, *Just the Funny Parts: And a Few Hard Truths About Sneaking into the Hollywood Boys' Club* (Dey St., 2018), 49.

a self-serious character: *Abbott Elementary*, from the episode "Light Bulb," aired January 4, 2022, on ABC.

70 **the bland opening sequence**: *Too Many Cooks*, directed by Casper Kelly (Williams Street, 2014).

Sam and Dave keep digging: Mac Barnett, *Sam and Dave Dig a Hole*, illustrated by Jon Klassen (Candlewick, 2014).

"a couple of janitors": Robertson Davies, *Tempest-Tost* (1951; Penguin Canada, 2015), 49.

"when your dad corners me to talk about sports": Samantha Irby, "Please Invite Me to Your Party," *New Yorker*, March 27, 2023.

Sideshow Bob on *The Simpsons* steps on a rake: *The Simpsons*, episode "Cape Feare," aired October 7, 1993, on Fox.

71 **"Funny Filters"**: Scott Dikkers, "Remembering All Eleven," *No Dikkering Around*, December 14, 2023, https://scottdikkers.substack.com/p/remembering-all-eleven.

"Upper Class Twit of the Year": *Monty Python's Flying Circus*, episode "The Naked Ant," aired January 4, 1970, on BBC1.

roommates are also different types of vampires: *What We Do in the Shadows*, directed by Jemaine Clement and Taika Waititi (Madman, 2014).

two young women rampage through Prague: *Daisies*, directed by Vera Chytilova (Barrandov, 1966).

72–73 **Chuck Jones talks about being inspired**: Chuck Jones, *Chuck Reducks: Drawing from the Fun Side of Life* (Grand Central, 1996), 226.

73 **a group of cowboys sit around a campfire**: *Blazing Saddles*, directed by Mel Brooks (Warner Bros., 1974).

The Art of Dramatic Writing: Lajos Egri, *The Art of Dramatic Writing: Its Basis in the Creative Interpretation of Human Motives* (Touchstone, 1960). Originally published 1946.

74 **"It was in my gut"**: Bob Newhart, interview on *WTF* podcast, hosted by Marc Maron, August 11, 2014.

78 **routine about a terrible ventriloquist act**: Albert Brooks, appearance on *The Ed Sullivan Show*, episode aired January 31, 1971, on CBS.

"Pre-taped Call-In Show": *Mr. Show*, episode "The Return of the Curse of the Creature's Ghost," aired December 5, 1997, on HBO.

79 **"Is it funny? Really, truly *funny*?"**: Bob Odenkirk, quoted in Mike Sacks, *And Here's the Kicker: Conversations With 21 Top Humor Writers on Their Craft* (Writers Digest Books, 2009), 122.

"No writer has ever lived": Jacques Barzun, *On Writing, Editing, and Publishing: Essays Explicative and Hortatory*, 2nd ed. (University of Chicago Press, 1986), 5.

80 **"I laugh in life"**: Steve Martin, *Born Standing Up: A Comic's Life* (Scribner, 2007), 73.

"Comedy is a distortion": Martin, *Born Standing Up*, 104.

"Dad Hands Phone Off to Mom": *The Onion*, May 30, 2017.

"Neighbor Arriving Home at Same Time": *The Onion*, June 25, 2017.

"It's harder being gay than it is being Black": Wanda Sykes, *I'ma Be Me*, HBO, 2009.

81 **"Seven Dirty Words"**: George Carlin, "Seven Words You Can Never Say on Television," track 9 on *Class Clown* (Little David Records, 1972).

81–82 **"Sometimes if you add 'ass' to something"**: Ismo Leikola, performance on *Conan*, episode aired January 22, 2018, on TBS.

82 **"so powerful is the charm of words"**: Gene Wolfe, *The Shadow of the Torturer* (Simon & Schuster, 1980), 151.

83 **"Sometimes I'll just throw one in there"**: Mitch Hedberg, *Comedy Central Presents*, episode aired January 5, 1999, on Comedy Central.

"football and soccer are like gimme the ball": @KimmyMonte, Twitter (now X), February 12, 2023, https://x.com/KimmyMonte/status/1624927477419151360.

Chapter 4

87 **one-panel *New Yorker* cartoon**: Edward Steed, *The New Yorker*, January 17, 2020, 39.

"primitive savagery": Philip Witte and Rex Hesner, *Funny Stuff: How Great Cartoonists Make Great Cartoons* (Prometheus, 2024), 19.

89 **"The more specific you are"**: Cristela Alonzo, interview on *Good One: A Podcast About Jokes*, hosted by Jesse David Fox, June 30, 2022.

"Around the corner, the citizens of Gettysburg": Sarah Vowell, "What He Said There," in *The Partly Cloudy Patriot* (Simon & Schuster, 2022), 1.

91 **Homer Simpson demands**: *The Simpsons*, episode "Boy Scouts in the Hood," aired November 18, 1993, on Fox.

Bugs Bunny's plummeting airplane: *Looney Tunes*, episode "Falling Hare" from the *Merrie Melodies* series, directed by Bob Clampett (Warner Bros., 1943).

91–92 **the spirit of Elora's newly dead grandmother**: *Reservation Dogs*, episode "Mabel," aired August 17, 2022 on FX on Hulu.

92 "**Basic Ball**": *A Black Lady Sketch Show*, episode "Your Boss Knows You Don't Have Eyebrows," aired August 9, 2019, on HBO.

"**Funeral Ball**": *A Black Lady Sketch Show*, episode "Anybody Have Something I Can Flog Myself With?," aired April 15, 2022, on HBO.

93 "**A man's body and his mind**": Laurence Stern, *The Life and Opinions of Tristram Shandy, Gentleman*, 1759–76 (1759, 1767; Wordsworth Editions, 1996), 109.

94–95 "**A comic goes through life**": Jimmy Carr and Lucy Greeves, *Only Joking: What's So Funny About Making People Laugh?* (Gotham, 2006), 120.

95 "**make connections, see parallels**": Gerald Mast, *The Comic Mind: Comedy and the Movies* (University of Chicago Press, 1979), 15.

"**Most of the people living on it were unhappy**": Douglas Adams, *The Hitchhiker's Guide to the Galaxy* (1979; Del Ray, 2009), 3.

97–98 "**The bully, his name was Clyde**": Percival Everett, *I Am Not Sidney Poitier* (Graywolf, 2011), 17.

101 "**We mine ourselves**": Chuck Jones, *Chuck Amuck: The Life and Times of an Animated Cartoonist* (Farrar, Straus and Giroux, 1999), 147.

102 "**With tech like that, you could cure cancer!**": Elliot Kalan, *Spider-Man and the X-Men* no. 2, illustrated by Marco Failla (Marvel Comics, January 28, 2014).

"**I am familiar with the works of Pablo Neruda**": *The Simpsons*, episode "Bart Sells His Soul," aired October 8, 1994, on Fox.

104 "**got all of America started on the hot new craze**": *The Daily Show with Jon Stewart*, episode aired January 7, 2009, on Comedy Central.

104–5 "**In real life, you're a person**": David Sedaris, quoted in Mike Sacks, *And Here's the Kicker: Conversations With 21 Top Humor Writers on Their Craft* (Writers Digest Books, 2009), 191.

106 "**The idea is that people in positions of power**": Lindy West, *Shrill: Notes from a Loud Woman* (Hachette, 2016), 179.

"**I truly believe that if you're a comedy writer**": Nell Scovell, *Just the Funny Parts: And a Few Hard Truths About Sneaking into the Hollywood Boys' Club* (Dey St., 2018), 25.

107 "**analyze *why* you like what you like**": Merrill Markoe, quoted in Sacks, *And Here's the Kicker*, 87.

107 "**You should constantly try to paint**": Pablo Picasso, quoted in Helene Parmalin, *Picasso: The Artist and His Model, and Other Recent Works* (H. N. Abrams, 1965), 43.

Chapter 5

112 "**We do not *decide* to laugh**": Steve Allen with Jane Wollman, *How to Be Funny: Discovering the Comic in You*, 1987 (Prometheus, 1992), 13–14.

113 "**Tone is everything**": Loren Bouchard, interview on *Bullseye* podcast, hosted by Jesse Thorn, August 5, 2022.

"**We at KidLuv**": George Saunders, "I Can Speak!," in *Persuasion Nation* (Riverhead, 2006), 10.

"**And so I thought I would take**": Saunders, "I Can Speak!," 3.

114 "**But if we get rid of the Confederate flag**": Roy Wood Jr., *Father Figure*, directed by Shannon Hartman (Comedy Central, 2017).

115 "**kill George Lucas with a shovel**": Patton Oswalt, "At Midnight I Will Kill George Lucas with a Shovel," track 11 on *Werewolves and Lollipops* (Sub Pop Records, 2007).

115 "**we were in the middle of a massive family crisis**": Sara Schaefer, *Grand: A Memoir* (Gallery, 2020), 57.

118 "**I love that you're so fucking fancy**": Samantha Irby, "Milk and Oreos," in *Meaty: Essays* (Vintage, 2018), 111–12.

120 "**Keaton's presence makes *The General***": Gerald Mast, *The Comic Mind: Comedy and the Movies* (University of Chicago Press, 1979), 9.

"**The Beach Boys were singing**": Richard Brautigan, "Pacific Radio Fire," in *Revenge of the Lawn: Stories, 1962–1970* (Simon & Schuster, 1971), 28.

121 "**When was the last time you touched your ceiling?**": Atsuko Okatsuka, *The Intruder*, directed by Tig Notaro (HBO, 2022).

"**human sacrifice, dogs and cats living together**": *Ghostbusters*, directed by Ivan Reitman (Columbia, 1984).

122 "**Everything was fine with our system**": *Ghostbusters*.

124 "**No, we never played cowboys and Indians**": Charlie Hill, quoted in Kliph Nesteroff, *We Had a Little Real Estate Problem: The Unheralded Story of Native Americans and Comedy* (Simon & Schuster, 2021), 158.

"**The Second Worst Kind of Camp for Jews**": Sarah Silverman, *The Bedwetter: Stories of Courage, Redemption, and Pee* (HarperCollins, 2010), 24.

126 **"Pregnant Women Are Smug"**: Garfunkel and Oates, "Pregnant Women Are Smug," track 3 on *All Over Your Face* (n.p., 2011).

"29/31": Garfunkel and Oates "29/31," track 4 on *Secretions* (n.p., 2015).

127 **"Life's a piece of shit"**: Eric Idle, "Always Look on the Bright Side of Life," from *Monty Python's Life of Brian*, directed by Terry Jones (Cinema International, 1979).

128 **"Everyone at a roast has consented"**: Jesse David Fox, *Comedy Book: How Comedy Conquered Culture—and the Magic That Makes It Work* (Farrar, Straus and Giroux, 2023), 236.

129 **"It is incumbent on the roasters"**: Fox, *Comedy Book*, 236.

"Comic insults are often playful": Richard Boston, *An Anatomy of Laughter* (Collins, 1974), 41.

130 **"I think we shared one of the worst nights"**: Marc Maron, *WTF* podcast, hosted by Marc Maron, September 25, 2023.

"I'm not great with roasting": Marc Maron, interview on *The Howard Stern Show*, episode aired February 15, 2023.

"Jesus Christ, they don't like me": Chevy Chase, interview on *WTF* podcast, hosted by Marc Maron, September 25, 2023.

Chapter 6

133 **"Specific words in specific order matter"**: Nell Scovell, *Just the Funny Parts: And a Few Hard Truths About Sneaking into the Hollywood Boys' Club* (Dey St., 2018), 96.

134 **"Artificial intelligence aces the Turing test"**: Elliott Kalan, "20 Things You Didn't Know About . . . The Future," *Discover*, January 11, 2011.

135 **"the ability to know where the top of the vocality"**: Mel Brooks, *All About Me! My Remarkable Life in Show Business* (Ballantine, 2021), 34.

136 **"The front of the truck is fine"**: Brooks, *All About Me!*, 56.

138 **"He's got a weak left hook"**: Jason Adam Katzenstein, "He's got a weak left hook . . . ," cartoon, *New Yorker*, March 7, 2022.

139 **"One of my best friends is a man"**: Jena Friedman, performance on *Conan*, episode aired February 8, 2018, on TBS.

"Everyone knows that Custer died": *The Royal Tenenbaums*, directed by Wes Anderson (Buena Vista, 2001).

140 **"Even the Zodiac Killer was polite enough"**: Josh Gondelman, *Nice Try: Stories of Best Intentions and Mixed Results* (Harper Perennial, 2019), 9.

141 **"Greeks were known to have made wicked fun"**: Mary Beard, *SPQR: A History of Ancient Rome* (Liveright, 2015), 198.

"One comedy of Plautus": Beard, *SPQR*, 202.

141–42 **"Man Walks on the Fucking Moon"**: Scott Dikkers, ed., *Our Dumb Century: The Onion Presents 100 Years of Headlines from America's Finest News Source* (Crown, 1999), 113.

142 **"Writing is embodied thought"**: Jacques Barzun, *On Writing, Editing, and Publishing: Essays Explicative and Hortatory*, 2nd ed. (University of Chicago Press, 1986), 32.

"Don't be afraid of saying things simply": Norm Macdonald, quoted in Nathan Heller, "Norm Macdonald Was the Real Thing," *New Yorker*, September 15, 2021.

143 **"There are going to be fewer but better Russians"**: *Ninotchka*, directed by Ernst Lubitsch (MGM, 1939).

144 **"Ah! A soul wishes to speak to you!"**: *HouseBroken*, episode "Who Ain't Afraid of No Ghosts?," aired July 23, 2023, on Fox.

145 **"What effect are you producing and at what cost of words?"**: Barzun, *On Writing*, 28.

"One word too many in a thing": Andrew Bergmanm, interview on *Gilbert Gottfried's Amazing Colossal Podcast*, hosted by Gilbert Gottfried, February 17, 2022.

146 **"I ordered French toast during the Renaissance"**: Steven Wright, quoted in Jimmy Carr and Lucy Greeves, *Only Joking: What's So Funny About Making People Laugh?* (Gotham, 2006), 75.

Chapter 7

151 **"Writing is not what you start"**: Nell Scovell, *Just the Funny Parts: And a Few Hard Truths About Sneaking into the Hollywood Boys' Club* (Dey St., 2018), 22.

"Everything we've done has happened with the three of us": Elaine May, quoted in Sam Wasson, *Improv Nation: How We Made a Great American Art* (Houghton Mifflin Harcourt, 2017), 68.

"Sometimes I think a joke is really funny": Steven Wright, quoted in David Wolinsky, "Steven Wright Gets in Touch with His Inner Deadpan," *The A. V. Club*, January 22, 2010, https://www.avclub.com/steven-wright-gets-in-touch-with-his-inner-deadpan-1798218826.

152 **"the artist goes from intention to realization"**: Marcel Duchamp, "The Creative Act," in *The Writings of Marcel Duchamp*, ed. Elmer Peterson and Michel Sanouillet (1957; Da Capo, 2007), 139.

152 **"the creative act is not performed by the artist alone"**: Duchamp, "The Creative Act," 140.

153–54 **"Do not make the mistake of assuming"**: Steve Allen with Jane Wollman, *How to Be Funny: Discovering the Comic in You*, 1987 (Prometheus, 1992), 46.

156 **"when the audience is ready to receive a joke"**: Jesse David Fox, *Comedy Book: How Comedy Conquered Culture—and the Magic That Makes It Work* (Farrar, Straus and Giroux, 2023), 77.

156–57 **"Clothes are funny when"**: Richard Boston, *An Anatomy of Laughter* (Collins, 1974), 54.

157 **performing before an audience of prisoners**: Mo'Nique, *I Coulda Been Your Cellmate!*, directed by Gary Binkow (Netflix, 2007).

158 **"You learned what the audience expects"**: Mel Brooks, *All About Me! My Remarkable Life in Show Business* (Ballantine, 2021), 45.

"Let's figure out which is the worst race": Ronny Chieng, "15 Minutes of Ronny Chieng," Netflix Is a Joke, April 22, 2022, https://www.youtube.com/watch?v=oUUVRa2SNWU.

160 **"The only safe thing is to take a chance"**: Mike Nichols, quoted in Sam Wasson, *Improv Nation: How We Made a Great American Art* (Houghton Mifflin Harcourt, 2017), 67.

163–64 **"It's just a process of editing"**: Tig Notaro, interview on *Good One* podcast, September 30, 2019.

165 **"The artist may shout from all the rooftops"**: Marcel Duchamp, "The Creative Act," in *The Writings of Marcel Duchamp*, ed. Elmer Peterson and Michel Sanouillet (1957; Da Capo, 2007), 138.

166 **"When a reader has a problem"**: Haruki Murakami, *Novelist as a Vocation* (Knopf, 2022), 100.

"Subjectivity works both ways": Scovell, *Just the Funny Parts*, 71.

167 **"These are just jokes"**: Larry Wilmore, quoted in Mike Sacks, *And Here's the Kicker: Conversations With 21 Top Humor Writers on Their Craft* (Writers Digest Books, 2009), 306.

"a dull comedy heaven": Steve Martin, *Born Standing Up: A Comic's Life* (Scribner, 2007), 203.

Chapter 8

174 **"Yes, they were funny, but they were also interchangeable"**: Alan Zweibel, *Laugh Lines: My Life Helping Funny People Be Funnier* (Abrams, 2020), 21–22.

174–75 **"Your stage self, for stand-up comedy"**: Steve Allen with Jane Wollman, *How to Be Funny: Discovering the Comic in You*, 1987 (Prometheus, 1992), 198.

175 **"As I am, so I see"**: Ralph Waldo Emerson, "Experience," in *The Essential Writings of Ralph Waldo Emerson*, ed. Brooks Atkinson (Modern Library, 2000), 323–24.

177 **"Good comedy arises from the ability"**: Chuck Jones, *Chuck Amuck: The Life and Times of an Animated Cartoonist* (Farrar, Straus and Giroux, 1999), 169.

"I need to find a way to show people": Maria Bamford, *Old Baby*, directed by Jessica Yu (Netflix, 2017).

178 **"As a person who's tried to kill themself"**: Maria Bamford, *Weakness Is the Brand*, directed by Robert Cohen (Comedy Dynamics, 2020).

"It takes years for the audience": Marshall Brickman, quoted in Mike Sacks, *And Here's the Kicker: Conversations With 21 Top Humor Writers on Their Craft* (Writers Digest Books, 2009), 152.

179 **"nobody actually learns any Black history"**: Wyatt Cenac, interview on *Good One* podcast, January 14, 2018.

179–80 **"I tend to write jokes as independent little things"**: Cenac, interview on *Good One* podcast.

Chapter 9

184 **"all the jokes were dependent on"**: Stephen Merchant, quoted in Mike Sacks, *And Here's the Kicker: Conversations With 21 Top Humor Writers on Their Craft* (Writers Digest Books, 2009), 21.

185 **"You have your own set of rules, as a character"**: Holly Hunter, interview on *Bullseye* podcast, February 16, 2021.

187 **"Humorous dialogue, we discovered"**: Chuck Jones, *Chuck Amuck: The Life and Times of an Animated Cartoonist* (Farrar, Straus and Giroux, 1999), 210.

188 **"Dead Parrot"**: *Monty Python's Flying Circus*, episode "Full Frontal Nudity," aired December 7, 1969, on BBC1.

191 **"three types of sketches"**: Robin Thede, interview on *Good One* podcast, June 23, 2022.

"Dylan's Burger": *I Think You Should Leave with Tim Robinson*, episode "You Sure About That? You Sure About That That's Why?" (Netflix, 2021).

192 **"Courtroom Kiki"**: *A Black Lady Sketch Show*, episode "Born at Night, But Not Last Night," aired September 6, 2019, on HBO.

"Happy Fun Ball": *Saturday Night Live*, episode aired February 16, 1991, on NBC.

193 **"Wells for Boys"**: *Saturday Night Live*, episode aired December 3, 2016, on NBC.

"Female Role Audition": Natalie Walker, @nwalks on Twitter (now X); videos no longer available but were originally posted starting in 2016.

194 **"Porcupine Racetrack"**: *The State*, episode aired February 11, 1995, on MTV.

Chapter 10

200 **a shark gets frustrated**: Elliott Kalan, *Sharko and Hippo*, illustrated by Andrea Tsurumi (HarperCollins, 2020).

202 **four animals wear the same item**: Sandra Boynton, *Blue Hat, Green Hat* (Boynton Bookworks, 1984).

203 **a father chicken is repeatedly exasperated**: David Ezra Stein, *Interrupting Chicken* (Candlewick, 2010).

204 **a dog assumes a horse is a big dog**: Elliott Kalan, *Horse Meets Dog*, illustrated by Tim Miller (HarperCollins, 2018).

205 **"To be a writer for the young"**: Margaret Wise Brown, quoted in Andrew Blauner, ed., *The Peanuts Papers: Writers and Cartoonists on Charlie Brown, Snoopy, and the Gang, and the Meaning of Life* (Library of America, 2019), 26.

206 **parody of "Take Me Out to the Ball Game" about poop**: Dav Pilkey, *Dog Man: Mothering Heights* (Scholastic, 2021).

"It was always most important to make the audience laugh": Joe Flaherty, quoted in Sam Wasson, *Improv Nation: How We Made a Great American Art* (Houghton Mifflin Harcourt, 2017), 188.

winter "hits fast" in the valley: Jeff Smith, *Bone* no. 1 (Cartoon Books, July 1991).

207 **"I am a monkey who taught myself to read"**: B. J. Novak, *The Book with No Pictures* (Penguin, 2014).

Isaac Newton sits under a series of fruit trees: *The Who Was? Show*, season 1, episode 4, released May 11, 2018, on Netflix.

208 **"the strip's surface concerns are children's"**: Bruce Handey, "It's Once upon a Time, Charlie Brown," in Blauner, *The Peanuts Papers*, 27.

209 **a child gets too silly while getting dressed**: Nikki Yektai, *Crazy Clothes*, illustrated by Sucie Stevenson (Bradbury, 1988).

the story of a pizza-loving raccoon: Adam Rubin, *Secret Pizza Party*, illustrated by Daniel Salmieri (Penguin, 2013).

Chapter 11

212 "**militant irony**": Northrop Frye, "The Mythos of Winter: Irony and Satire," in *Satire: Modern Essays in Criticism*, ed. Ronald Paulson (Prentice-Hall, 1971), 233.

"**Satire must break through the crust of familiarity**": Frederick Kiley and J. M. Shuttleworth, eds., *Satire: From Aesop to Buchwald* (Odyssey, 1971), 1.

213 "**Throw the Jew Down the Well**": *Da Ali G Show*, episode "Peace," aired August 1, 2004, on HBO.

214 "**The content of satire is criticism**": David Worcester, *The Art of Satire* (Harvard University Press, 1940), 16.

215 "**One is wit or humor**": Frye, "The Mythos of Winter," 234.

216 "**changed the way that I do satire**": Ruben Bolling, interview on *Blockhead: Cartoonists Talk Comics* podcast, hosted by Geoff Grogan, July 30, 2024.

217 "**The power depends on the depth of the artist's insight**": Ralph Waldo Emerson, "Art," in *The Essential Writings of Ralph Waldo Emerson*, ed. Brooks Atkinson (Modern Library, 2000), 276.

219 "**full appreciation of satire can take place**": Steve Allen with Jane Wollman, *How to Be Funny: Discovering the Comic in You*, 1987 (Prometheus, 1992), 157.

220 "**one of the most heroic acts of the last fifteen years**": Adam McKay, quoted in Mike Sacks, *Poking a Dead Frog: Conversations with Today's Top Comedy Writers* (Penguin, 2014), 128.

221 "**you could argue that it's not particularly edgy**": John Kruse, interview on *9/12* podcast, hosted by Dan Taberski, September 8, 2021.

"**There were a lot of jokes that got thrown out**": Carol Kolb, quoted in Sacks, *Poking a Dead Frog*, 190.

222 "**it flirts dangerously with its own literal content**": Claude Rawson and Ian Higgins, introduction to *The Essential Writings of Jonathan Swift* (Norton, 2010), xxiii.

"**it fails because it loses control**": Kiley and Shuttleworth, *Satire*, 3.

222 “**A man can’t write successful satire**”: Mark Twain, quoted in Kiley and Shuttleworth, *Satire*, 2017.

223 “**Without a clear indicator of the author’s intent**”: Wikipedia, “Poe’s Law,” last modified December 23, 2024, https://en.wikipedia.org/wiki/Poe%27s_law.

his book appeared on the American Nazi Party’s recommended reading list: Norman Spinrad, *Science Fiction in the Real World* (Southern Illinois University Press, 1990), 158.

225 “**the gorilla channel**”: @pixelatedboat, Twitter (now X), January 4, 2018, https://x.com/pixelatedboat/status/949100087350710272.

226 “**Every one of Swift’s rhetorical victories**”: Peter Steele, *Jonathan Swift: Preacher and Jester* (Clarendon, 1978), 54.

“**If a magician puts a curse upon you**”: Alan Moore, “Storytelling: Course Notes 2.0,” *BBC Maestro*, 2022, https://assets.bbcmaestro.com/writing-exercises-and-more.pdf?version=1655041745.

227 “**We were just trying to reflect what everybody was going through**”: Todd Hansen, quoted in Mike Sacks, *And Here’s the Kicker: Conversations With 21 Top Humor Writers on Their Craft* (Writers Digest Books, 2009), 145.

a brilliant satire of military chaos: Joseph Heller, *Catch-22* (Simon & Schuster, 1961).

208 **a Black man becomes a successful telemarketer**: *Sorry to Bother You*, directed by Boots Riley (Annapurna, 2018).

Chapter 12

231–32 “**my way of feeling like I’m part of the world**”: Hallie Haglund, “Is Our Fate Written in the Standardized Stars?,” *That Hurts My Feelings*, Substack, February 8, 2024, https://halliehaglund.substack.com/p/is-our-fate-are-written-in-the-standardized.

233 “**Consider how many of your problems would go away**”: @anniew, Twitter (now X), December 13, 2022, https://twitter.com/AnnieW/status/1602589440895062017.

“**Hustle hard and become highly skilled!**”: @iconawrites, Twitter (now X), August 21, 2022, https://x.com/iconawrites/status/1561404681439559680.

234 “**I’m sorry Ms. Jackson**”: @JNalv, Twitter (now X), February 20, 2013, https://twitter.com/JNalv/status/304345341535338496.

235 **"Eventually, I believe, everything evens out"**: Jack Handey, "How Things Even Out," in *What I'd Say to the Martians: And Other Veiled Threats* (Hyperion, 2008), 2.

"need someone in or around geigertown, philadelphia": @dril, Twitter (now X), February 2, 2011, https://x.com/dril/status/32882019272753152.

237 **"Food $200"**: @dril, Twitter (now X), September 29, 2013, https://x.com/dril/status/384408932061417472.

238 **"He was a man whose significance"**: Zadie Smith, *White Teeth* (Random House, 2000), 10.

239 **"Often, we have to stand behind"**: Sarah Vowell, "Pop-A-Shot," in *The Partly Cloudy Patriot* (Simon & Schuster, 2022), 61.

240 **"Unlike the game of basketball itself"**: Vowell, "Pop-A-Shot," 64.

"'I'm hungover'": @DrakeGatsby, Twitter (now X), November 20, 2022, https://x.com/DrakeGatsby/status/1594329373670539272.

242 **"The sordid experience of sharing the stage"**: Ricky Jay, *Learned Pigs and Fireproof Women* (Villard, 1986), 14.

244 **"Omg did you see what Vaush said"**: @doulbedoink, Twitter (now X), March 16, 2022, https://x.com/doulbedoink/status/1504165271724044291.

Chapter 13

247 **"no limits of tongue, vocabulary, or grammar"**: György Kepes, *Language of Vision* (1944; Dover, 1995), 13.

250 **"a couple of hours away"**: *Dr. Brown*, episode "First Outing," Channel 4, May 24, 2012, https://www.youtube.com/watch?v=XfONJQ7DudQ&t=53s.

253 **"Each panel should be regarded"**: Will Eisner, *Comics and Sequential Art* (1985; Norton, 2008), 163.

"The success or failure of this method": Eisner, *Comics and Sequential Art*, 7.

253–54 **Calvin looks out a window**: Bill Watterson, *Calvin & Hobbes*, strip published February 21, 1988.

254 **"dead inventory of optical facts"**: Györy Kepes, quoted in Reid Mitenbuler, *Wild Minds: The Artists and Rivalries that Inspired the Golden Age of Animation* (Grove Atlantic, 2020), 275.

255 **"Don't just rely on stock generic features"**: Scott McCloud, *Making Comics: Storytelling Secrets of Comics, Manga, and Graphic Novels* (HarperCollins, 2006), 27.

256 **Fozzie Bear trips and falls**: *Muppet Babies*, from the episode "Fozzie's Last Laugh," aired September 28, 1985, on CBS.

heroic action cops . . . leap off a roof and fall: *The Other Guys*, directed by Adam McKay (Columbia, 2010).

256–57 **Django shoots the villain**: *Django Unchained*, directed by Quentin Tarantino (Columbia, 2012).

257 **a shotgun blast throws the suspicious wife**: *A Simple Plan*, directed by Sam Raimi (Paramount, 1998).

the Hulk picks up Loki and slams him repeatedly against the floor: *The Avengers*, directed by Joss Whedon (Marvel, 2012).

259 "**Comedy is not opening a funny door**": Ed Wynn, quoted in Chuck Jones, *Chuck Reducks: Drawing from the Fun Side of Life* (Grand Central, 1996), 35.

Chapter 14

264 "**we laugh loudest over incidents we experience or observe directly**": Steve Allen with Jane Wollman, *How to Be Funny: Discovering the Comic in You*, 1987 (Prometheus, 1992), 57.

265 "**Porthole of Time**": *The Flop House* podcast, hosted by Elliott Kalan, Dan McCoy, and Stuart Wellington, August 15, 2010.

271 "**Hair Party**": *Birthday Girls Club* podcast, hosted by Beattie Edmondson, Rose Johnson, and Camille Ucan, May 11, 2022.

Conclusion

276 "**the two primary rules of all creativity**": Chuck Jones, *Chuck Amuck: The Life and Times of an Animated Cartoonist* (Farrar, Straus and Giroux, 1999), 36.

278 "**If you can look at anything you do and be satisfied with it**": Chuck Jones, *Chuck Reducks: Drawing from the Fun Side of Life* (Grand Central, 1996), 162.

279 "**If I am not for myself**": Pirkei Avot 1:14.

Index